Penguin Books

LAWYERS

Born in Montreal, Jack Batten studied law at the University of Toronto, where he graduated in 1957. After practising law for four years, he turned to free-lance writing. He has been a staff writer for *Maclean's* and *The Canadian,* managing editor for *Saturday Night* and a film critic for CBC Radio.

In addition to many magazine articles, Jack Batten has written fourteen books, among them *Lawyers, In Court, Honest Ed's Story* and a young adult novel, *Tie-Breaker*. His biography of J.J. Robinette was published in fall 1984.

Lawyers

Jack Batten

Penguin Books

Penguin Books Canada Ltd., 2801 John Street,
    Markham, Ontario, Canada L3R 1B4
Penguin Books Ltd., Harmondsworth, Middlesex,
    England
Penguin Books, 40 West 23rd Street,
    New York, New York 10010 U.S.A.
Penguin Books Australia Ltd., Ringwood,
    Victoria, Australia
Penguin Books (N.Z.) Ltd., 182-190 Wairau Road,
    Auckland 10, New Zealand

The material in this book was drawn from two previous
books, *Lawyers* and *In Court*, both originally published
by Macmillan of Canada.

First published by Macmillan of Canada,
A Division of Gage Publishing Limited

Published in Penguin Books, 1985

Copyright © 1984 Jack Batten

All rights reserved.

Manufactured in Canada

Canadian Cataloguing in Publication Data
Batten, Jack, 1932-
    Lawyers

ISBN 0-14-007390-6

1. Lawyers – Canada.   I. Title.

KE395.B38 1984   349.71'092'2   C84-098579-7

Except in the United States of America, this book is sold
subject to the condition that it shall not, by way of trade
or otherwise, be lent, re-sold, hired out, or otherwise
circulated without the publisher's prior consent in any
form of binding or cover other than that in which it is
published and without a similar condition including this
condition being imposed on the subsequent purchaser.

For Marjorie, with love

Contents

Contents

Introduction

The documentary television series about Canadian lawyers that the CBC has fashioned, using my books *Lawyers* and *In Court* as part inspiration and part point of departure, began — and almost ended — with a telephone call that I didn't return.

The man who placed the call was Cameron Graham, a CBC-TV public affairs producer, working out of Ottawa, with a lengthy and distinguished record. It was Graham who presided over such documentaries as *The Canadian Establishment* and *The Diefenbaker Years*. Just before Christmas of 1980, he hit on an idea for his next project. It would be a series of programs that examined the legal profession in Canada. He'd arrived at the notion as he was reading *Lawyers,* which had been published a couple of months earlier. The way the book came into his hands was, like everything else in the early days of the project, a piece of happenstance that was almost frighteningly casual. In the fall of 1980, Graham's son entered first year law at Queen's University. As a Christmas gift, he asked his father for a copy of *Lawyers*, a book that chronicled the on-going careers of a number of Canadian lawyers in all the disciplines from corporate law to criminal law. Graham bought the book. He began to wrap it, then decided to take a look at it first. He read, a light went on in his head, and the next day, in the week leading up to Christmas, he put in the telephone call from Ottawa to me in Toronto.

I wasn't home. My son took the message.

"Call a Mr. Graham," he wrote on a piece of paper. "CBC. Ottawa."

"Drat!" I said when I saw my son's note. I'd just

returned from a cross-country tour to promote *Lawyers* and couldn't face the prospect of another radio or television interview, which was what I thought Graham's message heralded.

I didn't return the call. In fact, persisting in rudeness, I didn't return a second message that Graham left with my son a few days later. Not another round of questions about the bloody book!

"I think there's a television series in your book," Graham said on the phone when he finally caught up to me a couple of weeks after Christmas.

"A *series*?!" I said, reaching with my free hand for the smelling salts. "Is *that* what you were calling about?"

"Didn't you get my messages?" Graham asked.

"Out of the country," I mumbled. "Out of my mind."

Over the following year, as I worked with Graham, a consummate gentleman and professional, in preparing an outline for the proposed television series, in speculating on which real-life lawyers would make the best subjects for the cameras, and in watching Graham's CBC-TV unit structure the initial logistics for the programs, I realized, looking back, that my long adventure with the legal profession had more than a dash of near-miss folly about it. I'd almost blundered my way out of the TV series in just the way that I had, in the first place, blundered through the practice of law.

I was called to the Ontario bar in June 1959, and the first time I appeared in court as a lawyer, not long after the call, my client was up on a charge of indecent exposure. He was a short, fat young man with a face that sent out waves of despair. The facts of the case were simple. And damning. He'd had a few beers with his buddies after work and was driving home alone when he noticed a girl, also alone, walking along a dark residential street. He parked his car several yards ahead of her, stood on the sidewalk with his pants unzipped, and, as she drew near, asked, "Do you wanna?"

She didn't.

She ran home and told her father, who returned to the scene of the proposition. My short, fat, sad client had remained in place. His pants had remained unzipped. The father summoned the cops and they hustled my client to jail.

"I'm guilty," he told me when I turned up in the police cells the next day. His mother had retained me early that morning.

"Wait a minute," I said.

"No, no! I don't know what came over me. I deserve what I get."

"Maybe you won't get anything if you listen to me. I'll ask for a remand and work out strategy. That's what your mother's paying me for. We'll plead a blackout or something. Drunkenness. Temporary insanity."

"I'm so ashamed," he said. "I undid my fly in front of that girl. I pulled out my . . . I mean, I exposed myself. I'm disgusting."

"Well, if you put it that way."

The trial lasted five and a half minutes. A policeman recited the facts. I called the mother as a character witness, and she told the court her son was a good boy who stayed home most nights playing pinochle with his father. As far as she knew, he'd never previously unzipped himself except in the privacy of the family bathroom. The magistrate fined my client two hundred dollars, and the last I saw of him, his face a portrait of remorse, he was in the gentle clutches of a Salvation Army officer who felt spiritual guidance was in order. I didn't have the heart to send his mother a bill for my lack of services.

That's more or less how my entire legal career proceeded. It was not so much disastrous as unfortunate. I practised in a Toronto firm that was downtown, medium-sized and — apart from such exceptional clients as the flasher — respectable. I handled mechanics'-liens actions and mortgage foreclosures, drew deeds and probated wills, collected unpaid accounts for a ready-mixed concrete company, and put together articles of incorporation for small businessmen. I didn't distinguish myself and seemed to be headed neither for disbarment nor for the annual list of Queen's Counsel published each New Year's Day in *The Globe and Mail*. Clearly, something about the practice of law eluded me, and in September 1963 I left the profession to make my way in the world writing magazine articles, newspaper reviews, and non-fiction books.

Fourteen years later, on November 26, 1977, fate and a defence counsel took me back to the very courtroom where I'd appeared so ineffectually on behalf of the fat young man. This time I was a witness at a preliminary hearing and, once again, not in sparkling form. The accused person in the case was the stuff of headlines, Keith Richards, guitarist and founding member of the Rolling Stones rock group. RCMP narcotics agents had arrested Richards at the Harbour Castle Hilton Hotel in Toronto and charged him with possession of heroin for the purposes of trafficking, an offence that could get him a long term in prison. Richards' counsel, a leading member of the Canadian criminal bar named Austin Cooper, wanted to demonstrate to the judge at the preliminary hearing that, although his client had been addicted to heroin, he was also gifted, famous, and wealthy, and therefore had no financial need to traffic in the junk. Cooper asked me to provide the testimony about Richards' gifts, fame, and wealth.

I had the qualifications. For five years in the late 1960s and early 1970s, writing first in *The Toronto Star* and later in *The Globe and Mail,* I had reviewed the rock bands that passed through Toronto on concert tours and nightclub dates. Cooper thought the combination I brought to the courtroom of lawyer and rock reviewer, admittedly unique, would impress the judge. Maybe it did. My verbal dexterity as a witness undoubtedly didn't.

Cooper, on examination-in-chief: "How long have the Stones been productive and functioning as a group?"
Batten: "That's probably one of the most remarkable things about them and about Mr. Richards is that rock and roll is a sort of a bit of fly-by-night business and as I observed in all those years of reviewing bands who got to be a sensation one week and then vanished the next week, but the Rolling Stones, unlike so many others, are still with us and still regarded as one of the very best today after sixteen, seventeen years."

The court reporter's transcript, as this exchange conveys, made me sound approximately as articulate on the witness stand as the Watergate Tapes showed Richard Nixon to be in the Oval Office. Still, Keith Richards' day in court had beneficial consequences for me as well as for him. He was eventually found guilty on a lesser offence of simple possession of heroin, and as his punishment — a mere slap on the wrist — he was directed to perform a benefit concert in aid of the Canadian National Institute for the

Blind, which was apparently the judge's favourite charity. Richards was grateful to the court. So, in a different way, was I.

The Richards trial made me think again about the legal profession. I admired the way Cooper handled himself and his case in court. He pointed out to the judge in a low-key and thorough closing argument that Richards had recently cured himself of his drug addiction. He had endured torment. Now he was clean and whole. What need to punish him further? Cooper was cool and resourceful and persuasive, all the things I hadn't been in my defence of the fat flasher. Cooper's style in court suggested to me the marvellous possibilities for a good lawyer in the legal profession. I wondered how I'd missed out on realizing in at least some small way the skills I was supposed to have learned. After all, adding up my time in law school, in articles, and in practice, I had devoted nine years to the profession. But where, in those nine years, had I failed to find a connection with the law and its practice?

I decided to root around for an answer. I would talk to Cooper and several other lawyers, approach barristers and solicitors in all the different fields, ask them questions about their work, follow them into the courtrooms and the boardrooms, discover what makes them tick, find out for myself where they and I had parted ways, them to go on to success in the profession and me into another profession altogether. I thought the answers I found would satisfy the part of my psyche that wondered about the failure in my past.

Besides, I also thought, there might be a book in the small voyage of discovery.

I was wrong.

There were two books.

For the first, *Lawyers,* I found myself peeking into every nook and cranny of the profession and covering much of Canada in looking for answers to my questions. I spent a week in the Northwest Territories with lawyers who struggled to bring order and justice to the Inuit. I hung around the glossy offices of a powerful downtown Toronto corporate firm. I bumped around the back roads of Huron County in southwestern Ontario with a general practitioner who took time away from the problems of his farmer clients to smell the flowers along the way. I passed long hours listening to a Calgary counsel with an outrageous sense of humour and a specialty in medical malpractice cases, who could tell hilarious and ghoulish stories about botched operations and doctors who crumpled on the witness stand. I stuck close to a crown attorney in Whitby, Ontario, as he prepared the case against a boy who had murdered another teenager, a young girl, in the most brutal frenzy of violence. I absorbed stories and legal lore from a lawyer whose clientele was made up of rock bands and other performers, from a lawyer in the Yukon whose practice nudged up against the frontier, and from a counsel in Toronto who went to court for the most vulnerable of all clients — children. I watched them at work, all of these lawyers, listened to them, and wrote down what I saw and heard in a book. That was *Lawyers.*

For the second book, *In Court,* which I worked on while the television series was going through its early filming stages and which the CBC eventually incorporated into the series, I concentrated on one branch of the legal profession. This was a book about the lawyers whose work takes them into the courtrooms — the counsel, the barristers, the most high-profile and colourful of all the people who practise law.

Again I ranged across the country. Again I poked into the various specialties that counsel immerse themselves in. I sat in court while the trial of two young men from Windsor, Ontario, charged with the murder of a police officer, unfolded over four weeks of counsel's cross-examination and argument. I visited veteran criminal lawyers in Vancouver, Winnipeg, and Toronto, and served as a grateful audience for their tales of drama and comedy in the courtroom. I stuck to the heels of a libel law specialist while he sweated through a crisis that might have crippled a leading Canadian publishing house. I recreated a couple of spectacular cases, one involving a suspected Russian spy and the other concerning an injured hockey player who sued his National Hockey League team, by reading each case's voluminous trial transcript and by analysing the testimony and evidence under the guidance of the counsel who won the cases. And I sat across the desk from the greatest of all Canadian trial lawyers, John J. Robinette, and took in his wisdom and reminiscences.

What I learned from the writing of the two books had much less to do with me than with the legal profession in Canada. I never found out why I'd struck out at law. The question that was in my mind as I began the research for *Lawyers* — why hadn't I turned out to be as skilled at law as Austin Cooper? — retreated in significance. Somewhere on the way through my research, I dismissed it. I was too busy discovering happy and exciting new details about the ways in which the law is practised in this country.

Lawyer's work, I recognized in my trips into Canadian law firms and courtrooms, isn't dull stuff. It isn't dry or esoteric or, to meet another charge levelled at lawyers, a necessarily devious business. It is — once past the routine chores of real estate deals, will probates, and the like, the sort of thing I handled in my own brief law career — consuming and wonderfully involving. A complex corporate deal, something that puts millions of dollars on the line, can become a thrilling piece of theatre, a truth that I learned in my weeks of prowling the corridors of Tory, Tory, Des Lauriers & Binnington in Toronto's Royal Bank Tower. A frontier lawyer, a man like Willard Phelps of Whitehorse, leads a life that's nervy and daunting. And when a libel lawyer is summoned into last-minute action, he must expect to spend several consecutive days on a tight rope that someone else has strung for him.

It was the counsel, the lawyers who glory in the courtroom, who offered the most revelations. It occurred to me as I watched dazzling performers like Dave Humphrey of Toronto and Bert Oliver of Vancouver and Harry Walsh of Winnipeg that we Canadians have rarely celebrated our gifted counsel. We read books about Melvin Belli and Louis Nizer and Richard "Racehorse" Haynes, Americans all. We see F. Lee Bailey, another American, on our television screens, and we sit through movies that hail the legend of Clarence Darrow, yet another American giant. But we've permitted few home-grown counsel to lodge themselves in our consciousness.

That's an omission in social history that I hope *In Court* helped to correct. Canadian counsel are as crafty and colourful as their American counterparts, as silver-tongued and spell-binding as the Darrows and Nizers of the U.S. Dave Humphrey can shift gears with the expertise of a Belli. John Robinette has towered over the profession in all of North America. And the others I wrote about rank alongside the acclaimed Americans in persuasive skills — smooth

Bert Oliver, relentless John Laxton, canny Joe Sedgwick.

The television series that Cameron Graham and his CBC-TV associates have put together documents and honours the work of these and other Canadian lawyers. So does this book. It's a compilation of the most representative material from *Lawyers* and *In Court*. All the legal disciplines are covered — not just the glamorous, highly visible counsel but also the corporate lawyers, the frontier practitioners, the family law specialists, the labour lawyers, the crown attorneys, the libel counsel. And they all rate our attention for the ways in which their talent, wit, and flair light up the many worlds of the Canadian lawyer.

CHAPTER ONE

Counsel to the
Last Frontier

On an August Sunday afternoon, Willard Phelps
steered his boat across the water with one hand and
drank red wine out of a tin cup with the other. The
boat was a 165-horse-power Starcraft, its name
painted across the stern: *Whiplash*. The water was
Bennett Lake. Drawn on a map, its shape looks like a
dolphin leaping out of the sea, head ducked down,
tail flying, flippers extended. Bennett Lake is forty-
five miles south of Whitehorse, close to the border
where the Yukon meets British Columbia.

"All those beautiful trees up there, they were
almost gone," Phelps shouted over the buzz of the
Starcraft's engine. He was waving with his right
hand, the one holding the red wine, at the steep,
rocky hills that surrounded the lake. The hills were
covered in pine and spruce, and they gave way to
snowy mountains in the high distance.

"Ottawa was behind it. I came back from law
school ten years ago and found that a big mining
company, Bermuda Resources it was called, had the
rights to cut down all the timber around Bennett and
Atlin and the other lakes in this chain. The decision
came from the bureaucrats in Ottawa, those buggers.
Bermuda could chop down the whole lot and ship it
to Japan. Well, hell, that would've destroyed the
ecology around here. It'd have taken 150 years to
retrieve the soil. Just a horror show. Anyway, fate

intervened. Bermuda went broke in some mining venture or other and never could afford to move into Bennett. We were saved, but God only knows what Ottawa could still visit on us. That kind of thing, worrying about Ottawa, trying to preserve what we've got in the north, getting the right to run our own lives, that means my practice has to suffer. I use my legal training to help fight the battles. It takes time. It sure as hell takes time."

Phelps's roots run almost as deep in the north as history permits. His grandfather, the original Willard Phelps and also a lawyer, arrived in the Yukon from Hamilton, Ontario, in 1898, only a couple of years after George Washington Carmack and his Indians pals, Tagish Charlie and Skookum Joe, found gold at Bonanza Creek and signalled the rush on the Klondike. Willard the First set up practice in Whitehorse. He had a business on the side, running the mail from Whitehorse to Dawson, and he sat in the Territory's Legislative Assembly for twenty-two years. He was part of Yukon history. He used to tell about the early days of Whitehorse, about sitting around in the school principal's log cabin exchanging lies with the fellow who worked at the Bank of Commerce. The bank clerk's name was Robert Service.

"My dad didn't follow grandfather into law. Engineering instead," Phelps said, drinking wine in the middle of Bennett Lake, not another boat moving on the horizon. "Dad learned to hunt and fish up here with the Indians, and when I was old enough, in the 1940s and early '50s, just growing up, he passed on what he learned to me. Those years when I was young were the years that broke the Indians in the Yukon. It was never the gold rush that hurt them. Nor the Alaska Highway. It was when the world fur market went belly-up around 1950. The Indians depended on furs for their living. The market collapsed, and the federal government came along to move the Indians out of the bush and into settlements. That was for the government's convenience. Made it easier to hand out the welfare cheques. But it was devastating to the Indians' pride."

Phelps turned the boat in a wide arc to the right and headed down a bay, a part of Bennett Lake that shows up on maps as one of the dolphin's extended flippers.

"The Indian kids I grew up with, people that are in their early forties or younger now, they were the first Indians to get criminal records in the Yukon. They were the first who were taken away from the traditional ways, from the forest, and they started drinking and getting in trouble with the law. I've acted for lots of them. Legal-aid work. Pitiful. The older Indians are honest people and well-balanced people, and then you get their children, my generation, and all of them have criminal records that are horrible. What's a lawyer supposed to do?"

Phelps circled out of the bay and across the lake to the dock in Carcross where he keeps his boat. Carcross is tiny and storied. Its name is a piece of shorthand for Caribou Crossing, and its proudest landmark is a cairn that celebrates the driving of the last spike in the White Pass and Yukon Railroad on July 29, 1900. The railroad took twenty-six months to build, 110 miles of it, from Skagway, the Alaska seaport, to Whitehorse, and it provided transportation for the thousands of dreamers who flocked in to pan a fortune in the Klondike. Carcross saw plenty of traffic in its earliest days.

"Biggest disappointment in my life was when that thing stopped running," Phelps said, pointing at a huge and dilapidated stern-wheel riverboat that rested at a tilt, high and dry and forlorn, on the Carcross beach. "The *Tutshi*. It ran up and down these lakes for half a century. You had to be fifteen to work on it in the summers. All my friends had their turn. I was waiting for mine and the summer I was fifteen, 1956, they took her out of service. Broke my heart."

As Phelps spoke, a train pulled through town. The White Pass and Yukon still operates, lugging tourists and small freight from Skagway to Whitehorse. The train looked cute and miniature, like something Jesse James might hold up in a Republic Pictures movie. Phelps led the way past the Caribou Hotel, built in 1911, and Watson's General Store, where they offer gold pans for sale. Beyond the post office and around the corner, he opened the door to the log cabin that has been in the family since Phelps's grandfather bought it in 1917.

"I have close ties to this land," he said, plunked in a big stuffed chair in the cabin's cluttered main room. He looked the part of a man of the north. Phelps wears a beard that's clipped like a shadow on his face. He's lean and dead-panned in the style of a hunter who'd have no trouble sneaking up on a moose, and his hands, not like any city lawyer's, are rough and scarred, the hands of someone who's baited his share of fishing lines.

He spoke a little of his history. Growing up in Whitehorse and Carcross. Leaving for the University of British Columbia where he took honours in philosophy and economics. Spending a few months working on a master's degree in philosophy at the University of Toronto. Rejecting it in favour of law at UBC. Getting called to the bar.

"I came back to Whitehorse and set up my practice," he said, sipping at the wine left over from the boat ride. "It wasn't easy to get established. I used to sit in my office on the second floor listening for footsteps on the stairs. The first four or five files I handled, I didn't get paid a nickel. It was work for the local ne'er-do-wells who dropped by my office really just for the company.

"The secret to getting started in Whitehorse is to win a few trials. That generates publicity. The thing is, Whitehorse has two daily papers, one weekly, a private radio station, and a private TV station. That's a lot for 14,000 people, and reporters'll look anywhere for a story. They love to give trials a big play. My chance came. My first criminal case. It was down in Atlin and my client was charged with buggery. I drove down with the crown attorney and I only had one question for him. "If I win this case, who's gonna drive the guy back to Whitehorse?" Well, I won, and the problem of transportation was taken care of because the guy turned out to be an escaped convict and they shipped him back east. But the trial got a lot of media coverage, people heard about me, and the business started to roll in. Corporate stuff for the companies that come up here to dig mines. Drawing contracts. Handling the disputes that the contracts sometimes produced. Court work. Enough of everything."

At the same time Phelps pitched in to community activities. He was elected to the Legislative Assembly for one term. He acted for the territorial government in negotiating Indian land claims. He helped organize the Progressive Conservative party in the Yukon ("there's a backlash up here against the Liberals because everybody associates them with the Ottawa bureaucracy that's done us in"). And he was one of three members of the Lysyk Commission. It held hearings throughout the Yukon in 1977. It visited seventeen communities and accumulated 750 pages of testimony. Its subject was natural gas, and finally, after all the visiting and the testimony, it came out in favour of constructing a pipeline to carry the gas from Prudhoe Bay in the north to the United States in the south by way of the Alaska Highway route. Phelps figures the Lysyk Commission contributed mightily to the Yukon's future.

"After I got out of law school," he said, working on the last cup of wine, "I could've stayed and practised down in Vancouver. But I looked around and realized that ninety per cent of my friends in the city were lawyers. That wasn't the way I grew up. I grew up with Indians and woodsmen and tough old ladies who made their living out of hunting and trapping. All sorts of odd ducks and real people. So I came back here. I didn't want to live an insular existence, and in the Yukon you're really no good as a lawyer unless you get out and mess around in the community with the rest of the characters. When I think about it now, I'm not sure whether I turned out to be a lawyer who hunts and fishes or a hunter and fisherman who happens to practise law."

He drained his wine cup.

"Doesn't make a hell of a lot of difference."

* * *

You can't miss the new courthouse in Yellowknife. It looks like a Brobdingnagian sardine can. It's six storeys tall, a skyscraper by Northwest Territories standards, and wrapped from street to roof in silver-colour aluminium. It glints and flashes in the sun and reflects light beams across the rest of drab downtown Yellowknife. According to one local lawyer, it was built this way, visually unmistakable, so that the Inuit and the Indians who are its most frequent customers wouldn't have any trouble locating the place.

Inside, the courthouse runs to a warmer look. The prevailing motif in décor, not surprisingly, is Eskimo Traditional. Tiles depicting Eskimo domestic scenes cover a large pillar in the centre of the building. Banners of jolly Inuit figures hang in the courtrooms. And inside a long glass display case against one wall of the lobby on the second floor, a series of small but commanding Eskimo carvings recreates significant trials from the Territories' judicial past.

One trial required three carvings of tiny, grim figures in parkas. The first shows a man with a rifle shooting another man in the back. In the second, a woman is stabbing the killer in the chest. And in the third, two children lie stricken on the ice. Beside the stark carvings, a printed card tells the story of the little figures.

Kikkik. Tried at Rankin Inlet on April 4, 1958. Half brother of accused killed Kikkik's husband, Hallow. Kikkik then killed the half brother and then out of food struck across the barrens in winter for help. Abandoned two smallest children in igloo. Charged with murder and with abandoning one child and criminal negligence in respect to one child who died. Not guilty in each case. Offences near Henik Lake.

"Those legal cases out there in the carvings," Jim Slaven explained, "you might say they're what got the law started in the north. Judge Jack Sissons heard them all. He was the first judge up here, appointed in 1955, and he was the guy who said we're gonna take the law to every man's door. He meant every Eskimo's door, and he put the court on the circuit, flying out of Yellowknife every month or so for a few days or a couple of weeks, as long as it took to hold trials in a bunch of communities distributed the hell and gone across the Arctic. He started it, Sissons, and we've still got the circuit with us to this day."

As he spoke, Jim Slaven sat chain-smoking in his office at the rear of the second floor of the courthouse. He's a hefty man in his early fifties, round face, short black hair brushed back from his forehead, spectacles, and a manner that's open and welcoming. Since 1974 he's been a Territorial Court judge, the equivalent of a Provincial Court judge in the rest of Canada, and he knows everything about that unique N.W.T. institution, the circuit.

"I put in about 40,000 miles a year flying around the Territories," Slaven said. "But it isn't the miles that wear you down. It's the hours. The planes are so damned slow. We fly in a Twin Otter or a DC-3, one of those old makes of plane, and by the time the court party piles on — the judge, court clerk, court reporter, crown counsel, and defence counsel, plus all our robes and typewriters and food and cases of beer — we're lucky if that plane gets up to eighty miles an hour. We're lucky if it gets eighty feet off the ground."

The circuit splits into two basic trips. One takes the court north from Yellowknife to the Mackenzie Delta, into Inuvik and its suburbs. The other is to the east, 1,300 miles to Frobisher Bay on Baffin Island, then around the Eastern Arctic. In all, the travelling court dishes out justice to Territories citizens spread over 1.3 million square miles. Most of those miles are forest, lakes, and tundra, but one hundred or more communities are tucked into the wilderness, home to 43,000 people. About 14,000 are Inuit, another 12,000 are of Indian ancestry, the rest are white, and slightly more than 10,000 of the 43,000 live in Yellowknife, the N.W.T. capital, 600 air miles north of Edmonton. But it's the people outside the metropolis who keep the circuit in operation.

"For the way the law is administered up here," Judge Slaven said, "you have to learn how to husband your energies. It's cold in those planes, forty-five below in winter, colder inside the plane than outside. And when you get where you're going, you can't count on a hot meal, not even a cup of coffee. Sardines and crackers. Sometimes I hold court in a schoolroom in some tiny dot of a place on the map of the Arctic on nothing but some sardines and crackers all day. *Day?* In winter, there isn't any day. Just twenty-four hours of darkness."

Judge Slaven shook his head at the wonder of it all.

"When I know there's a grind ahead," he said, "I don't take a drink."

He shook his head again. "Amazing," he said.

What's amazing is that under such hectic, even primitive, conditions, the system, in one strange way or another, seems to generate justice.

"Sure it works," Slaven said, and by way of illustration he proceeded to tell the story of the sad and troubled young man of Rankin Inlet.

Like several other northern communities, Rankin Inlet is an artificial invention. It sits on the west shore of Hudson Bay several hundred miles north of the Manitoba border, and until the early 1950s it existed only for a couple of dozen Inuit. Its isolation ended when nickel was discovered in the area, and by 1957 North Rankin Nickel Mines Limited was in business. The mine recruited Eskimos from camps and communities for hundreds of miles across the land west of Hudson Bay. They were people of different backgrounds, styles, cultures, and languages. They worked at the mine, thereby pushing the population of Rankin Inlet from almost scratch to over 1,000, until the nickel ran out in 1962. Many of the Inuit returned to their old home grounds, but a few hundred stayed on in Rankin, living off hunting, fishing, and government relief payments. The community floundered for years until Rankin was designated the regional headquarters for the N.W.T. District of Keewatin. That made it a minor centre for local government, transportation, and communications. New jobs turned up, many Inuit freed themselves from relief, and the population climbed back to almost 1,000.

Then, one shocking day in 1978, much of Rankin was burned to the ground. The damage added up to several million dollars. Arson, everybody recognized, and it didn't call for intensive police work to nail the arsonist. He was a young Inuit, mentally retarded. He was arrested, charged, and held for Judge Slaven.

The court party arrived in Rankin by plane from Yellowknife at noon on the trial date. It was an autumn day in 1978 and Judge Slaven was ready to proceed. But a group of Rankin people — Inuit — asked him to delay proceedings. They were calling a community meeting to talk about the young man and his fate.

"It was the first time such a thing had happened in Rankin," the judge said, "the first time the local people had ever sat down together. You see, coming from all various backgrounds the way they had, different strains of Eskimo, they'd never merged as a real community. There was a professor up there, fellow named Williamson from the University of Saskatchewan, who'd been going to Rankin every summer for eighteen years, and he said this was the old traditional Inuit way of doing things, meeting together and looking after their own. Well, hell, under those circumstances the court was pleased to stand aside for a few hours. That might sound ridiculous to a judge in the south, but northern justice is different.''

The Inuit met and the judged waited. "Had some sandwiches and cold coffee for dinner," he said. "My wife was along because it was our wedding anniversary. I told her, 'You can't say I didn't take you out for dinner on our anniversary.' "

The meeting broke up and Judge Slaven convened court. He took a guilty plea from the young man's lawyer and then listened to nine Rankin people testify, representatives chosen at the meeting. They talked of the young man's problems and his character and his family, of their wishes to care for him, to find him a job, to ease his troubles. Judge Slaven sat into the night. The witnesses' testimony was translated from Inuit into English and his comments and questions were translated from English into Inuit. The judge waited.

"Once I had to stop the trial and send for the local nurse," the judge said. "It was the boy. He was picking at scabs on his arm. They started to bleed."

The testimony ended and Judge Slaven announced his verdict. Arson calls for a jail term. No jail term, Judge Slaven told the court. Instead, probation. He put the young man in the care of the community.

"Down south," he said, "that'd raise a few eyebrows."

LAWYERS

It was past midnight when the court party climbed on the plane to fly home to Yellowknife.

"You get better justice in the north," Judge Slaven said, lighting up another cigarette in his office at the Yellowknife Courthouse. "Look, when we go on the circuit and land at Pangnirtung or Whale Cove or Tuktoyaktuk or one of those remote spots, the defence counsel along on the trip is going to be seeing his clients for the first time. Maybe a fellow's charged with something serious — rape, or even murder — and people might think, well, hell, how's that lawyer gonna give his client a decent defence on such short notice? Easy, I say."

The judge leaned back in his chair and ticked off his reasons. "Number one, the defence counsel has more concentrated time with his client. No phones ring on the circuit. Nobody has to keep office hours. The client probably ends up with more attention from his lawyer than he'd get in Toronto. Number two, the crown attorney up here shares his whole file with the defence, which is something pretty damned unique to the north. The defence doesn't have to worry about the most remote sort of surprise. And number three, if the accused person objects, says he hasn't had enough time to consult his lawyer, I say, okay, take your time, we'll wait till tomorrow or the next day."

Judge Slaven let out a long stream of cigarette smoke. "Down south," he said, "the courts are like sausage factories, cranking out the cases. Up here, we take our time. Hell, why not? There's no place special anybody's going."

The Mackenzie Valley Pipeline Inquiry, better known as the Berger Inquiry after its commissioner, Mr. Justice Tom Berger of the British Columbia

Supreme Court, began its hearings in a large public room at the Explorer Hotel in Yellowknife on March 3, 1975. Its mandate was to look into the engineering and construction of a proposed Arctic gas pipeline and to measure the impact of such a pipeline on the human, physical, and living environment of the north. The pipeline, according to plans proposed in 1975 by Canadian Arctic Gas Pipelines Limited, one of the two companies competing for the job (Foothills Pipe Lines Limited was the other), would run about 2,600 miles from Prudhoe Bay north of Alaska across the top of the Yukon and up the Mackenzie Valley to markets in the south. It would cost seven billion dollars to build, making it the largest free-enterprise development ever attempted anywhere in the world. Mr. Justice Berger spent a year and a half listening to witnesses debate the pipeline's merits. He ended up with 32,353 pages of testimony from formal hearings. He travelled into thirty-five communities in the Northwest Territories and the Yukon to hear the views of local residents, and their words added up to another 8,438 pages of testimony. When all the talk was finished, Mr. Justice Berger wrote his report to the federal government. It was dated April 15, 1977, and it recommended that, in order to protect birds, whales, and other wildlife, no pipeline should be built through the Mackenzie Delta and that the construction of any pipeline through the Mackenzie Valley should be postponed for ten years, enough time to settle the claims of native peoples to compensation for their lands and enough time to develop an orderly program for the building of the pipeline.

The years of the Berger Inquiry were years for lawyers to shine. "Other than the Indian people themselves," says Doug Sanders, a professor at the

University of British Columbia law school who concerns himself with the north, "lawyers were the most visible actors in the inquiry." The motives of some of the inquiry lawyers might have been mixed. Work for native peoples, for one motive, carries with it a decided cachet. Professor Sanders thinks it has done so for a couple of decades.

"Indian work has never been disreputable," he says. "A lawyer told me in 1973 that he was doing work at cost for one of the Indian organizations because he wanted a judgeship. He thought it would look good on his record. Indian work today is probably more respectable than work for labour unions."

Then, too, many of the lawyers who appeared before Mr. Justice Berger were southerners from big firms in Toronto and Calgary. To carry the burden of its argument, Canadian Arctic Gas Pipelines turned to Pierre Genest, a prominent counsel at Cassels, Brock in Toronto and a dedicated Liberal party backroom boy. The four counsel to the commission itself came from another Toronto firm, Cameron, Brewin and Scott, where the politics, like those of Mr. Justice Berger, who was a New Democrat MP and a leader of British Columbia's NDP before his appointment to the bench in December 1971, tend to be socialist. These lawyers, outsiders to the Territories, exerted a significant influence on the inquiry — and therefore on the north — and the north reciprocated in kind.

"I spent two winters with the inquiry," says Stephen Goudge, a slim, clean-lined, intense young lawyer from the Cameron, Brewin firm, "and when I came away, I realized what a constraint the environment has on every part of your life up there, physical, mental, social, all kinds of ways. At one point, I went into Inuvik for three weeks in winter, and for three weeks there was no sun. None. It's amazing the impact that has on your psychology. I came out of there and I flew straight to Florida."

But Goudge feels the experience left him with an enormous admiration for the lawyers who practise year round in the north.

"They're dealing with problems in an area that is really the country's last frontier," he says. "There's a reordering of relationships going on between white people and native peoples up there. It's a social problem, but many of the materials they have at hand to deal with the reordering are legal tools. So lawyers are deeply involved in the crucial changes in the north, and from what I saw of them at the Berger Inquiry, they're special people."

John Bayly, for instance. He's a lawyer in Yellowknife, a crown attorney now, but during the inquiry he appeared as one of the counsel for COPE — the Committee for Original People's Entitlement — representing Inuit from several communities in the Mackenzie Valley.

"I led all the evidence for COPE at the inquiry," Bayly says, "and I handled all its cross-examination of witnesses. I knew the evidence better than anybody except Berger."

When Bayly speaks that way, as he frequently does, it's not out of conceit but out of passion. He cares about the north and about the people who'd been living off its hard land for thousands of years before the white man began dropping in. Bayly's love of the Territories sneaks out in quiet ways. He's a phlegmatic man, dark and lightly bearded, in his mid-thirties, and he seems to enclose himself forever in pools of calm. But when he talks in his studied, level way, his concern for the north gradually becomes irresistible. He isn't one of the lawyers whom Professor Doug Sanders speaks of, the cynics who take on native clients as a career booster. Bayly cares.

"A story," he might say. "In the north, among the native people, no one knocks on doors. You walk into the house and you sit down. Nobody makes a fuss about it. Certainly not the people whose house it is. Perhaps they may not speak to you immediately or perhaps they'll pour you a cup of coffee right away or hand you a beer. It doesn't matter. All right, suppose in a community like that, where all the doors are open, a fellow walks into someone's house and nobody's at home and he sees a dollar bill or a bottle of beer and that he takes it away with him. Technically that's breaking and entering, which is a serious crime with a stiff sentence. But, as a crown attorney, I instruct the police not to lay such a heavy charge. Treat it as simple theft. Call it unlawfully in a dwelling house. The point is to be aware of the difference in cultures up here. White people may not approve of friends and strangers walking uninvited into their houses, but Inuit welcome it. And we can't permit the white man's law to intrude on such a charming custom."

Bayly's background makes him an unlikely candidate for the role of passionate spokesman for ancient northern ways. He grew up in southern Ontario. His father was a deputy minister in the provincial government, and young John attended private schools — Upper Canada College and Trinity College Schools. Before his call to the bar he articled with a large downtown Toronto firm, and after his call he spent nine months as a crown attorney in Thunder Bay, Ontario.

All along, though, he carried on a romance with the far north. He worked at a federal government job in Rankin Inlet for six months in 1967. In 1972 he took a canoe trip from Great Slave Lake to the Arctic and back. "I'm an outdoors jock," he says. "I like to paddle my canoe in the summer and run behind my sled and dogs in the winter." In the winter of 1974 he decided to test his affection for the north. He joined a private practice in Yellowknife.

"I got called to the Territories bar at 8:30 on the morning of January 21," he remembers, "and by nine I was on a plane to Inuvik. It was my first circuit. It didn't pay much. The circuit never does for a defence lawyer. It's all legal-aid work. You do it because it's fun."

And there are other quaint compensations.

"I'd arrive in a community and people would be at my door. Would I draw a will? Could I take a divorce case? Fix up a partnership agreement? There's always business on the side, and I'd get paid in odd ways. A free hotel room. A pair of snowshoes. Some Eskimo carvings. I'd come home with my pockets full of trinkets. For me, that's the north."

Bayly Burrows is the north, too. It is, as the sign at the side of the road leading into the property proclaims, the Bayly homestead. It lies a few minutes north of Yellowknife near the road that turns off to Giant Mine, one of the two gold mines — Cominco at the south end of town is the other — that are among Yellowknife's major employers. The Burrows takes up a couple of acres of sloping land, enough for a summer vegetable garden, for a large pen to enclose eight sled dogs, for an area to let the three Bayly kids romp around in, and enough for the small house that snuggles up to Back Bay, a gracious body of water that eventually leads into Great Slave Lake down around the corner to the south.

"COPE consumed my life for as long as the Berger Inquiry went on," Bayly said late one summer afternoon, sitting back in a stuffed chair in the living-room of the house, sipping cups of tea, utterly at ease amid the jumble of books, toys, and Eskimo artifacts. "It was a strong little grass-roots movement, and it knew how to confront the government from past battles it had with oil companies. COPE's idea was to take the pipeline application and go into the communities and explain to the people what its coming would mean to them and to the land. These native people weren't simple. Some of them had worked on oil rigs and understood the stakes. But they were naive in the sense that they thought that if the pipeline went through, they could pull their skidoos up to its stations and fill them with gas."

COPE went into communities spread over 4,500 square miles. It assembled teams of Eskimo field workers and white consultants — biologists, sociologists, geographers, lawyers — and visited each house in each community. The visitors documented the native people's experiences and reactions. Then they returned to each house in each community a second time. No resident was left untouched by COPE's researchers. Bayly and his fellow experts prepared COPE's brief for Mr. Justice Berger and then went back a third time to the communities to search out residents who would testify before the inquiry, bringing to immediate life the information that Bayly and the others packed into the brief.

"The pipeline," Richard Nerysoo of Fort McPherson near the Mackenzie Delta told Mr. Justice Berger, "means more white people who will be followed by even more white people. White people bring their own language, their own political system, their economy, their schools, their culture. They push the Indian aside and take everything.''

"Another thing I accomplished," Bayly said over his tea, "I got Berger to go with the inquiry into Inuvik for two months so he could see how hard it is to work in the cold and dark of the winter. People do silly things in those conditions, and the lawyers from the inquiry were no different. They did silly things. Bickering. Arguing. Pointless disputing. I protected myself. I took my family in for the two months."

When the Berger Inquiry ended, Bayly left COPE to return briefly to private practice and then to join the Attorney General's office as a crown prosecutor. He did not take a gung-ho spirit into his new job; in fact he carefully avoided the role of a crusader bent on ridding his bailiwick of all crime. This attitude, he thinks, found its beginnings on the day he spent in court in Tuktoyaktuk. He was working with the Berger Inquiry at the time, had a couple of free hours, and, since the court happened to be sitting in Tuk, he went by to absorb the litigious atmosphere.

"I was dismayed at how little the community was affected by the comings and goings of the court party," he explained. "It isn't a scandal in the Territories to be called to face a court. It's just something you have to go through at a certain stage of your life. It's part of the white man's way of doing things. I remember the judge made a speech to the court about the seriousness of some crime or other, about a sentence he was passing. The lawyers listened, and the police and the court officials listened, but the community people didn't think it was terribly important that some of them must go to jail or bear a criminal record. So when I came back from working with COPE, I asked myself, where's the great social significance of what I'm doing?"

One episode in the courtroom at Tuktoyaktuk left its mark on Bayly. "The main case that the community was concerned about was a bootlegging charge. This man had come into Tuk with bottles of whiskey and sold them at thirty dollars apiece. He pleaded guilty and was fined fifty dollars. The community was very upset at the lenience because they were trying to keep liquor away from the young people. They hated bootleggers but somehow the court was oblivious to the feeling in the community."

These days, as a crown attorney, Bayly comes down hard on bootleggers. "I try to send them to jail." On the other hand, he's soft on nuisance crimes, on crimes that, in his view of northern life, arise out of Inuit customs, out of, for example, their aversion to locks on the doors of their houses.

"The RCMP doesn't always understand what I mean," Bayly said, sipping at yet another cup of tea in the casual, throw-away comfort of his living-room. "You see, the policeman has changed up here. It used to be that the Mountie was the guy who went out fishing and hunting with the people. He gave the Eskimos' dogs their needles. He spoke the language. Now the RCMP doesn't even have any dogs of its own. Men aren't allowed to volunteer for service in the north. They're assigned here as part of their tour of duty, and if one of them develops an affection for the place, he's assigned somewhere else in a hurry. Can't let the police get too friendly with the natives."

Bayly shifted in his chair. "I'm in the middle between the police and the court. The way I see my job, it's to make sense of a situation before the judge gets into the picture. If there's a serious crime — murder or rape — I start the machinery turning. But for cases that I think are essentially frivolous, I'll stay proceedings or ignore the situation altogether or say to the RCMP officer who's laid the charge, look, just go back and tell the guy not to do it again. I mean, why should the court and all its apparatus charge off a thousand miles to prosecute someone for allowing dogs to run at large? All it takes is common sense to apply the criminal law to the north."

Bayly walked slowly across the living-room to the long windows at the back. On one side of the room his small son lay stomach down in a playpen, stretching a shaky arm at a dangling string of coloured beads. On the other side his wife sat with her teacup under a reproduction, unframed and Scotch-taped to the wall, of an Andrew Wyeth painting, *Christina's Way*. Bayly looked straight ahead, across Back Bay. The water was flat, without a ripple, and the land beyond it was scarcely less level. Only a few scattered spruce poked against the horizon. There were no boats in sight, no people, no movement, no disturbance. The view stretched to eternity.

"What's up here," Bayly said, "the land and the people and the culture, they're all worth preserving. And preserving is part of a lawyer's work."

Judge Slaven leaned his head and shoulders into his courtroom, the Territorial Court on the second floor of the Yellowknife Courthouse, from the side door, the judges' entrance.

"Greyeyes?" he asked of any one of those scattered through the room — court clerk, court reporter, crown attorney, a couple of defence counsel, a half-dozen others in the public seats. "Greyeyes shown up yet?"

The crown attorney spoke. "Nothing." He was a young man in a tan suit and he didn't bother to stand up from his chair. "No Greyeyes, your honour, and no word."

21

The judge grunted around the cigarette in his mouth and disappeared back into his office. He looked half-dressed, wearing his vest and dickey but no gown. Judge Slaven doesn't run a tight ship.

"This Greyeyes," he said, settled behind his desk, "he got banged up pretty bad in some kind of hullabaloo with one of the guys out there in the courtroom, the accused. He's charged with assaulting Greyeyes, but the crown's got no case unless Greyeyes shows up to testify against him. The really complicating factor is that Greyeyes has a civil claim in the works for money to get himself fixed up. He looks something fierce, I understand, but his civil claim may go down the drain if the guy out there isn't convicted on the criminal charge. I'm not supposed to stick my nose in all of this, but dammit, I'm sending a search party out for Greyeyes."

In the courtroom next door, the Supreme Court, Mr. Justice Calvin Tallis was listening to a witness, a smartly dressed, handsome white man in his late twenties, who delivered his testimony in sentences that rose at the end to question marks.

"So Napatchie had the baby, Patrick, in her arms sitting in the passenger seat of the truck? And on the way to the airport, I was driving, and she opened the door as if she was going to jump out and harm herself and Patrick, and I had to keep one hand on the wheel and grab her back with the other? We were right at the corner where Yellowknife Motors is, going thirty miles an hour?"

It was a custody case. Robert Fitzgerald, the handsome witness, and Napatchie Sagiaktook, an Inuit woman from the Eastern Arctic, had been lovers. On March 17, 1977, a child was born, Patrick, but the couple's relationship soured. Fitzgerald worked long hours, establishing his own carpet business in

Yellowknife, and Napatchie, feeling abandoned, threatened to kill herself. Fitzgerald allowed her to leave Yellowknife to return to her people in Frobisher Bay, taking Patrick with her. A few weeks went by, and Napatchie phoned Fitzgerald. She had a new boyfriend. He didn't want Patrick. She was going to give the baby to another family.

"What did you do when you got the phone call?" Fitzgerald's lawyer asked him. The lawyer's name was Susan Green, a pretty, long-haired, blonde woman wearing large tinted glasses, wide brown pants, high-heeled sandals, and a black gown. "How did you react to the call?"

"I flew to Frobisher and had supper with Napatchie's family at their house? It was crowded, thirteen people and two puppies in three bedrooms, and when I left, I brought Patrick with me?"

Napatchie Sagiaktook sat across the courtroom with her lawyer. She was a short, chunky woman. Her black hair was pulled tightly back. Her face, broad and flat, was sinking into itself in the centre. When she smiled, her mouth became a small scar.

"Once," Fitzgerald told the court, "Napatchie swallowed half a bottle of aspirin?"

In his office Judge Slaven put on his gown, and the court clerk called the Territorial Court to order.

"I've got partly to the bottom of this," the judge said, speaking directly to the crown attorney. "A woman who used to be one of our court reporters, native woman, seems to have told Greyeyes that it wasn't necessary for him to appear today. Don't know where she got the notion, but Greyeyes has gone into the bush."

He shifted his attention to a man sitting in the public benches. "George," the judge said. The man stood up, a black man as tall as a basketball centre, erect and dapper and poker-faced. "George, you're acting for Greyeyes on the civil end. See if you can track him down, and in the meantime I'm adjourning for another half-hour."

Robert Fitzgerald's wife testified in Mr. Justice Tallis's courtroom. She was a schoolteacher, a composed and proper woman. She'd married Fitzgerald a few months earlier. She put Patrick in a day-care centre each school day, she said, answering Susan Green's questions, and she and Robert spent the evenings and weekends playing with the boy.

"Patrick especially likes outdoor games," she said.

Napatchie nodded slowly in a motion that seemed as ancient as the north.

Judge Slaven was on the phone. "Well, George, if he can't come out of the bush, that's the end of it. The accused's from outside, as you know, Edmonton or some place, and I can't drag him back up here again for the trial, all that expense." He paused to listen. "I worry about Greyeyes, too, George." He hung up and let out a soft moan.

Mr. Justice Tallis adjourned the custody case to Frobisher Bay at a date five weeks later. Napatchie, her lawyer told the court, was also recently married. Her husband, a Hudson's Bay store manager at Wakeham Bay in Northern Quebec, couldn't afford to fly all the miles and hours to Yellowknife. Frobisher, a ninety-minute flight from Wakeham Bay, was more convenient. The husband wanted to testify that he and Napatchie could make a good home for Patrick if they were awarded custody of the boy.

"That's the court's policy," Susan Green told the Fitzgeralds after Mr. Justice Tallis had left the courtroom. "The court travels to the witnesses instead of making them come to it."

Judge Slaven's court was again called to order.

"Greyeyes," the judge said, "has got a job in the bush. George Carter spoke to his employers and they'll fly him out if that's what he wants, but there's no telling whether he'll still have the job when he goes back. So he'd better stay put."

The judge looked at the crown attorney. "What does the crown have to say?"

"The crown is offering no evidence in this matter, your honour."

"Very well. The crown offering no evidence, the charge is dismissed."

Judge Slaven banged his gavel and whisked out of his chair in one swift, practised motion.

"You can't help it up here," he said, back in his office. "There's bound to be some collision between the whites' and the native peoples' cultures. The industrial system coming into the north and all the rest of it, the liquor, and now the Montreal drug dealers are doing their business over in Frobisher. How're Indians and Eskimos supposed to cope with that? How's an ordinary fella like Greyeyes supposed to figure out what the courts are trying to do for him? Bound to be collisions."

Mr. Justice Tallis's court flew to Frobisher Bay and sprang a surprise. The judge was impressed with Napatchie Sagiaktook's husband and his testimony. He thought that Napatchie and her husband were fit parents for her young son, that they should have a chance to raise him. Custody of the boy, Patrick, Mr. Justice Tallis announced, was awarded to his mother.

As for Greyeyes, he vanished into the bush.

Judge Jack Sissons' work and reputation are in the process of being shredded. It was Sissons, appointed the first judge in the Territories on July 1, 1955, who handed down the original body of judicial decisions that attempted to adapt the white man's laws to keep alive the customs and culture of the northern people. Sissons, a stubborn, independent Scots-Canadian, was moved by an immediate affection he found in himself for the Inuit. "Eskimos," he wrote in his memoirs, "have as much promise for Canada as Scots have had for the rest of the world." And during his eleven years on the Territories bench he was partly successful in his campaign to preserve the Inuit way of life. But in recent years other lawyers and judges and civil servants have begun to rethink his decisions, and Judge Sissons, now dead, is a man whose proudest monuments are being torn down.

"What's happening with Sissons' laws," John Bayly says, "reflects the changes in attitudes to the people up here. Sissons was famous because he bent the rules to fit the northern situation. Now we're trying to pretend that the north is no different from the rest of Canada."

Sissons was a lawyer and judge from the Peace River country of Alberta. He was a Presbyterian and a Liberal. He walked with a limp from a childhood attack of polio, and he rejoiced in his mother's family relationship — cousins — with David Livingstone, the African explorer. When the federal government asked him to take over the Territorial Court he was sixty-three years old. He said he welcomed the adventure.

From the beginning, Sissons announced that his would be a travelling court, taking justice to the people, and from the beginning, too, he showed his compassion for the Inuit he encountered on the circuits.

Kikkik, the woman whose ordeal is charted in the small carvings on display at the Yellowknife Courthouse, felt Sissons' compassion. At an isolated winter camp near Henik Lake in the Eastern Arctic, Kikkik's half-brother shot her husband dead. Terrified, Kikkik stabbed the half-brother and set off with her five children for a Hudson's Bay Company post twenty miles across the tundra. Partway on the journey, out of food and moving too slowly, she left the two smallest children under caribou skins and an improvised shelter of blocks of ice. She reached the post, but five days later when she returned to the makeshift igloo, the youngest child was dead. Kikkik was charged with murder, criminal negligence, and abandoning a child.

"Justice," Judge Sissons said in his address to the jury at Kikkik's trial, "demands that we revert in our thinking to an earlier age and try to understand Kikkik and her life and her land and her society."

He suggested to the jury it might find that Kikkik had acted in self-defence and in defence of her children.

The jury's verdict: not guilty on all charges.

So it went with Judge Sissons. In the case of Noah, he held that marriage by Eskimo custom, without ceremony or legal sanction, was still valid in Canadian law. In the case of Kolitalik, he found that three men, Amah and Avinga and Nangmalik, had, as charged, assisted the old and sick chief of a camp of fine Inuit hunters on Igloolik, an island off the northeast coast of Melville Island, to commit suicide, but he suspended sentence against the three because, he told the court, he had no wish to break up such a splendid community. And in the cases of Jimmy Kogogolak and Michael Sikyea and Matthew Koonungnak and Francis Kallooar, he held that the

27

Inuit and the Indians are not subject to the hunting ordinances which restrict white men and that their ancient rights to hunt and fish for food remain unbounded.

The judgments in the hunting cases began the reaction against Sissons. "Crackpot law," David Searle says of the judgments. Searle is entitled to his opinion, since he had a close-up view of Sissons in action. He served as the Territories' crown attorney for five years, 1962 through 1966, when the judge was blazing his trail of controversial decisions.

"Sissons was a hard guy to be in daily contact with out on the circuit," Searle remembers. "He was forever taking reporters along — Farley Mowat, people from *Life*, a reporter from the *Globe and Mail*. He'd play to the media, and he'd trample all over established law to make himself the protector of the Eskimos."

These days, Searle is the senior partner in the biggest law firm in the Territories. It's called Searle, Richard and Kingsmill, and it practises out of smart offices in the Gallery Building on Franklin Avenue, Yellowknife's main drag. Searle handles a big load of corporate and commercial work on behalf of the mining and development companies that are moving into the north. He appeared for the Northwest Territories Chamber of Commerce at the Berger Inquiry, and he's a director of Pacific Western Airlines. Searle is as visible and as influential as a lawyer can get in the Territories.

"Oh, but I still take a couple of capital cases every year," he says. "The life on the circuit gets into your blood no matter what nonsense you have to put up with."

He laughs. He's a hearty laugher. He's a large, convivial man in his mid-forties. He's restless. He prowls the room when he talks, and when he reaches the punch lines of his stories, he hovers over his listener waiting for the reaction. Then he laughs.

"Sissons used to load the dice against the crown," Searle says. "He'd look through the reports from justices of the peace around the Territories for convictions of Eskimos on charges of hunting out of season. Then he'd instruct an appeal to be brought before him, and he'd promptly acquit. It was a no-win situation for the crown."

That wasn't Searle's only complaint.

"We wanted to take Sissons' decisions to the court of appeal, but he'd fox us. He'd hold in those hunting cases that we hadn't proved any facts. You can only appeal on matters of law, not on the facts. So he'd rule we hadn't proved the identity of the accused. He'd rule we hadn't proved that the accused shot the musk-ox. He'd rule we hadn't proved that the musk-ox *was* a bloody musk-ox. We had no case at all when Sissons had finished with us, nothing to apply any law to and no law to appeal on."

The frustration ended one day in July 1964 when an Eskimo named Sigeareak from Whale Cove on Hudson Bay shot some caribou, cut out their tongues, sliced off a few other pieces of meat, and left the rest of the caracasses to rot.

"A blatant case," Searle says, happy at the memory. "A blatant, lovely case. Just took the tongues. A great delicacy. Tasted them myself. Absolutely delicious."

Sigeareak was charged with "killing and abandoning game fit for human consumption contrary to section 15(1)(a) of the game ordinance". But before his trial, Searle called on the magistrate who was to hear the case, an experienced northern hand named

Peter Parker, and suggested a piece of strategy designed to outfox Sissons.

"I wanted an acquittal the first time round. That's odd for a crown counsel, eh? But it was part of the plan. I wanted Peter Parker to find that all the facts had been proven, that it was Sigeareak who'd shot the caribou and abandoned them. Then he had to find that on the basis of Sissons' decision in *Regina v. Francis Kallooar,* one of those damned pieces of law that said Eskimos aren't bound by the game ordinance, he had to acquit Sigeareak."

Which is precisely what Magistrate Parker ruled.

"Then the crown, which was me, appealed by way of stated case. That's where you appeal against any proceeding in a magistrate's court on the ground that what he held was erroneous in law."

The appeal from Magistrate Parker's decision went before Sissons in a stated case that asked the question: "Was the magistrate right in holding that the game ordinance and particularly section 15(1)(a) thereof does not apply to Eskimos?"

"Ah, it was diabolical," Searle says. "I knew we had Sissons. He had to affirm Parker's decision, which he did, and then at last we had some law to take to the court of appeal."

On the appeal, William Morrow acted for Sigeareak, thus in effect arguing Judge Sissons' view of the law. Morrow was a distinguished counsel from Edmonton who was later to follow Sissons on the bench in the Territories and even later to be appointed to the Alberta Supreme Court. But in the Sigeareak matter he was unsuccessful in protecting Sissons' string of decisions in the hunting cases. The court of appeal upset Sigeareak's acquittal, and so, on further appeal, did the Supreme Court of Canada.

"I think it is desirable to say specifically," Mr. Justice Hall wrote in the highest court's judgment, "that insofar as *Regina* v. *Kallooar* and *Regina* v. *Kogogolak* hold that the game ordinance does not apply to Indians and Eskimos in the Northwest Territories, they are not good law and must be taken as having been overruled."

Judge Sissons was heart-broken.

"With the words of Mr. Justice Hall," he wrote in his memoirs, "it seemed . . . that my campaign had failed and the seven years' war had gone to the bureaucrats."

"Oh yeah, he was furious," David Searle says today. "In one fell swoop we reversed all his earlier decisions. And he never knew who the Machiavelli was behind the whole plan. I never told him it was me and he went to his grave not knowing. But, lord, I'd had my gut full of all those years of taking his crackpot law."

Searle's delight in his ultimate triumph over Sissons doesn't spring from revenge realized or any other malicious motive. Uh-uh, he says. The point, according to Searle, is that Judge Sissons, good-hearted man that he may have been, wasn't reading the drift of the northern times correctly.

"All right," Searle says, "maybe twenty years ago people in Baker Lake and all those other places were living in ice houses. But that was ending in Sissons' day, and now everybody has a home made out of wood and bricks. The young people speak English. They don't know the Eskimo tongue. And hunting and fishing, my lord, it's only the very old people who live off the land in this day and age. The era of bringing up defences for Eskimos that Sisson raised is long gone."

Even the notion of the circuit, as established by Judge Sissons, is falling at least partly into disrepute. John Bayly thinks so.

"Sissons was right to have the court go into the communities," he says. "But it's got out of hand. Now we fly in for trivial matters when we shouldn't. It'd be better for the people if they called on the travelling court much less and if the local justices of the peace handled everything except fraud and rape and murder."

Alas, there are problems. The JPs, to cite one difficulty, are reluctant to judge their neighbours, especially at the fees they're paid. How come, the JPs argue, they get five dollars per case while the judge from Yellowknife gets $35,000 a year in salary, and gets to fly in a big plane and to wear a beautiful gown?

"So," Bayly says, "the justices of the peace are refusing to sit whenever anybody enters a not-guilty plea, and our court is kept on the road. It gets silly. Once, two little boys in a community in the Eastern Arctic got into some mischief, set fire to a tree, and fed the dogs some fish that had glass in it. Instead of scolding the boys, the community called in the court. It cost $5,000 just to put the plane in the air. That's what Sissons started for us."

But at least some of Sissons' work remains intact and on display. Mike Sikyea's duck, for example. Mike Sikyea is an Indian from Yellowknife who shot a duck six miles north of the city one day in the summer of 1962. Unfortunately for Mike a Mountie happened on the scene and charged him with hunting a duck out of season contrary to the Migratory Birds Convention Act. The charge came before Judge Sissons, who ruled that the Act didn't apply to Indians engaged in their age-old right to hunt for food in all seasons on unoccupied crown lands. The crown attorney appealed, and over the next few years the case wound its way up to the Supreme Court of Canada, where Sikyea was ruled guilty of the offence. The case, appeals and all, cost the crown $250,000 to pursue.

The duck that gave rise to the charge, the duck that prompted Jack Sissons' decision and the crown's appeal, has been stuffed and placed in the glass case on the second floor of the new Yellowknife Courthouse. And these days, whenever Mike Sikyea pours himself a few drinks, he leads his friends on a brief conducted tour of the courthouse.

"That duck up there," he'll say, stopping in front of the display case, "that's my quarter-of-a-million-dollar duck."

"Absurdity," John Bayly says, "pervades a lot of what the law and lawyers do up here in the Territories."

CHAPTER TWO

The Country Lawyer

Paul Ross is a loving man. In the mornings, he wakes up his thirteen-year-old daughter with hugs and kisses. When he reads *Babar* to his five-year-old son, he turns on different voices for all the characters, W.C. Fields inflections for Cornelius, a quaver for the old lady, sensible tones for Babar. And he tells his wife she's beautiful in a way that makes you think her beauty is a fresh daily delight to him.

All of which — his openness and generous spirit — may explain why Paul Ross chose to practise law in the town of Clinton. Population: 3,200. Atmosphere: tranquil. Clinton is in Huron County in the far southwest reaches of Ontario. The surrounding countryside is given over to prosperous farming — dairy products, poultry, some beef — while Clinton itself functions mostly as a service centre for the area. The hospital is in Clinton. The Board of Education operates from the town. It's got an Ontario Provincial Police detachment, a library, three taverns, a factory that makes parts for pianos, and not much else. Local citizens tend to amble when they're out on the street, and the wise men of town — the editor of the weekly *News-Record*, the fellow who runs the IGA, and a few others — get together for a slow cup of coffee twice a day at Bartliff's Restaurant and Bakery. Clinton, all things considered, is a place where there's time to sniff the flowers. That's what brought Paul Ross to town.

"Things aren't angry like they are in a city law practice," he says. "This part of the world's got so much geographical room that you don't have people disputing for their own personal space. The larger spaces absorb all the aggressions."

Ross knows about the city. He grew up in Toronto and practised law there for several years. But on visits to Huron, he was seduced by the county's peace. He struck a deal with Beecher Menzies, the lawyer with the longest service in Clinton, and in January 1976, when Ross was thirty-eight years old, he entered into a new partnership. Menzies, Ross, 49 Albert Street, directly across the road from Bartliff's.

Ross and Menzies make a vivid contrast. Ross, the big-city boy, has wavy red hair, freckles, cord suits, and too much energy to suppress. He may be the fastest walker in the county. Menzies is large and amiable. He's a three-piece-grey-suit lawyer and has the kind of Old Ontario face, hearty and shrewd, that wouldn't look out of place in a portrait of the Family Compact. He grew up in Clinton, the son of the United Church minister, and returned from law school in 1955 to buy the town practice from a lawyer who was moving up to the bench. Menzies knows the territory.

"Beecher," Ross says, "has practised here long enough that he has the history of practically every piece of Huron property off by heart. When he's got a real-estate deal, he doesn't need to check the title. It's in his head."

There's a third lawyer in Clinton, Gerald Hiltz, a young man who started up a practice about a year before Ross came to town. Hiltz is meticulous, a worrier, and on real-estate deals with Beecher Menzies he'll submit detailed lists of requisitions, asking Menzies to clear up genuine or feared flaws on the property titles. Menzies ignores Hiltz's letter until Hiltz, a few blocks down Albert Street, telephones in exasperation.

"Don't you ever open your mail?" Hiltz asks.

"Aw, Gerry, the title's as good as gold," Menzies says.

"But my *requisitions*!"

"Gerry, do you want to close the deal or don't you?" Menzies says.

"That's *it*," Ross says. "When I hear Beecher talk like that, that attitude, I know why I'm here. None of the tension about a simple real-estate deal that I used to feel in the city."

"Tension? Over real estate?" Menzies says just before he strolls across the street for coffee with the other wise men at Bartliff's.

By mid-morning, the late October day had come up shiny and clear, and Ross decided to hit the road. It's a now-and-again habit of his to steal a few hours away from the office in the middle of the day and mosey through the back lanes of Huron County.

He checked the files stacked on both sides of his desk. Any emergency about to erupt? Not likely. There was the employment contract he was drawing for the new manager of the Little Inn over in Bayfield. There was the farmer east of Clinton who was getting an unfair deal from the Workmen's Compensation Board. There was the Draper Brothers and Reid purchase, a group of local men who were buying the old Heintzman piano factory. And there were the family-law cases, a specialty that Ross was developing in Huron, arranging adoptions, launching custody actions, drawing separation agreements.

, "This one I call my Caspar Milquetoast file," he said, lifting a bulky folder with two hands. "My client is a simple farmer, a guy with manure on his boots, and he's married to a woman who's got a university education. She gives him a hard time until one day he snaps and walks out and ends up in this office. It's the first time in twenty years of marriage he's struck back against the wife. Only trouble is she's sitting on the farm and he's out in the cold. The farm is a $350,000 operation, but it isn't worth a penny unless somebody's running it, which nobody is with my guy off the property. I move fast. I get a court order. It puts my guy back on the farm. It gives the wife $50,000 to clear off. She does. He stops being Caspar Milquetoast. He's running his farm and nobody's hassling him. The wife's at some institution of higher education working on a Master's and hanging out with people who don't have manure on their boots. Happy ending."

Ross surveyed the stack of files. "I might've laughed at this stuff when I was a lawyer in the city. Maybe I'd have called it small potatoes. But now it makes me feel good. The Caspar Milquetoast, I'm really proud of that one."

Five minutes later, Ross's brown Chevette was on a two-lane highway running north out of Clinton through farmland that rolled just enough to take away the threat of boredom. Ross had a comment for each farm, each clump of woods, each grocery-store-and-gas-pump village. On the back roads of Huron County, he was part tour guide, part social historian, Baedeker crossed with Vance Packard.

"The farmhouse over there," he said, "all that old grey stone, it's lovely, you know, but inside the people've destroyed it. The idea of fine décor out here is a lot of flocked wallpaper over every surface. You look at the design they choose, and if you saw it on a Rorschach test, you'd say it was a row of naked female pelvises.''

He pulled onto the shoulder of the road opposite a farm that smacked of money. The chicken-houses, long barracks two storeys high, showed fresh paint. The grass around them was clipped to the tidiness of a golf-course fairway, and men moved across the property in strides that said they were on profitable business.

"Know what the farmhouse on this place has?" Ross said. "Great big swimming-pool. Indoors. Some of the farms in the country are worth a million bucks. It's a matter of quotas, which is something country lawyers have to bone up on. Every farm comes with its own quota. Take milk. The federal government subsidizes dairy farmers, and it sets a big over-all quota of how much milk is going to be produced in the entire country in any given year. Then it parcels out the quotas to the provincial governments and the provincial governments parcel them out to individual farmers. If a farmer gets a big quota, he's laughing. He can earn a lot of money. But if he goes over his quota and produces too much milk, he gets penalized. And the whole thing is complicated by the fact that there are different kinds of quotas. You have to understand all this intricate stuff — they don't teach it in law school — to be able to handle the job when a farm sale comes into the office because we're talking here about a pretty large legal fee.''

Ross drove on down the highway.

"I didn't know anything about the economics of farming when I moved to Huron," he said. "So for six weeks I used to get up early and help a farmer milk his cows and listen to him talk before I went in to the office. Every morning I stood behind cows and watched their tails flick in my face. Cows' tails, one thing I learned about farming, are soaked in cows' piss.''

Ross took his sweet time. He turned down dirt roads, stopped to check out properties that had for-sale signs posted on them, steered into a farmer's front yard to buy two pumpkins and a couple of Spy apples, price: $1.75. Everywhere he drove, the land had the feel of thrift. Huron had been settled a century and a half earlier by people who were hard-working, tight-fisted, and low church — Scotch Presbyterians, Congregationalists, and Methodists from the north of England. The Dutch came later, an even more conservative and strict people. They worship at the Dutch Reformed Church and send the kids to their own Clinton District Christian School where there's little truck with the evils of modern ways and plenty of emphasis on fundamental values. Huron County has no room for slackers.

"Things aren't *entirely* moral out here," Ross said. "Farmers' sons are still known to sneak into the barn and have relations with sheep."

Ross drove up a steep hill into Goderich. It's the largest town in the county, almost 8,000 people, the headquarters for Huron's municipal government and courts. It's a town that might have been put together on order for a Walt Disney movie. It is pretty and miniature and ideal. It has a town square and a district where the best houses look down a steep hill to the Maitland River and to Lake Huron beyond it, and everyone who comes to town remarks on its magnificent sunsets. Goderich, by and large, stands still. John Galt and Tiger Dunlop, two early Ontario go-getters, had great hopes for the town when they organized it in the first part of the nineteenth century. But since then, Goderich has been content to get by on its salt business, a couple of foundries that manufacture agricultural equipment, the municipal government offices, and the tourists who crowd in during the warm months. The sunsets really are magnificent, and that's almost enough for everyone in Goderich.

"The *London Free Press* stopped carrying its Goderich section the other day," Ross said. "It's the biggest daily newspaper in the area. Runs weekly reports from all the more important communities around here. Now it's dropped Goderich. Maybe it's trying to tell us something."

For lunch, Ross decided on the Albion Hotel in Bayfield, a few miles south of Goderich. Bayfield bustles in the summer and empties in the fall. It's a village of cottages and small shops and restaurants and marinas on Lake Huron, and summer people, many of them Americans from Michigan, just naturally take to it. The Albion stays in business through the slack season and on this day the fat and friendly waitress said the special at $3.50 was trout fresh out of the lake. She'd cleaned it herself that morning. Anything for you, Mr. Ross, she said. Ross had acted for her in a custody action.

"A lawyer's fee," Ross said, discussing the nitty-gritty of his profession over the trout and a beer. "What the fee depends on is not the time a lawyer puts into a file, not the amount of work he has to do on it, not the result he gets for his client. It's none of those things. The truth is — this came to me since I moved down here — a lawyer's fee really depends on the standard of living he decides he wants to maintain. He charges his clients whatever amount is going to give him and his family the right-sized house, the proper number of cars, enough holidays in Florida. Like that."

He asked the waitress if there was another piece of fish, just a tiny piece more. There was.

"Okay," he went on, "what does my theory about fees mean to me personally? It means I can afford to charge less and earn less than I could in the big city. We don't have any fancy restaurants in Huron, no sixty-dollar lunches with clients. We don't need big cars and a different suit for every day of the week. And recreation? It's mostly outdoors. It's mostly free. A lawyer like me, handling an ordinary practice, can earn $30,000 to $40,000 a year, ball-park figures, and stay happy. That sounds like peanuts by Toronto standards, but in terms of life-style it goes as far as the salary of the downtown lawyer who hustles his ass off for one hundred grand a year."

Ross finished his lunch and walked across the hall to the Albion's bar, where the waitress was washing glasses. He asked her about the aftermath of the custody action. She took a long fifteen minutes to relive the episode in her life and to analyse her emotions. Ross folded his coat on a stool, leaned on the bar, and listened until she wound to the end of her story.

"Glad you're happy," Ross said.

The fat and friendly waitress smiled a lovely smile.

Back in the Chevette, Ross steered through a series of sharply curved dirt roads that led past the basin for the Bayfield Yacht Club to a beach edging on Lake Huron. Enormous brown waves broke against a pier that reached out from the beach. On the pier, a single Canada Goose hopped in the spray from the waves. He was alone and he was baffled. Where had the other geese flown to? Where were his friends?

"Oh my God, that's terrible!" Ross said, his voice loud in the small car. "He looks so little. He's so vulnerable. That's the most pathetic thing I've ever seen."

At that moment, the way Ross spoke of the Canada Goose and its predicament, he might have been as concerned for it as he was for any of his clients, for Caspar Milquetoast, for the fat and friendly waitress.

"Maybe," he said, "there's time out here to be concerned for all kinds of strange things."

When the subject of the Truscott case surfaced, as it inevitably had to, it was at the lawyers' luncheon table in the Bedford Hotel. The Bedford fronts on Goderich's town square across the street from the courthouse, and each noon the grey-haired waitresses in the pink uniforms hold the dining-room's best table for any of the county's lawyers and judges — there are about thirty of them in all — who happen to be in the neighbourhood. A dozen usually show up, and conversation over the fried-egg sandwiches and coffee and the occasional beer centres on lawyerly gossip, lightweight stuff. But this day somebody mentioned Steven Truscott, the boy who was convicted of murder in the courthouse across the square.

He was fourteen at the time, and the victim of the crime, Lynne Harper, was twelve. She was raped, then strangled with her blouse, one June evening in 1959 in a woods near the old RCAF base at Clinton. Truscott was sentenced to be hanged. His age, and Lynne Harper's, made the case a sensation around the world. So did the prospect of the rope for a fourteen-year-old. Truscott's sentence was commuted to life imprisonment. He served ten years and was paroled, but the sensation lingered on.

Truscott insisted he was innocent. The locals had railroaded him. "It would be hard to match the bigotry, hate, and vindictiveness of the citizens of Huron County," he wrote in a book published in the fall of 1979. "I considered the people of Goderich and Clinton little better than a lynch mob."

At lunch this day, talk started off as usual. MacEwan Egener who practises in Goderich reminisced about the famous curling party that members of the bar threw a few years back at the arena up in Walkerton. There was as much drinking as curling, and when time came to adjourn for more celebrations at the County Court judge's house six miles down highway number four in Hanover, the legal profession had a transportation crisis on its hands. Who was sober enough to steer a car in traffic? Somebody influential phoned the OPP.

"The police used their cruisers to block off all the side roads," MacEwan Egener said, big smile in place. "Allowed no cars into the area. By the time our bunch set off from the curling rink, that highway was as clear as Main Street at four in the morning."

Alan Mill, a partner from a firm in Wingham, brought up the aging lawyer from over east of the county who got himself disbarred for a violation of the Mann Act in the United States. It seemed the aging lawyer liked to invite young girls to accompany him on visits to horse shows in Pennsylvania and Ohio and New York State. Somehow the visits invariably ended with hanky-panky in motel rooms. One of the young girls blew the whistle on the elderly solicitor, and he lost his right to practise when he was convicted of taking female persons across state lines for immoral purposes.

"Unfair," Alan Mill added jokingly. "Doing that sort of thing with young girls at his age, two or three

43

times a night I understand, they shouldn't have disbarred him. They should have awarded him a Q.C. on the spot."

Then somebody got around to Steven Truscott.

"Any place you go outside the county," Beecher Menzies said, "they hear you're from Clinton and they say, ah, the Truscott case, as if you're personally responsible for some notorious miscarriage of justice."

"That's so," Dan Murphy from Goderich said.

"The boy had a million dollars' worth of counsel," Bill Cochrane said, the judge of the Provincial Court. "Frank Donnelly at the trial here in town, John O'Driscoll on the appeal, Arthur Martin when the case was heard all over again in '66 by the Supreme Court in Ottawa. All three of those men got appointed to the Ontario High Court later on. Counsel like them, if there was a chance the boy was innocent, they'd have persuaded the courts he was."

"Hmmm," Dan Murphy murmured.

"The thing the Truscott people got wrong," Beecher Menzies said, "was making Glenn Hays out to be a monster. Glenn was a fair and decent crown attorney, that's the truth. If he went hard in prosecuting Truscott, well, it was his job to do so."

Dan Murphy nodded.

"They called Glenn bloodthirsty," Menzies said.

Murphy nodded again, and everyone considered Menzies' words.

"By a great coincidence," Murphy started in, "I arrived in Goderich to start practising on the day before the Truscott case began. I stayed out at the Donnelly cottage, lovely weather, too, end of the summer, y'know, and every morning, Mr. Donnelly, Frank, would get up, shave in cold water, and drive down to the courthouse. I went with him and never missed a day of the trial. Wonderful drama. Frank didn't put the boy on the stand, but when he was finished with his cross-examinations, there was something wrong with the crown's case. There were little pieces of timing that were out — the times when witnesses saw the boy, when the girl must have died, when the boy arrived back at his home. Didn't fit together. To my mind, Frank Donnelly raised a reasonable doubt that that boy murdered that girl."

Murphy took a sip of coffee and wiped his mouth with a paper napkin.

"Nine juries out of ten," he said, "nine out of ten would've acquitted Truscott. But he had one piece of bad luck."

Murphy took a slow look around the table.

"He got the tenth jury."

Judge Bill Cochrane's desk was bare except for his chequebook. Middle-of-the-road pop music filled the office from a walnut-finished radio-and-stereo set. The wall-to-wall broadloom muffled outside noises, and when the judge was finished with his desk work — signing a few personal cheques — a book waited, Peter Newman's *The Bronfman Dynasty*, hardcover edition. It was 2:30 p.m. on a Thursday and, as usual, there was no afternoon business for the Provincial Court (Criminal) in the County of Huron.

"I've been two years in this job," Judge Cochrane said, "and for seventeen years before that I was the county's crown attorney. In all that time I've handled five murders, two bank robberies, and three rapes. That's all the big crime Huron's known."

The judge sat erect in his chair, a fastidious man, silver hair brushed back, silver moustache clipped to a fine line, grey suit fresh and creaseless, his manner old-world and courtly.

"It's easily explained about the lack of crime," he said. "We have no ethnic groups. No large centres of population. No place for a criminal to hang out. There were 50,000 people in the county twenty years ago and there are 50,000 today. The place never changes, not for the worse anyway."

Besides, the judge went on, Huron's native criminals, the few who turn up, tend to be short on the wiles of big-city crooks.

"Bob Smith decided to rob the bank over in Brucefield," the judge said. "This is a few years ago when I was the crown. Brucefield looked a good bet. Just a village. Bank only visits one day a week, Thursdays, to take care of the farmers. Good volume, though. Well, Bob cut the barrel off his dad's shotgun, got himself a balaclava to cover his face, and drove up to the bank on the Thursday after New Year's Day. His being short of funds over the holiday season was what prompted the adventure in the first place. Bob drove up to the bank in his old black-and-yellow car with the broken door on the driver's side wired shut and he came out with nine thousand dollars.

"He got across the back road as far as Seaforth, six or seven miles, and ran out of gas. Bad planning on Bob's part. But he pushed the old black-and-yellow car to a service station, bought gas out of his loot, stayed to chat awhile with the attendant, and went on up to Kitchener, another sixty miles. That's where he ran into his pal who owned a brand-new Camaro. Trouble was the brand-new Camaro had been repossessed by the dealer back in Exeter, which happens to be just south of where Bob had done his robbery. Didn't matter. The two lads drove to Exeter, Bob peeled off some more bills, and the friend let him drive the Camaro on his getaway to the States.

"No doubt from the start who the guilty party was. Bob had the only black-and-yellow car with the driver's door wired shut that anyone around here could recall. The OPP knew Bob pretty well anyway. They'd turned him down when he applied to join the force. But it was Bob who sealed the case himself. He took a holiday in the Caribbean and dropped a line back to his friend the Camaro owner arranging to meet up with him in Nashville, Tennessee, at the Grand Ole Opry. Bob signed the letter, 'Your friendly bank robber'.

"FBI were waiting for Bob when he walked into the Opry and they shipped him up to us. Bob received five years. It wasn't a difficult case to prosecute. Not many are in Huron."

Judge Cochrane excused himself to sign another cheque.

Heather Ross is Paul Ross's second wife. She's the mother of five-year-old Quinn, a tornado of a kid, and stepmother to thirteen-year-old Tagen, a blonde who would drive Humbert Humbert to distraction. Before Heather married Paul, she worked at interesting jobs in Toronto, at the CBC radio program *This Country In The Morning* and at *The Canadian Magazine*. Before that, she grew up in the interior of British Columbia, and in 1970, when she was twenty, she was elected Miss Kelowna. Her loveliness isn't the standard stuff of beauty queens. It is surprisingly English. She is small and porcelain. Her nose is Audrey Hepburn and her dark eyes never blink. She radiates serenity.

She is also tough-minded. That made it no accident when she involved herself in the Great Huron County Book-Banning Fuss of 1978. It began when Lloyd Barth, a retired high-school teacher from Blyth, objected to three novels that the Huron Board of Education permitted as optional reading for grade thirteen students at the county's five high schools. The Catholic Women's League of Knightsbridge took up Barth's cause, and Renaissance Canada, an evangelistic pressure group from just outside Toronto, parachuted in its support. They asked that the board protect Huron's adolescents from the three books — Salinger's *Catcher in the Rye*, Steinbeck's *Of Mice and Men*, and Margaret Lawrence's *The Diviners* — and the board listened.

"Just by chance," Heather explained one morning as she baked a coffee cake in her kitchen, "I heard on a Friday late in the spring that the board was going to rule on the books the following Monday. That's how things happen out here. Very quietly. Well, I phoned some people and we got the board to postpone its decision and started writing a brief to show the anti-banning position. It wasn't a situation where the whole county was excited. There was a small group against the books, a small group in favour, and a big majority that didn't care. That's also how things happen out here."

Heather's friend Alice emerged as chief spokesperson for the pro-books faction, Alice Munro, the author and winner of two Governor General's Awards for her stories about small-town people. She grew up in Wingham in the north of the county and now, at almost fifty, lives in Clinton. Her days are marked by privacy and old-fashioned good manners. She stays at home, "looking at the wall, with nobody to notice," she says, waiting for the stories to come. When she feels it's time for a luncheon with Heather, she communicates a week in advance by polite note.

"In this kind of society," she has said of southwestern Ontario, "everyone has a different idea of who you are, so you learn to keep quiet and preserve yourself with the least possible trouble.''

Still, Munro made herself visible on behalf of Heather's cause. She gave interviews to Toronto newspapers and TV stations, and she took a seat on the platform in the Clinton High School gym for a meeting organized by the Writers' Union of Canada to explain the anti-banning position. Five hundred citizens turned out. One man brought a Bible and told the gathering it was the only book that a high-school student needed to be taught. A couple of others led prayers for the county's soul. Alice Munro tried to talk of literature. It was an awkward gathering and, not long afterwards, Munro got a new unlisted phone number at home.

The Board of Education allowed time at a meeting one summer night for representations on the books issue. Heather intended to read her group's brief. But, attacked by nerves, she turned to her husband the lawyer, the man trained to persuade.

"Maybe I saw it as part of my role in the community to speak my piece," Ross says. "When Beecher set up practice here, he joined the Lions Club. I go down to the Board of Education and defend books that my neighbours think are dirty."

His appearance before the board wasn't encouraging.

"Oh, they *listened*," Ross says. "But the chairman had already bragged that he hadn't read any of the books and didn't intend to. He could make up his mind on the basis of the excerpts that Renaissance Canada passed around."

On August 21, 1978, the board announced its decision. *Catcher in the Rye* and *Of Mice and Men* passed, but *The Diviners*, winner of the 1975 Governor General's Award for fiction, was struck from the Huron County high-school curriculum.

"Loss of respectability is important to middle-class people," Alice Munro said afterwards. "Maybe they shouldn't be educated out of it. Some of the values they hold are working very well for them. There's a great deal of comfort in a rooted permanent society where everybody knows what's expected of them."

Heather found that the books fuss caused her to take a deeper look at her life in the country and her place as a country lawyer's wife.

"I'm not sure that many of the lawyers around here would admit it," she says, "but their wives are very important to their practice, more important than city lawyers' wives by far. Meg, for example, Beecher's wife, Meg is a dynamo. She's a substitute teacher at the high school and does work at the hospital. She makes contacts all over the place. She's the one who asks people from out in the country over to their house for dinner, people that it would never occur to Beecher to entertain. Really, in an indirect way, Meg recruits clients for Beecher and helps keep them steady clients."

Heather is content with a lower profile and a more independent role. For a couple of years she ran the Arbor, a gift shop in Clinton. Now she looks after the kids, cooks, reads, thinks about getting back to the painting she used to do.

"I like the country very much," she says. "But there are two things I miss about life in the city. One is being able to tear off on the spur of the moment to a movie or to a good cheap little restaurant. You can't do that in Huron."

And the second thing she misses?

"Friends, the kind of friends where so much is understood between you without having to express it. Out here, I find that I always have to explain myself."

Late one night, Paul Ross poured a Scotch on the rocks. He put a record on the stereo set, a Mozart concerto for flute and orchestra, and pulled his chair close to the low fire in the grate in his living-room.

"The lawyers out here are good," he began. "Beecher is what you'd call the pillar of the legal community, and Donnelly and Murphy — that's Don Murphy and Jimmy Donnelly, the son of the guy who defended Truscott — are such excellent counsel that they've got a lock on the litigation work in Huron *and* they get retained by firms to act in cases outside the county."

He sipped at his Scotch.

"Dan Murphy. There's one of my favourites. He's a lot of what Huron County's all about. He's a gregarious guy. He likes his white wine. He laughs all the time. He lives in one of those big houses in Goderich that look over the Maitland River. He's also a Catholic. He's got seven kids. He doesn't want any school to tell them they can read *The Diviners*. That's the mix you get in the man, smart and straight, a little outrageous, and very, very conservative. People in the county speak that language, and Donnelly and Murphy do terrific business."

Ross poured just an ounce more Scotch into his glass. He isn't a naturally generous drinker.

It's not easy for an outside lawyer to break into a community like Clinton. It's an eggshell situation at first. You walk softly. I had some work for a real-estate agent in town, and through absolutely nobody's fault the deal fell through. I said to him,

51

'Well, you win some and you lose some.' He didn't like that. Hasn't brought me any business since I made the crack. You wait a while before you enjoy the privilege of kidding around about money in Huron.''

Ross turned over the Mozart.

"The first time I got myself involved in the town came when the Minister of Health down at Queen's Park said the provincial government was closing the Clinton hospital. That really struck at the heart of the community. They never move as a group here, they're individuals, but the hospital issue brought them together. The Minister, Frank Miller, came to town to make a speech about the reason the province had to close the hospital. Try and smooth things over. The people threw snowballs at him. That's how mad they were and how united. Well, I was a little reluctant to get into the situation, being new in town and everything, but I knew I had a feel for what should be done. At one point in my life I took eight months out of law and worked as a speech-writer for Cabinet ministers in Bill Davis's government. Anyway, I got in touch with people I'd met at Queen's Park and I figured out the lawyers to talk to in Toronto. In the end, our side went to court and argued that the provincial government didn't have the power under the Hospitals Act to shut the Clinton hospital. The court looked at the Act and agreed. The hospital stayed open. It still is. That felt good.''

Another ounce of Scotch, another small log on the fire.

"Almost everything feels good to me these days. No matter what else the practice of law *is* in the country, what it *isn't* is a battle. In Toronto, you look good to a client by making somebody else look not good. That doesn't have to happen in Clinton."

A sip of Scotch.

"Out here — this is one of the bottom lines for me about a country practice — you don't have to destroy the lawyer on the other side."

The Mozart concerto floated away on a soft flurry of high notes.

CHAPTER THREE

Anatomy of a Law Firm

Wellington's Court Restaurant in downtown Toronto is a place of maroons and browns and muffled atmosphere. It's favoured by corporate lawyers who like quiet and discretion with their lunch. Let the high-profile corporate guys eat at Winston's where the proprietor, John Arena, guarantees a flurry of attention for anyone with a Name. John Turner has a favourite Winston's table. Jim Arnett of Stikeman, Elliott, Robarts and Bowman prefers Wellington's Court and generally begins lunch with a soda-water.

"I got into corporate law because I had a romantic notion of it," he said one noon hour, waiting for his soda-water. "You're involved in power. You're involved in the corporate planning process right alongside the senior management of multinational companies. You really see what's happening in the business community. You have the perspective that maybe, say, a deputy minister in Ottawa has. It's heady stuff. It's like I thought at the beginning. Romantic."

Jim Arnett is a slim man in his late thirties with a quality of purity about him, something hard and clean and exact in his personality. He studied law at the University of Manitoba ("worst law school in the Commonwealth"), took classes at Harvard, including some Henry Kissinger seminars, and then went searching for a career. He spent a year at the Department of Justice in Ottawa, entered private practice in Winnipeg, and defected briefly to the advertising game with the Vickers and Benson agency in Toronto ("I decided advertising was frivolous") before he arrived at the Stikeman firm and romance in 1974.

"Of course, there's no way to get around working long hours in this end of the law," he went on. "You're not cutting the mustard unless you show up at the office on weekends. It's the unspoken pressure that makes you put in the time. You have to keep track of the hours you spend on all your files. That's for the purposes of billing the clients. You bill by the hour. All the statistics, that's the hours and billings and so forth, are fed into a computer. Which means that everybody else in the office can check at a glance on how much you're working. There's the unspoken pressure."

He took a swallow of his soda-water. "In any corporate firm a junior lawyer, the person just getting off the mark, is expected, or *required,* to show 1,600 billing hours a year. You don't chalk up big figures like that by working day to day. It stands to reason there's a disproportionate number of workaholics among corporate lawyers."

Arnett ordered a julienne salad and talked of his firm's history. It began in Montreal in the 1940s with Heward Stikeman, the first lawyer in Canada to make a reputation as a tax expert. He built a formidable Montreal firm, then looked to expansion. First, an office in London, England ("A gold mine of business for us with the multinationals," Arnett says. "Fifty per cent of my time is on London work"). Next, Toronto. In the 1960s Stikeman opened a Bay Street firm, now up to two dozen lawyers, in partnership with John Robarts, who brought with him the contacts of ten years as premier of Ontario.

"The big corporations we have as clients rate lawyers on the basis of how fast they can move paper around," Arnett said, forking his salad. "Multinational executives think in terms of logistics. It's all very well to have a document properly drawn, but if it isn't in the right place at the right time, then it's no good. What it means is that we only spend half our time on substantive stuff and the other half on things like how to get a paper signed in Vancouver and on somebody's desk in Ottawa a day later. It gets complicated when your client has a head office in London, a branch in Tampa, Florida, a tax accountant in New York City, and turns out his products on the west coast. But that's corporate law."

Arnett asked for another soda-water. "In multinationals it's hard to find who's running things. The executives do a lot of ass-covering. They're always drawing memos to set down their position on any given situation just in case there's a bomb that might go off and blow them out of the water. They look for lawyers to buttress them. One executive'll phone a lawyer in our firm and report back to his company that the lawyer said to go ahead and follow XY course of action. Another executive'll phone another lawyer in the firm and report back that he said to take YZ action, something very different. What's happened is that the first executive has talked to somebody in the corporate end of things over here and the second executive has talked to somebody on the tax side. There may be two quite different reasons, corporate and tax, for taking two different courses of action. There's a lot of politics at work in the situation, what with the two executives jockeying for their positions, and it's part of the law firm's job to make sure that things don't fall between the cracks. We have to provide the overview so that the tax and the corporate reasons for taking different steps get reconciled in the best interests of the client. The client, you know, isn't really a monolith. It's individuals."

Arnett had vanilla ice cream for dessert. No coffee, thanks. "Hardware's important. Crucial, in fact. Telex, computers, word-processing machines. Some days my secretary spends three or four hours at the telex. That's how you get things done. Using the hardware. It's the major revolution that's come along in corporate law in these last few years, but to me it's second best. Marshall McLuhan, you know, says you don't need to talk personally to anybody these days because the phone and telex and the rest are contemporary man's substitute. But nothing's as good as a face-to-face meeting, not even a bunch of people on a conference call. It's not the same dymanics. Some element escapes you."

Arnett polished off the ice cream. "Corporate lawyers are different from other lawyers. We aren't concerned with justice. We're solicitors. That's the starting point, and then it's almost as if we're becoming part of the international business bureaucracy. Not quite, but we're getting there."

Arnett walked out of the dim of Wellington's Court into the shiny glass and silver metal of the skyscraper above the restaurant, the Commerce Court West. He rode an elevator to the forty-ninth floor, back to Stikeman, Elliott and the romance of moving paper.

* * *

The New York businessman was in a hurry. He wanted to wind up the deal, the acquisition of a

Canadian company, in time to avoid an American tax deadline that was not much more than a week away. He arrived in Toronto and rushed to his Canadian lawyer, Jim Tory, at Tory, Tory, DesLauriers and Binnington. It was a small gathering in the Tory offices — the American businessman, Jim Tory, a couple of lawyers from his firm, and the president of the Canadian company which was to be the subject of the swift acquisition. The Canadian president had been summoned to the meeting on such short notice that he hadn't brought along his own lawyer. That worried him.

"I don't know," he said. "It looks like a good deal, but the speed of it all kind of gives me concern. I don't have anybody here advising me."

He looked at the deed of sale on the table in front of him, freshly drawn and lacking only his signature.

"I'll tell you what," he said. "I respect Jim, and if Jim says I should sign the deal, I'll sign."

Tory shifted in his seat.

"Well, I've got to point out there are certain negatives in the sale from your side," he said to the Canadian president, and over the following few minutes he proceeded to outline the "negatives".

"Yeaa-ahh," the president said, stretching the word into a couple of syllables. "I didn't recognize any of those things myself, not till you put your finger on them."

He nudged the deed of sale across the table.

"In light of all this," he said, "I don't think I'm going to sign the deal."

He left the meeting.

"Wait a minute," the New York businessman said to Tory, "whose lawyer *are* you anyway?"

And he went home to New York without his Canadian acquisition.

Tory, Tory, DesLauriers and Binnington is a remarkable institution for two reasons. To begin with, it is a "hot" firm, Canada's consummate corporate-commercial law firm of the 1970s and early '80s. Its lawyers, over fifty of them in mid-1980 with the body count threatening to rise, act for, among other distinguished clients, Wood Gundy (stocks and bonds), the International Thomson Organization (newspapers, oil, and sundries), Reichhold (chemicals), Rogers Cable Telecommunications (radio and television), and Simpsons-Sears (merchandising). It provided the legal brains behind the key corporate takeovers of recent years: the Bronfman family's conquest of Brascan, the Thomson purchase of the Hudson's Bay Company and the FP newspaper chain. It dispatched senior partners on assignment, both temporary and permanent, to run some of the country's most powerful corporations and public bodies, Jim Tory's twin brother John to the Thomson organization, Trevor Eyton to Brascan, Jim Baillie to the Ontario Securities Commission. Tory, Tory, DesLauriers and Binnington is, in short, omnipresent in the Canadian corporate world. That constitutes its first point of distinction. Its second, perhaps surprisingly, is that it is a firm of lawyers who are honest and responsible and decent. Tory, Tory is, also in short, a place of nice guys.

"Jim and John Tory," Trevor Eyton says, "don't have a mean bone in their bodies, and they're the people who established the standards the firm goes by."

Dick Gathercole agrees. He teaches at the University of Toronto Law School after a career in practice that included a half-dozen years at the Tory firm, and although his personal politics (middle left) make him a natural debating opponent for Eyton (far right), he too recognizes "the personal integrity of the Tory brothers. The spirit and excellence of the firm come from them, and so do the things that make it such a *good* place to work."

It's Jim Tory who is chiefly responsible for setting the moral tone, at least since John departed in 1973 to serve as senior financial advisor and all-round *éminence grise* to Kenneth Thomson, the second Lord Thomson, in the management and expansion of the empire he inherited from his father, Roy, the first Lord Thomson. John's name remains in the firm title and he stays in regular communication with Jim on matters legal, business, and social. But it's Jim who heads the firm, and for a standard-bearer and shining example to his peers and juniors he is a curiously anonymous man. He is fifty, has blond hair, a roundish face, a shy smile, and an unfailing talent for hiding his light under a bushel. (John is darker, slimmer, and almost equally self-effacing.) Jim's suits, no matter how freshly pressed in the morning, look slightly rumpled by noon hour. His notion of the ideal Saturday is to put on his thick old white wool sweater-coat and take his wife Marilyn shopping at the St. Lawrence Farmers' Market, then settle in at a modest restaurant called the Old Fish Market for a lunch of beer and scallops. His private life — "private" in the sense that Margaret Trudeau would never grasp — is all of a piece. When he and John turned fifty in March 1980, friends organized a party of celebration at an inn in a development ninety miles north of Toronto for family skiers called Cranberry Village. The party invitation, written by one of the friends, read "Dress: T-shirts. No gifts." The wording seemed appropriate on every count.

What Jim Tory, with his probity and, to be sure, his brains (he was the silver medallist in the year of his call to the bar), has most significantly managed to shape at Tory, Tory is a true community of corporate lawyers. The firm displays among its members a series of interconnections and mutual passions and a commonality of interests that are almost uncanny and that beyond question contribute to the firm's *esprit* and success. Bill DesLauriers and Art Binnington grew up three houses apart on Hillhurst Boulevard in an unpretentious North Toronto neighbourhood. The two Torys, DesLauriers, and Binnington were University of Toronto fraternity brothers at Psi Upsilon, not a frat of the first, snobbish rank but one that mixed jock activities, gregarious weekends, and ties that bind. The list of items-in-common, large and small, among Tory, Tory partners runs on from past to present: Paul Moore is the Akela, scouting language for adult leader, of his son's Wolf Cub pack in Mississauga, and Brian Shields used to hold the same title and responsibility, dressing up one night a week in the costume decreed decades ago by Lord Baden-Powell, for *his* son's pack at Lawrence Park Community Church.

Ah, Lawrence Park. It's another piece of togetherness that several members make their homes in Lawrence Park, a subdued, leafy residential district on the outer fringes of Toronto's north end that in recent years has unobtrusively slipped past Forest Hill and Rosedale as the city's most desirable address. Shields lives in Lawrence Park. So do Bill DesLauriers and John Tory. Jim bought his Lawrence Park home in 1959, a comfortable-old-shoe of a house, substantial and three-storey, that's handy to a park, the subway, and the Rosedale Golf Club. Tory uses all three. It's gratifying, too, but hardly essential, that Ross Le Mesurier, corporate finance chief at Wood Gundy, lives next door to Jim, and that Dick Thomson, chairman and chief executive officer of the Toronto-Dominion Bank, has a house around the corner.

But the factor that binds Tory, Tory's senior partners most intrinsically is their common beginnings at the University of Toronto Law School during the years — the 1950s and early '60s — when it was tiny and renowned for its legal scholarship. Of the firm's eight pace-setting members from the period around 1960 — the Tory brothers, DesLauriers, Binnington, Eyton, Shields, Jim Baillie, and Gordon Coleman — all but one, Shields, who studied at Osgoode Hall, proceeded downtown from the U. of T. Law School. It was no coincidence. The Tory firm had a self-appointed talent scout at the school — Bora Laskin. In the years long before his ascendancy to the Supreme Court of Canada, Laskin lectured in labour law, property law, and constitutional law at the university law school, and his concern for the bright students who passed under him was genuine and abiding. The Tory boys ranked among his favourites, and in the years when they were building the firm, Laskin operated as a faithful recruiter.

Trevor Eyton was one of the recruits. Eyton is a husky man — he puts on a Santa Claus suit for the annual Tory Christmas parties — with unblinking eyes that could look holes through a corporate adversary, and he remembers that Laskin was single-minded when it came to Tory, Tory.

"It was a custom in third year at the law school," he says, "that all the students would go to Bora and he'd give each one a list of three or four law firms that he thought would be appropriate places for them to article. He'd say, check out these three or four and make a choice among them. Bora was very well-

connected downtown. He knew every firm and he
knew his students. He had a sense which students and
which firms would mix.

In my third year, I waited until three-quarters of
the class had been to Bora before I went to see him. I
sat down in his office. He had this enormous room,
but the desk was positioned right up at the door,
which was always open, so he could see the students
passing by and call them in for a chat. I sat down and
he leaned over and patted me on the knee and said,
'You go to Tory's.'

" 'But what about a few other firms?" I said.
"What about Blake, Cassels or McCarthy and
McCarthy?'

" 'Never mind the others,' he said, and he patted
me on the knee again.

" 'Tory's,' he said.

"Of course he was right. Bora Laskin is one of my
heroes."

At the other end of the pipeline, down at Tory's, it
was John Tory who took charge of the hiring for
several essential years. "If you look down the list of
the first twenty-five names on the firm letterhead
today," he says, "you'll see my handiwork." He
used two criteria in selecting students and young
lawyers. Marks came first. "That may be élitist," he
says. "But by taking the students with the best
marks, I knew I was starting with people who'd
already proved they knew how to work. I used to
phone up the secretary of the law school — she was a
wonderful woman and very good to me — and I'd
tell her to send me down the top twenty-five people
from third year. I guess I had kind of an inside track
there, an advantage over the other firms."

The second criterion was more amorphous. It had
to do with nerve and personality. "Corporate

lawyers have a closer relationship with their clients than other sorts of lawyers," Tory says. "A person charged with a criminal offence doesn't have to *like* his lawyer. He just wants somebody who's going to do something to get him off. But in corporate law there's so much give and take, back and forth, exchange of ideas, intimacy, and so on, that lawyers and clients have to get along. That's what I looked for in students and juniors, all-round types who showed the potential to hit it off with company presidents and corporate executives." Those people, after all, don't like to suffer fools gladly.

What has emerged from the various links, from the coming together of lawyers who have shared over the years an educational institution, a neighbourhood, good deeds, and one another's respect, is a law firm that boasts more rah-rah than most college football teams. The spirit pervades the office — partners gather each Friday afternoon in a small conference room off the main boardroom for drinks and conviviality — and it extends outside the firm to the clients that Tory, Tory elects to take on.

"You might as well work for people you have respect and affection for," Eyton says. "If I don't like a client, I'll send him to someone else in the firm — or more likely out of the firm. The point is, you're going to be working hard, you're going to be working through the night on many, many occasions, but you never think about the effort when you're tied into clients who are appreciative and supportive. When the client sees you pressing yourself to the limit, he'll remember it and like it. And he'll have a short memory when things don't end up right. That's the way it goes at the firm. Jim Tory, the man at the top of the list, the senior guy, he feels the pressure of doing the job. He *feels* it. The clients recognize that, and in return the corporate world is full of people who'll do anything for Jim.''

The man at the top, Jim Tory, typically waves aside anything that hints at personal glory and prefers to speak in praise of the "team concept" in the practice of corporate law. He elaborates:

"Suppose we're into an important transaction at the firm, a takeover or something. Well, you start off with the lawyer who's the over-all director of the deal. He's the generalist. As a lawyer, I'm a generalist. I don't think I'm an expert in anything, but I know a little about a lot of branches of commercial law.

"So, on the deal, the generalist seconds to himself a tax man and a securities man, people in the firm who are specialists in those areas. Some lawyers do nothing but securities work. They know all about the stock exchange, about what the Ontario Securities Commission will permit, about how many days you have to accomplish certain aims. They're experts. Maybe the generalist'll also need a person from the real-estate department in the firm to handle a land aspect of the deal. If some sort of opposition is expected in the course of the operation, he'll get a litigation man to stand by. He'll pull in two or three young fellows, junior lawyers, who can draft all the paperwork that's inevitably involved. Pretty soon we'll have maybe eight to ten lawyers gathered together, and they'll be devoting seventy per cent of their working time to one transaction.

"That's what the team concept amounts to. I don't know how it feels at other firms, but to collaborate with good people from our office, go along with them on a deal that's important to a client, the whole thing amounts to, ah, a very satisfying experience."

"*Satisfying* to work with people at Tory's?" Trevor Eyton says. "I'll put it this way — of the eight or nine or ten people in the world I most respect and love, the high percentage are at that law firm."

Paul Moore may be the quintessential Tory, Tory partner. He has been a member of the firm since his call to the bar in 1967. He ranks as one of the senior Tory men on one prime account, Wood Gundy. And he's a lawyer who registers as positively evangelical when talk turns to the grandeurs of corporate practice.

"I want to be a productive member of society," he explains. "When I was in law school, I was torn between criminal litigation and commercial law. I had a conversation with a crown attorney and he told me ninety-five per cent, maybe more, of the people who come up in criminal court are flat guilty. How could I be a productive member of society defending guys who're already guilty of something? I joined Tory's and burned the midnight oil learning about corporate securities work. That was a very right decision on my part. It's the business aspect of Canadian life that produces the country's wealth. I mean everybody from the Avon lady to the guy who runs a Becker's store to the Bronfman family. I work for those people. I'm loyal to business. That means I'm socially useful. And it doesn't hurt to get paid well for it either."

Moore's personal pride in the Tory firm is immense and specific. "I can name on the fingers of both hands the number of law firms in Canada who do the sort of work we do," he says, "and I can name on the fingers of one hand the number of lawyers who are really good at it. Most of the latter are in this firm.''

His pride begins when he surveys the elegant Tory offices. They're on the thirty-fourth and thirty-fifth floors of the Royal Bank Building, which is plainly the jewel among Toronto's downtown towers. On the outside it has a shimmery copper gleam, and, rather than being of a conventional boxy shape, it boasts exterior walls that take off in cunning zigzags. Inside, the entrance lobbies are all mirrors and potted plants and splashes of colour from the tapestries of Jack Bush and Jack Shadbolt. The effect is one of calm and order, a peace altogether alien to the commerce that is the building's reason for existence.

Upstairs, the Tory floors maintain the building's mood. The atmosphere is muted. The hallways are not in the usual bowling-alley style but repeat the zigzag patterns of the outer walls. The colours of the carpets and the interior surfaces run to beiges and pale browns. A pair of contrasting landscapes, a traditional A.J. Casson oil and a large, ethereal work by Takao Tanabe, face each other over the knubby blue chairs and couches in the clients' reception area. Paintings catch the eye everywhere; Tory, Tory owns enough Canadian art, tastefully chosen, to make a serious collector wince in envy. The individual offices, also slightly eccentric in shape, come in three sizes: large for a few senior men, medium for the middle-level partners, smaller by a degree for juniors and students. Most of the senior and middle-level offices face south over a splendid view of Toronto's harbour and islands. Paul Moore's office, medium-sized and next door to Trevor Eyton's (now rarely occupied while he presides over Brascan Limited), looks slightly east.

"There's a reason why I chose this location," he said in the office one bright November afternoon. Moore, chunkily built, likable, and a natural enthusiast, is in his early forties and could pass for ten years younger. His face has clung to boyishness. A lick of reddish-brown hair falls over his forehead. He likes to chew gum. "The reason is, the sun shines in from the south, and that does two things, drive up the temperature in the offices and blinds you to the view. I wasn't keen on either prospect."

Moore pays attention to such matters of detail in his life. "In the mornings, I pace myself through the *Globe and Mail*," he said. "Front page and comics at home. On the bus ride from the house to the commuter train I chat with my neighbours. The quiet half-hour on the train, which I treasure, I use for a quick look at the sports and for studying the *Globe*'s "Report on Business" section. That's essential. I'm behind if I don't read the ROB. It tells me what the Ontario Securities Commission did the day before, what other corporate lawyers are up to, what new ideas may be floating around the business community. I get off at Union Station and I'm ready for the day until I catch the 6:23 train back home at night."

Moore was an outstanding student at the University of Toronto Law School. He stood number one in first year and again in second year. In third year, he scored five A's and two B's on the final exams. So did Dick Gathercole. But Gathercole's marks were marginally higher and he finished first in the class, Moore second. Moore went downtown to article with a well-regarded commercial firm, Campbell, Godfrey and Lewtas, while Gathercole, along with another top graduate from the U. of T. Law School, Gar Pink, proceeded for his articles to the Tory firm.

Gathercole, a man whose social views put him much in contrast with Paul Moore, pops up in illuminating ways in Moore's early legal career. When Moore took his call to the bar and was casting around for precisely the right firm to practise with, he spent an hour chatting in John Tory's office. He took immediately to Tory's solid ways. Tory found Moore long on intelligence and efficiency and short on stuffiness, surely a man for Tory, Tory. But was there room to take on a new junior when the firm had already elected to hire Gar Pink and another articling student, Bob Torrens? Ah, but Dick Gathercole, a third candidate for the firm, was leaving for a year's study at the London School of Economics. Room was made, and Moore joined Tory's. Twelve months later, so did Gathercole. He wasn't enthusiastic about corporate work and concentrated on the firm's new litigation department. He resigned in 1971 to work for a free legal-aid clinic, then for the Ontario Attorney General's office, then for his old law school. Unlike Paul Moore, Gathercole, a big, soft-spoken man, given to sweaters and corduroy pants, bright, an idealist, was not at heart a Tory, Tory lawyer.

"Those offices in the Royal Bank are like a sealed spaceship," he says. "That's how they strike me when I visit my friends at the firm. At least when I look out my window at school I see other people. They look out and see other buildings full of other lawyers. The office is cut off from the real world, and it explains why the lawyers in it don't understand that certain problems exist — for example, that in Ontario most ordinary citizens have no real access to the legal profession."

Gathercole makes clear his respect and affection for the Tory partners as lawyers and as people. But corporate law, put simply, isn't his bag. "It's typical of Jim Tory," he says, "that he let me do work on firm time for Digger House, a place for kids with drug problems, and Theatre Passe Muraille, a sort of adventurous theatre company. In fact, he encouraged me. But I've never been enamoured of multinational corporations. I couldn't see the significance in two huge companies fighting it out. I didn't really care who won. To work at the Tory firm successfully, you have to believe in the capitalist system."

Paul Moore, a capitalist without apology, takes satisfaction in his dealings with big corporations and the men who run them. "I was at a meeting over in the Wood Gundy boardroom not long ago," he said. "Some senior Wood Gundy people were there and a few executives from a corporation that we were working out a deal with. We had complicated matters to go over and the hours crept along until it was getting to six o'clock and nothing was close to being wound up.

" 'Listen,' I said finally, 'it's six, this is Tuesday, and I have to leave the meeting.'

"Why? Naturally they wanted to know why.

" 'Because Tuesday is my Cubs night. I'm the Akela of the pack and I have to be there.'

"Well, we're in this magnificent boardroom, we're talking a $5 million deal or something with very important businessmen, and the next thing that happens is Ross Le Mesurier, one of the head people at Wood Gundy, is down on his haunches, the way kids do at Cubs, with his fingertips spread out touching the carpet and he's giving the Cub yell: 'Dib, dib, dib, Akeee-la!' Right in the boardroom. He remembered his Cub days. Some of the others did too. I left the meeting and everybody understood."

Moore chewed on his gum. "The businessmen I deal with aren't the fat cats you might imagine if you went by the wheeler-dealer standards of a TV show like *Dallas*. They're friendly and decent and have all their brains in place. No profanity. No drunkenness. They're the people who make the products and furnish the jobs in this country. They run the companies, and corporate lawyers are the guys who provide the grease that keeps the companies carrying on business. Corporate-commercial law is all about getting things done."

Which, according to Moore, isn't as routine as it sounds. He has put in his share of consecutive round-the-clock sessions to wrap up a transaction for a client. He sets aside one hour at home each evening to retreat to his den, a room that *does* look directly over Lake Ontario, to check office files. He reads in his field constantly — the *Economist* ("for its politics, not its economics"), the *Financial Post* and the *Financial Times* ("to find out what my partners are doing"), the *Canada Business Law Report,* the *Canadian Tax Journal*, the bulletin from the Ontario Securities Commission ("because the law changes so rapidly in my field"). And he keeps up with the barrage of new and revised federal and provincial statues, the Securities Act, the Business Corporations Act, the Income Tax Act, the Bank Act, the Foreign Investment Review Act.

"Where the pleasure comes in my practice is in being innovative," he said, slumping into a comfortable posture in his chair. "You never do the same deal twice. You always think of new ways of accomplishing the client's objective. If you repeat yourself, then your practice is getting old hat. There's bound to be some fresh twist."

He offered an example.

"In the last couple of years, traditional corporate financing has dried up. So if one corporation wants to acquire another, that route is closed off. But what's replaced it is the takeover business, and there

are all sorts of variations on it. One way is for the
buying company to offer to purchase all the shares in
the target company and be successful in getting 90
per cent of them. Then, by statute, the offerer can go
to court and get an order directing the other shareholders, the people holding the 10 per cent that didn't
accept the original offer, to sell to the offerer.

"Okay, we had a deal where our client wanted to
make a takeover by this method, but we knew that a
large block of stock in the target company, 25 per
cent of it, was in the hands of one shareholder. That
could have been bad news. Suppose we started buying stock around the majority shareholder but didn't
get him. We'd be in a bidding war. So what we did
first was approach the majority stockholder and take
an option on his shares. It was subject to certain conditions and time limits and so on, but we had him tied
up. Then we went after the other shares. We got 93
per cent of them, including the one guy's 25 per cent.
Then we squeezed out the remaining 7 per cent. Our
client started with nothing and ended with 100 per
cent of the target company."

Moore shifted position in his chair, swivelling to
look out his window, the panorama of the city to the
east free of glare. "If the squeeze-out method isn't
available, there's the amalgamation tactic. What
happens there is that the client company sets up a
subsidiary company and it enters into an agreement
to amalgamate with the target company. You only
need to get two-thirds of the target company's shareholders to approve the amalgamation for it to be
binding on the minority one-third. That makes it
relatively simple, but there are plenty of variations
you might have to work on the transaction. Maybe
you'll offer the holders of shares in the target company redeemable preferred shares which are

redeemed in cash. That makes it inviting for them. Offering cash in some circumstances is innovative. The cash has interesting capital-gains implications. Everything depends on the mix, whether you offer money or shares. You work out the tax consequences and make it appealing to the shareholders in the target company. That's what lawyers are for.

"In one case," Moore went on, his boyish smile turning on at the memory, "we did a deal where we used takeover *and* amalgamation. These were two separate transactions but we packaged them. We sent to each shareholder in the target company a cash offer conditional on the amalgamation's being approved. It was an innovative idea. It worked. Our client got control of the company he needed to round out his business picture."

Moore was still smiling. "The way I feel after a deal of that kind is the way I always expected to feel in law. Like a productive member of society."

Robert and Anorah Tory worked a farm at Guysborough, Nova Scotia, in the mid-nineteenth century. Along with their crops they raised three sons whose lives read like chapters from Horatio Alger. James Cranwich Tory became Lieutenant-Governor of Nova Scotia. Henry Marshall Tory founded the University of Alberta, took office as its first president, and was later head of the National Research Council in Ottawa. John Alexander Tory, born in Guysborough in 1869, went into insurance with Sun Life of Canada. "Life insurance," he once said, "is something that enables one generation to hold out a helping hand to the next, and so assist the carrying out of the Divine purpose of humanity's progress toward the ideal." That lofty philosophy peddled a record number of policies for John A. He moved to

Toronto in 1908 and built his Sun Life division, the
Western Ontario Branch, into the most remunerative
life-insurance agency in the British Empire. When he
stepped up to a Sun Life directorship in 1938, his
branch was too lively for one successor to manage.
Western Ontario had to be split into six branches.

John A.'s son inherited his father's energy and his
uncle Henry's scholarship, and threw in his own dash
of flamboyance. John Stewart Donald Tory, born in
1904, graduated at the top of his class at Osgoode
Hall Law School, 1927's gold medallist, and the
following year took a doctorate in law and business
administration at Harvard. He went into practice
with the venerable and respected Toronto firm
headed by W.N. Tilley, a legend at the Toronto bar.
By 1941 Tory had acquired the expertise and confidence to strike out on his own. He formed a new
firm with his name at the front end. Its specialty was
corporate law and it thrived.

It was J.S.D. Tory who tended to Massey-Harris's
corporate work in that company's great years. Tory
shared the load of legal advice to the E.P. Taylor
interests with another firm, Fraser, Beatty, and when
Taylor formed the Argus Corporation in 1945 he
placed Tory on the board. Tory looked after Abitibi,
the colossus in pulp and paper, and in 1952 he shep-
herded Simpsons through its merger with Sears,
Roebuck and Company of Chicago. He was at his
zenith in the early 1950s, a member of the boards of
over thirty companies in fields as diverse as aviation
and publishing, oil and life insurance (Sun Life
naturally), and he reigned as indisputably the most
sought-after lawyer-director in the country.

J.S.D. lived well. He bought five hundred acres of
land in King, an area of rolling hills and gentleman
farms northwest of Toronto. He stocked his spread

with Aberdeen Angus and Guernsey cattle and with Yorkshire hogs. He kept horses, too, and each morning J.S.D. would rise with the sun, take a long canter, then settle in for a session of general reading — books, magazines, some legal documents — until it was time for his car and driver to transport him to the firm's offices on King Street in downtown Toronto where he'd go about the business of spreading his influence.

"J.S.D. Tory was a rare man, like one of those old-time tycoons you saw in the movies," one of his former law associates says. "He liked his drink and liked his pleasures, but most of all, I think he enjoyed the exercise of power."

Trevor Eyton remembers a small but all-so-typical sample of J.S.D.'s flourish when it came to wielding power.

"Mr. Tory and some other leading Toronto businessmen, very big names, wanted to put together a charity to help a university in the Caribbean," Eyton says. "The problem was that to get a deduction for the charity with the beneficiary outside of Canada, they had to get status as a charity inside Canada. A slightly tricky business, establishing exemption from the usual charitable status. Mr. Tory called me into his office — this was around 1960 when I was still a student — and turned the job over to my humble talents. I embarked on a program of correspondence with civil servants in Ottawa and I got exactly nowhere. I was crushed; here I was failing all these important Toronto businessmen, and after four months, I went back to Mr. Tory and confessed my failure.

"He sat me down in his office and had his secretary put him through to the Deputy Minister of Revenue in Ottawa. The Deputy Minister came directly on the line. That was the first thing I noticed. The second thing I noticed was that Mr. Tory called the Deputy Minister by his first name and the Deputy Minister referred to Mr. Tory throughout as 'Mr. Tory'.

" 'Are you against communism?'

"Those were the first words Mr. Tory spoke to the Deputy Minister, and naturally the answer was, 'Yes.'

" 'The only way we're going to keep communism out of the Caribbean,' Mr. Tory said, 'is by giving those people down there some university education.' And he went on to explain about the charity he and his friends wanted to establish and he asked the Deputy Minister what he intended to do about it.

"There wasn't any hesitation from the other end. 'I'll put your charity on the exempt status, Mr. Tory,' the Deputy Minister said, and I walked out of Mr. Tory's office with a better understanding of what power is all about."

J.S.D. and his first wife had twin sons, John Arnold Tory and James Marshall Tory, born March 7, 1930. The boys' mother, Jean Arnold Tory, is in her different way as remarkable as their father. A woman of pride and industry, she has given much of her life to community work: "not just sitting on boards," one of her friends says, "not showcase performances, but going out and slugging for her causes." To this day, in her seventies, Mrs. Tory keeps active — she plays golf several times a week at the Rosedale club, pulling her own cart around eighteen holes — and conducts herself with immaculate style. "A lot of the sons' definitive genes come from her," the friend says, "the ones that have to do with decorum and grace and that side of life."

Jim and John went to the University of Toronto Schools, a fiercely competitive high school for brainy kids. At UTS, the yearbook for the Tory boys' graduating class quoted John as planning a career in medicine. A son of J.S.D. Tory evading the law? Hardly. Indeed, the haste with which the boys were pointed into law school bordered on the unseemly. They took only two years in arts at the University of Toronto, then switched to the university's law school, taking advantage of a regulation that permitted enrolment in law without an undergraduate degree.

"I'd never do it again, miss out on a complete background in the arts," Jim says. "But it was, well, *suggested* to us that it'd be a good idea at the time.

The brothers got their call to the bar in 1954 and entered the firm founded by their father. It was a period of flux. Jim and John were absorbing the intricacies of corporate-commercial law through the late 1950s, while in the same years J.S.D.'s health and his enthusiasm for practice were on the wane. A couple of important clients — A.V. Roe Ltd. was one — took their business elsewhere. The firm endured upheavals. In 1957, a group of lawyers left the Torys to form a new firm, Miller, Thomson, Hicks. In 1961 — the firm was then titled Tory, Arnold, Wardlaw and Whittaker — Wardlaw and Whittaker departed. They tried to persuade a pair of the Tory firm's young whizzes, Trevor Eyton and Jim Baillie, to join them. The pair declined. Perhaps they saw the glory years ahead under Jim and John.

Failing health and all, the senior Tory never lost his panache. In 1965, facing death, he scheduled four short board meetings for one day, gatherings of directors of companies he had served and guided for years. At the conclusion of each meeting, he walked around the table and shook hands with his fellow directors.

"Thank you," he said to every man. He was driven home, and not long after, he died. Responsibility for the firm passed finally and officially to J.S.D.'s sons, thirty-five years old at the time, an outrageously tender age by the ancient standards of Bay Street.

"On the day Mr. Tory died," Eyton remembers, "four or five of the leading businessmen in the country phoned John and Jim and said they'd leave their accounts with the firm. That's a measure of the respect they'd had for the old man. But there was an unspoken rider on the commitment — the firm had to do the job of keeping the clients happy."

"Hectic" is how John Tory remembers the years immediately after his father's death. "With everybody leaving the firm or dying," he says, "there weren't many of us left, about eight or so lawyers. The firm was small and very young. The work got absolutely hectic but it was exhilarating. Enough hours in the day were the problem. I used to come home at night and sit in a chair in the den and read over letters of opinion that junior lawyers had drafted for clients. I'd suggest changes, write in new proposals, kind of redraft the letters, and next day I'd tell the juniors to get the letters retyped and be sure to send them out under *their* signatures. It wasn't that I didn't have pride of authorship in what I'd written. It was just that when the client called back I wanted him to phone the lawyer who'd signed the letter. I didn't want him to phone me. There weren't enough hours in the day."

Despite the burden of youth, the Torys and their partners delivered the corporate goods. Through the late 1960s they gave their clients intelligent advice, long hours, a deep helping of integrity, and, it seems clear, some additional measure of service, something with a touch of mystique. The extra ingredient, in John Tory's view, is nothing less than "creativity".

"People don't realize what's involved in the process of corporate law," he says. "Other lawyers, the ones in criminal law or civil litigation, deal with problems. There's nothing creative about that because what they're in fact dealing with is something that's already happened. In corporate-commercial law, on the contrary, you tangle with events that haven't yet occurred. *That's* creative. You've got a corporate reorganization or a corporate acquisition coming up, and you have to project yourself into the future and visualize all the possibilities, good and bad, that might happen and then figure out the ways to avoid the bad and capture the good."

Tory took his lessons in corporate finesse from an old master, Roy Thomson. It was Thomson who came out of Northern Ontario in the 1940s to put together an empire based initially on a chain of Canadian newspapers but later including everything from insurance companies to *The Times* of London, from travel agencies, truck lines, and Scottish television to North Sea oil. Roy Thomson and J.S.D. Tory enjoyed a close business and social relationship, and by the mid-1960s Thomson, by then Lord Thomson of Fleet, had begun to hand on direction of his empire to the two men's sons, Ken Thomson and John Tory.

"Talk about creative, that was Roy Thomson," Tory says, "and he forced me to be the same way. I was a young lawyer and he'd come to me and say he wanted to accomplish a certain end in a business deal, an acquisition maybe. I'd look into it and tell him it couldn't be done the way he wanted to do it. 'Find another way,' he'd say. And I'd have to. Roy never accepted that something couldn't be done. He was like most corporate clients — he knew where he wanted to end up. He knew where he wanted to go at the end of the road. It was my job, the lawyer's job, to find the road-blocks along the way and pick a route through them. I think that's not a bad metaphor for creativity.''

One problem, according to Tory, is that there's just a single way to acquire a corporate lawyer's thinking processes. "Not from law school. The only training you can count on is the kind that comes from working with corporate lawyers and clients who already know the ropes. Under those circumstances, corporate-commercial practice gives the most scope of any kind of law for people to demonstrate creativity, even people who aren't at all naturally creative. That's strange but true. Law school, though, fills in none of the background for that. You get called to the bar and you start from scratch.''

J.S.D. Tory, for his part, liked to compare law school to a boxer's training-camp, a place to get in shape and develop an edge. It wasn't, however, the real arena. It wasn't the marketplace where the corporate lawyer has to confront and sell. Corporate law, J.S.D. said, was selling. He had another theory: he kept in his law office a complete set of *Fortune* magazines, and he used to insist that any man could make himself into a sound corporate lawyer if he did nothing except read every issue of *Fortune* from cover to cover. That done, J.S.D. contended, a man would develop an understanding of how commerce works, how management functions, how presidents think, and how corporate lawyers sell themselves.

Trevor Eyton tends to agree with J.S.D.'s approach to corporate law. "Actually I'm appalled at how little we lawyers really know," he says, "and how well rewarded we are for the small areas of work we cover. But commercial lawyers, if I was summing us up, have to be persuasive. We have to be people who can look other people in the eye."

Looking people in the eye, Tory, Tory grew. Some favoured keeping the firm small and specialized, an impossible aim. Too many factors compelled it to expand almost in spite of itself. The ambitions of such Tory clients as the Thomson organization demanded that the firm hire new lawyers to handle the fresh volume of business. The increasing complexity of government regulations affecting large corporations called for more manpower at the firm. And the swelling reputation of Tory, Tory inevitably attracted new clients. New clients meant more lawyers.

"The firm had to expand in ways nobody might anticipate," Jim Tory says. "For example, our litigation department. For a long time, whenever one of our clients got into something that called for litigation advice, we'd send them over to another firm, Kimber, Dubin, where they specialized in that sort of law. But after a while we felt that wasn't good enough. We had to be in a position to give our clients the whole range of service under one roof."

Thus, in the late 1960s the Torys reached for another old classmate from the University of Toronto Law School. He was Frank Callaghan, who had been for years a counsel in the office of the Ontario Attorney General. Almost immediately the provincial government retained Callaghan and his new associates at Tory, Tory to handle a complex pollution lawsuit against the Dow Chemical Company. The litigation department needed more bodies. When Callaghan left in the early 1970s to become deputy attorney general, the Tory firm absorbed Kimber, Dubin with its five litigation specialists. When Charles Dubin left to take a seat on the Ontario Supreme Court, the firm hired Lorne Morphy, a counsel with a strong reputation based on years of outstanding court work at a variety of major Toronto firms. Today Morphy heads a litigation department that numbers a full dozen lawyers.

"At first we were just used to having litigation people around," Jim Tory says. "Now we've got a department that's about as good as anybody's."

For all its diversity of services, it is of course Tory, Tory's skill in corporate-commercial law that distinguishes it. Corporate takeovers, corporate acquisitions, corporate restructuring — the firm blankets the field. Peter Bronfman, for one, knew who to turn to when he and his brother Edward, nephews of the late and mighty Sam who launched the Bronfman dynasty, developed a yen in 1979 to take over Brascan Limited. He turned to Trevor Eyton.

The Bronfman vehicle for the Brascan adventure was Edper Equities Limited. It is two-thirds owned by the Bronfman brothers and one-third by Patino N.V. of the Netherlands. Eyton, who dished up legal guidance to the Bronfmans almost from the beginning of his Tory career, had introduced the Bronfmans and the Patinos, just another piece of astute lawyerly service, and the two families hit it off. Edper's assets included Place Ville Marie in Montreal, assorted shopping plazas across Canada, and some choice Calgary real estate, but the Bronfman-Patino-Eyton forces figured Brascan was ripe for plucking. It possessed, as one attractive feature, a hefty bank account. Brascan, a Canadian company that dated back to 1899, had originally built itself on investment in the power utility of Brazil and later expanded to take in a variety of holdings in Brazilian and Canadian companies (John Labatt, Consumers Glass, London Life). In late 1978 it sold off its ownership in Light-Servicos Electricidada S.A. of Brazil for $447 million. That put cash in its bank account. That made it appealing to Edper. .

On April 5, 1979, Eyton met with Brascan's chairman of the board, Jake Moore, and his legal advisor, a senior man from Blake, Cassels and Graydon (over one hundred lawyers, offices in the Commerce Court West), in a suite at the Royal York Hotel. Eyton looked Moore in the eye and told him Edper intended to pursue a controlling interest in Brascan. Moore, none too happy and prepared to resist, contented himself with a noncommittal expression. End of meeting and commencement of what was later variously described as "the largest and most controversial deal in recent Canadian busines history" (*Maclean's* magazine) and a "ruthless takeover" (*Toronto Star*).

The struggle, "testy" at times in Eyton's word, lasted for almost three months, but it was essentially a no-contest affair. Edper had on its side too much nerve, moxie, and money. On April 30, Edper purchased 2.4 million Brascan shares on the American Stock Exchange in New York, the largest single transaction ever in AmEx history. Edper kept buying — 3.3 million shares from various sources on May 1 — until it had spent $340 million, cash on the barrelhead, for 13 million Brascan shares. Other large shareholders in Brascan, correctly reading the drift, cast their lot with the Edper team, and by June 14 Edper had passed the 50-per-cent mark in its holdings of Brascan stock. Takeover, in·effect, completed.

Jake Moore stepped aside as Brascan's chairman of the board on June 29, taking with him payment of a year's salary ($250,000) and a juicy lifetime pension ($100,000 per annum), and later in the summer Eyton moved his talents from the thirty-fourth floor of the Royal Bank to the forty-eighth floor of Commerce Court West as Brascan's new president. He trimmed the company's staff by 50 per cent, streamlined the enterprise, and completed the conversion of Brascan from an operating company to a holding company. Eyton knew where he was going. He's always known where he's been headed.

"When I was in high school, Jarvis Collegiate in Toronto," he said one winter morning after he'd occupied his Brascan chair for six months, "the guidance counsellor asked me about my plans. This was all part of the routine in discussing your ambitions and future occupation and so on. I looked at the guidance person and said, 'I'm going to be a corporate lawyer for the CPR.' I don't know about the CPR part, but I got the rest of it right. At the time, I was thirteen."

In the same years as the Edper action, in 1979-80, the Thomson organization was spending some of its money in the interests of corporate reorganization. It bought 75 per cent of the Hudson's Bay Company for $641 million in April 1979 and it purchased FP Publications Limited for $165 million in January 1980. Both transactions involved struggles, with Galen Weston (of the Weston conglomerate that includes Loblaw's, National Tea, Weston Bakeries, and another half-hundred subsidiaries) over the Bay, and with Howard Webster (a Montreal financier who once owned the *Globe and Mail*) over FP. Both were engineered by John, with the support of Ken Thomson and the constant legal ministrations of Tory,

Tory ("On the Bay deal," John says, "my brother and Gar Pink and a couple of other fellows did practically nothing else for a whole six weeks"). And both were part of a larger scheme to bring a chunk of the Thomson money and authority from the United Kingdom back to Canada.

"The corporate restructuring of the Thomson organization has taken me two years," John Tory explained one Sunday afternoon in March of 1980, sitting with a drink by a grate fire in the den of his Lawrence Park home. "I had to consider corporate implications and tax problems. I had to look at everything from the U.K. standpoint and the Canadian standpoint. And I had to use lawyers from both countries to work through the maze. I'm a lawyer, but in this case, over the two years, I was looking at the job as a client. What I was doing — this made me feel pretty good — was asking lawyers to be what clients used to ask of me. To be creative."

The Tory, Tory success story shows no indications of running short on future chapters. "The young guys," John Tory says, "the young lawyers they send up to me from the firm to help on different deals, are smarter than they used to be in my days at the firm. They haven't got the experience or the flexibility, but they've got the brains. They amaze me."

One of the young guys happens to be John's son, John Jr., who entered practice with the family firm on March 3, 1980. Jim has a son at law school. He also has a daughter who is a chartered accountant and another daughter who spent much of 1979-80 in a community outside Peking pursuing her research in Asian studies. But for now it's John Jr. who's the prime candidate to carry on the Tory legal tradition. He has already recorded an intimidating share of accomplishments, a range that includes seven years as an on-air announcer at Toronto radio station CHFI and management of two federal election campaigns, one win, one loss, for Ron Atkey, Joe Clark's immigration minister. At his high school, UTS — where else would a Tory prep himself? — the school's director of Student Counselling Services, Clare Pace, once asked John Jr. the same question Trevor Eyton's guidance counsellor had directed at him. Where was he headed? What was his ambition?

"I'm going to be prime minister of Canada," the boy answered without a modest moment of hesitation.

Clare Pace thinks John Jr. might make it.

CHAPTER FOUR

Defending the Bad Guys: Profiles in Criminal Law

Caroline Lindberg's face belongs on a cameo. It is pale and heart-shaped and serene. Her hair is light brown and pulled loosely back from her forehead. She has a long, graceful neck and she wears white blouses. She is ladylike, a young woman whose presence has a naturally civilizing influence. She is a lawyer, called to the Ontario bar in the spring of 1981 when she was twenty-five years old. Her appearance suggests her practice would run to wills and trusts and pieces of property, perhaps assisting a senior partner in a large firm in advice to elderly gentlemen on the disposition of their estates. But appearances deceive. Caroline Lindberg is a criminal lawyer.

"A couple of years ago," she says, "I didn't think I'd be spending my time alone in a room talking to a guy who's charged with incest or indecent assault or eight counts of intercourse with a female under fourteen. But those kinds of people are my clients now. I'm happy with them as my clients. And I worry about them. Especially I worry about the ones in custody waiting for their trials, the ones who can't make bail. Sometimes I can't stop from going over in my head all my clients who are somewhere in a jail."

Lindberg practises on her own. After her call to the bar, she negotiated a line of credit from the Royal Bank for fifteen thousand dollars and spent part of the money to rent space in a small downtown Toronto firm. For about a thousand dollars a month she gets the use of the firm's library, part of a secretary's time, and an office not much bigger than the cells that are home to some of her clients. She lives alone in a tidy one-bedroom apartment near the University of Toronto. Once in a while, when she finds a spare thirty minutes, she walks up to the university's athletic complex for a swim. She enrolled in a yoga class but made it to only half the sessions. She used to see two or three movies a week; now it's one or two a month. Her criminal practice and those worrisome clients have somehow moved into the space she once called her own.

Richard White is a James Dean throwback in looks, all sulky face and wavy hair. He's nineteen years old, and by the time he became Lindberg's client early in the summer of 1981, he showed seven convictions for theft and for breaking and entering, and he'd done one stretch of three months in jail. He had a record, and he wasn't very bright.

"He's like so many of my clients," Lindberg said of White. "I don't act for master criminals. The people I get are the kind who answer 'I don't know' to most of the questions I ask them. They're not very good at articulating their thoughts. But intuitively they have a lot going for them. They remind me of characters from a William Faulkner novel."

The police figured they had a case of assault and robbery nailed shut on White. According to their scenario, the crime began when two fifteen-year-old girls hailed a taxi in downtown Toronto about three a.m. on a late-spring morning. The girls directed the cab driver on a route that ended in the underground garage of an apartment building. One of the girls got out of the cab, leaving the second girl in the front seat with the driver. The two were alone for a few minutes — during which time some sexual activity may or may not have commenced — when two men jumped into the cab, one through the left rear door and the other, scrambling over the girl, from the front passenger door. The man in the rear held the cabbie around the neck while the other frisked him for his money — about $100 — and his wallet. The mugging of the cab driver was shocking and swift, and within ten seconds the two men and the girls had vanished from the garage.

One night a couple of weeks later, as the same cab-bie was tooling through the same downtown streets on the lookout for a fare, he spotted the two girls. They were passengers in a car directly in front of him. He radioed his dispatcher to summon the police and set after the car in a surreptitious chase. Six miles later, a police cruiser joined the pursuit and pulled the girls' car to the curb.

"Yeah," the cab driver said, "they're the right broads."

He checked the other passengers in the car.

"Hey!" he said, pointing to a man in the back. "It's the guy from the garage. He's the one that grabbed my cash."

The guy was Richard White.

While the two girls were taken away to be dealt with by juvenile court, White was held overnight in a cell at a midtown police station. At 8:30 the next morning, two officers questioned him. Nah, White said, I don't know about any underground garage. We got a positive identification on you, the officers said, and they told White they were laying charges of assault and robbery. At three o'clock that afternoon, White was driven a few blocks to Metro Toronto

Police Headquarters, where he sat alone on a bench on one of the upper floors waiting to be photographed and fingerprinted.

"Hi ya." It was a policeman in uniform. He joined White on the bench, and according to the policeman's later story, he and White fell into an open and easy chat.

"You're gonna be printed in a couple of minutes," the policeman said.

"What am I charged with anyway?" White is supposed to have asked.

"Assault and robbery," the policeman answered. "Two counts of each."

"*Two*? I never assaulted another guy."

"Well, this one guy, the cab driver," the policeman said. "Did you get both the money and the wallet?"

"Yeah, I did," White said. "But, y'know, he was just out to get himself fucked by the girls, so he deserved to be ripped off."

No one, neither family nor friends, would put up bail for White, and he passed seven weeks in jail waiting until his trial date. The York County Legal Aid Society assigned him a lawyer, a man in his early thirties, and on the morning of the trial in Provincial Court, he appeared on White's behalf. The crown attorney called two witnesses, the cab driver, who said he had a "momentary glimpse" of White in the garage, and the uniformed policeman, who repeated the conversation he claimed to have had with White at police headquarters. When the crown had completed its case, White's lawyer asked for more time to prepare a defence. The judge gave him a week, but a day later, for reasons known only to White, he fired his lawyer.

The Legal Aid Society assigned Lindberg to pick up the pieces. She interviewed White in jail, a couple of long and thorough sessions, and the night before the case was scheduled for completion, she sat late in her office organizing her presentation. She struggled to feel hopeful, but the odds against her seemed formidable. She had no witnesses except White, and he wouldn't strike an impressive figure. She knew that Toronto judges traditionally come down hard on the accused in cases of violence against cab drivers. And she thought the judge on the White case presented special difficulties, a crown-oriented judge who had once been a crown attorney himself and before that, early in his career, a cop.

At 1:30 in the morning, still at her desk, Lindberg phoned the White home. When he wasn't in jail, Richard lived in the suburbs with his parents, who ran a janitorial service which Richard worked for. Lindberg spoke to White's younger brother, a seventeen-year-old who had one theft conviction of his own. Lindberg was fishing, trying to get a handle on White and his background, looking for anything that might give her an edge in her arguments to the judge. She was eager. She talked to the brother for an hour but ended up learning little that was new or helpful, and it was three in the morning before she put aside her papers and her disappointment and went at last to bed.

The trial was at the Collegepark Courts on the second floor of the building that was once Eaton's College Street department store. It's a 1930s art deco creation, and the courts, makeshift and homely, seem an intrusion on the building's graceful architecture. The courts — Provincial Courts — are in effect poor people's forums, hearing-places for desperate and low-life crimes, shop-lifting and mugging and breaking in, and the air in the corridors and the courtrooms is leaden with tension and bad breath and the stink of poverty.

Lindberg called White to the witness stand. His answers came in monosyllables, but in his five minutes of halting testimony, Lindberg got him to deny that he'd committed the assault and robbery. He agreed that he'd talked to the uniformed policeman at headquarters but he hadn't said anything that implicated him in the crime. White returned to the prisoners' box.

"Make your presentations, Miss Lindberg," the judge said. He was a man in his mid-fifties with a rubbery, humorous face and a flat voice.

Lindberg's manner in court, the product partly of her personality and partly of her inexperience, blends intensity and reserve in an attractive mix. Her voice is soft, but some quality in it, a sense of urgency, demands that it be heard. She comes across as undeniably sensible when she stands in front of a judge. She may be young and new to the game, so her manner says, but she carries the credentials of dedication and sound thinking and concern for the right legal principles. That, it's implied, ought to count for something.

On Richard White's behalf, she went straight to the weaknesses in the crown's case. Purposely she avoided much reference to the identification evidence, intuiting that the cab driver's "momentary glimpse" of his attacker wasn't by itself enough to convict White. She analysed the uniformed policeman's testimony. Did it make sense, she asked, that White, who had been told earlier on the day of his arrest that he was charged with assault and robbery, would ask another policeman what he was charged with? And why, come to that, would White speak so frankly to a policeman at all? Especially to a policeman in uniform? And what about the wording of the policeman's question to White, "Did you get *the* money and *the* wallet?" Doesn't that sound suspect? Doesn't it smack of coaching?

"As to the identification of the accused," the judge said, giving his verdict as soon as Lindberg had finished, "it doesn't satisfy me beyond a reasonable doubt. However, I'm accepting the police officer's evidence. It goes beyond a reasonable doubt, and there'll be a conviction against the accused."

Lindberg asked that sentencing of White be put over until the following morning, and that night she read through earlier assault-robbery cases, checking the jail time that judges handed out in such crimes. It was heavy, usually more than the two years needed to send a man to the penitentiary. She made notes for her remarks to the judge, and around midnight she phoned White's mother.

"I'd like you to come to court tomorrow," Lindberg said.

"Can't help you," the mother answered.

"Look, I don't want you to testify or anything. I just want to be able to tell the judge you're sitting in court. Your son could go to the pen, and one thing that might keep him out is if the judge knows you care enough to come to court."

"Can't," the mother said. "We're moving to a new house tomorrow and it's gonna take all day."

Next morning in court, the judge seemed impatient, and Lindberg spoke quickly. Richard White is too young to be sent away to a penitentiary, she said, only nineteen. The most time he's ever done in jail until now is three months. This is his first violent crime. And he's already spent seven weeks in jail waiting for his trial. Lindberg got it all out, all her points, in a smooth, even rush of words.

"Twenty-two months," the judge said. Since the sentence was under two years, it would put White in a reformatory, not the pen.

Lindberg spoke briefly to White in the holding cells before he was taken away to begin his time.

"He didn't show any reaction" she said when she came out of the cells. "He *never* shows any reaction. But twenty-two months is a very good sentence."

Lindberg went back to her office, balancing her optimism.

"Working for people like Richard," she said, "I'm beginning to feel distanced from just about everybody else in the world. Like, my mother will read of a crime in the newspapers and say, oh, look at the horrible thing this person has done, and I think, well, that person could be my client. But I don't make judgments about the person, not about Richard or any of my clients. What happens is that when I'm somebody's lawyer and he's charged with a crime, I'm the most positive element in his life at that point. That means my relationship with him develops in good ways, and it becomes difficult for me to identify with the rest of society who thinks the forces of law and order are working for the common good and these other people, the criminals, are evil. That isn't necessarily true. The police don't always deal with my clients in straight ways. Look at Richard and the policeman who testified against him."

Lindberg's mind scurried between ideas. She's given to close analysis of her thoughts and emotions, and she was keen to put her reactions to the events and people of her lawyer's life — cases, trials, bail hearings, clients, cops, crown attorneys — in immaculate perspective.

"Most of my clients aren't entirely rational. Maybe if they were, I'd find the work boring. My clients are people who act impulsively. They hardly ever sit down and plan what they're going to do. They just act, and it's always the things people do impulsively that get them in trouble. Those kinds of acts are never in a person's own best interests. So why do my clients pull these impulsive crimes? I'm fascinated to find out. I talk to them and ask questions and get involved. And I like it. My friends say to me, oh, you'll get over *that*. They think when I have an emotional response to my clients it's inappropriate and undesirable. They think I'll be happier when I get *over* these feelings. But there are things in life that I don't want to get over, and being fascinated by my clients is one of them."

Lindberg flashed back to Richard White. "What made me feel the worst all day about his case was telling him that his parents wouldn't be in court. Parents are always saying to me how much they love their children and then they don't show up in court to support the kids. It's common, but that doesn't make it any easier to tell a person like Richard that he's on his own."

Lindberg brightened.

"Twenty-two months, though, that's an okay sentence. I feel good about that."

Lindberg used two thousand dollars of the Royal Bank's loan to buy a second-hand car. It was a yellow Volks Beetle, and on a Monday morning in midsummer four days after she took possession of the car, she set off for the East Mall Courthouse, where she was to plead a client guilty to one charge of breaking and entering. The East Mall Courthouse is in the Etobicoke suburb of Toronto close to Highway

427, and as Lindberg came off 427 by way of an exit ramp, she saw a red light against her up ahead at the three-way intersection of the ramp and a four-lane main street. She pumped her foot on the brake. Nothing. The brake had failed. The pedal plunged to the floor, and the Beetle hurtled through the red light, past four lanes of oncoming traffic, and bounced over the curb on the far side of the main road. Lindberg was headed in a direct line for a brick house. The house's garage had wooden doors. Lindberg aimed for the garage. She crashed through the doors. Would there be a parked car on the other side? Lindberg braced herself. No parked car. But the garage was stacked with furniture and boxes. The Beetle crunched against them and came to rest in the litter. Lindberg checked herself. Nothing broken or bruised. But she could hear a funny fluttering sound in the garage. She opened the Beetle's door and looked up. The garage was filled with frantic pigeons. They'd been nestling in cages hung from the ceiling until the Beetle disturbed their peace. Lindberg got out of the car and stood amid the crushed boxes, the fluttering pigeons, and the forlorn Beetle. She felt less like a lawyer and more like an extra from a Laurel and Hardy movie. She telephoned the police and a tow truck and hurried to the courthouse. Too late. Her client's case had been called, and when Lindberg failed to appear, he was remanded back into custody. Lindberg took a taxi downtown and ordered two fast drinks for lunch.

"It's so bad about my client," she said. "He's come up for sentencing four times already, and every time something happens to put it off. This, though, *this* was the worst."

Lindberg didn't feel an early mission to practise criminal law. When the call came, it arrived late, more or less out of the blue in her third year of law school. There seems to be a pattern in her life, she thinks, of apparently random choices that turn out to be definitive discoveries about herself.

She chose an arts course in Carleton University because, as someone who had grown up in many parts of Canada — Prince Albert, Saskatchewan; Sudbury in Northern Ontario; Toronto — she liked the notion of Ottawa's stability and tidiness. "But when I got there," she says, "everybody looked and acted like everybody else in the city. I discovered I can't stand uniformity." After two years of Carleton and a few months of bumming around South America, she chose the University of Toronto Law School. "But I hardly looked into the future. It wasn't until I took my articling year in the Ontario Attorney General's office that I knew I wanted criminal law. What I didn't enjoy was law school itself, and after I discovered my feelings about criminal, it was a relief to realize that it seemed to have been worth while taking law after all."

At the Attorney General's office, she worked on a complicated fraud case, the prosecution of a Mafia figure, a couple of murder trials, several appeals to the Ontario Court of Appeal, and three appeals to the Supreme Court of Canada. She absorbed a lot of law. "I didn't get much court experience of my own, but that was okay. The crown attorneys wanted me to become thoroughly familiar with the cases they were working on so that I could sit down with them and talk the cases through. That way, they could pick up on the holes and weaknesses in their prosecutions. And me, I was getting exposed to case law and statutes and interpretations and court strategy of all kinds.''

It was this intense experience that helped Lindberg land a role in a high-profile trial a mere four months after her call to the bar. The work that came her way in the first weeks of practice was confined, as she expected, to cases like Richard White's and other relatively minor-league matters. But on a Monday in mid-August, a Toronto defence lawyer named Will Hechter took her on as his junior counsel in a case that was definitely major league.

"Caroline bowled me over," Hechter says. "I've never met anyone so young who has such a terrific knowledge of the law. Mention a legal point and she'll quote you a case. The other thing about her is that it was *she* who approached *me* about this job. She learned about it and phoned me and insisted that nobody else could handle it except her. I'd never heard of her before the call, but she talked her way on the case."

The case, as it happened, was murder: Lindberg's first homicide trial.

On December 30, 1980, Gary Fitzgerald and Joe Schoenberger, eighteen and seventeen years old respectively, left their homes in Windsor, Ontario, in Schoenberger's 1974 Dodge Duster and headed for the Mattawa area in the most northerly tip of Southern Ontario, where, according to Fitzgerald's plan, they would steal some guns and sell them to raise money for a trip to Hawaii. "I hate cops," Fitzgerald said at a party before the trip, "and if one gets in my way, I'll kill him." The two reached George Richards' home near Mattawa on New Year's Day — Richards was a second cousin of Fitzgerald's — and later, about eleven p.m., while several other people in the house slept, they loaded the Duster with guns and knives that belonged to Richards and drove into the night. One of the weapons was an AR-7 Explorer semi-automatic twenty-two. Over the following few hours, Fitzgerald would use it to kill two men and wound a third.

Shortly after midnight the Duster pulled into the Ultramar Gas Bar in Emsdale, about seventy miles down Highway 11 from Mattawa. Chester Blackmore, the station's fifty-year-old attendant, pumped $16.01 in gas into the car's tank. Neither Fitzgerald nor Schoenberger had any money, and when Blackmore moved forward to collect his payment, Fitzgerald shot through the open window and hit Blackmore twice in the face.

The Duster sped further south on Highway 11 until an Ontario Provincial Police cruiser signalled it to pull over. Constable Richard Verdecchia, thirty-five and alone in the cruiser, hadn't heard about the shooting back in Emsdale. What attracted him to the Duster was its broken tail-light. He stepped out of his cruiser, and Fitzgerald shot him through the chest. Fitzgerald walked to the fallen body and fired three more shots in a cluster around Verdecchia's right eye.

Several more miles down Highway 11, OPP Constable Neil Hurtubise was next to spot the Duster's broken tail-light. Hurtubise, forty-five and also alone in his cruiser, knew of the Blackmore shooting and was aware that Verdecchia wasn't answering radio calls for some inexplicable reason, but he didn't associate the Duster with either Blackmore or Verdecchia. On foot, he approached the driver's side of the Duster. Fitzgerald opened fire.

"You don't have to shoot me!" Hurtubise screamed.

He turned back to the cruiser. Fitzgerald's shots caught Hurtubise in the side and the shoulder, neck and cheek. He stumbled to his car radio.

"Officer shot!" he called as the Duster pulled away. "Officer shot!"

Hurtubise's signal set off the largest police hunt in Ontario history. Several dozen officers, a fleet of cruisers, a helicopter, and a tracking dog named Max set after the car that Hurtubise described. Three hours later, police found it in the parking lot of the Sundial Motor Hotel on the outskirts of Orillia twenty-five miles south of the spot where Hurtubise was shot. The Duster was empty — apart from nine guns, some rounds of ammunition, four knives, and two bayonets. Max, the dog, caught a scent and led his masters down a nearby set of railroad tracks and across a field to Kerr's Auto Body Shop. Fitzgerald and Schoenberger were asleep in the back of a dilapidated Volkswagen van on the lot, Fitzberald with the AR-7 Explorer beside him. The police woke and arrested the boys. It was 7:08 on the morning of January 2, 1981, barely eight hours from the time the two left George Richards' house in Mattawa.

The crown attorney's office charged both Fitzgerald and Schoenberger with first-degree murder in the killing of Constable Verdecchia because he was a policeman and with second-degree murder in the Chester Blackmore case. (The crown laid charges of attempted murder of Constable Hurtubise, then withdrew them; the charges would, however, resurface several months later.) The crown's case against Fitzgerald seemed open and shut; he had, as he admitted to the police with a touch of pride, fired all the shots from the AR-7 Explorer. But under a complicated section of the Criminal Code, Joe Schoenberger was equally guilty of murder if the crown could prove that he had aided or abetted in the shootings and knew or ought to have known that death would follow from Fitzgerald's actions.

Will Hechter thought he could head the crown off. Schoenberger's parents retained him to act for their son a few days after the shootings. Hechter was an energetic, friendly man in his late thirties who had entered private practice only six months earlier after experience as a crown attorney in both Winnipeg and Toronto, and he formed an early opinion about his new client from which he never wavered in the tough weeks ahead.

"I decided," he says, "that Joe had been nothing more than a boy who happened to be in the wrong place at the wrong time."

Schoenberger's background showed him to be a model teenager. No criminal record, solid student at school, popular among his peers. He held down a job in the shoe department of a Windsor store after school hours, and he played drums in the Scarlet Brigade, a local marching band that performed during the half-time show at the 1980 Grey Cup football game.

"Joe met Fitzgerald only a couple of months before the killings," Hechter says, "and somehow got caught up in his orbit. In the end, on the night of the murders, Joe was so afraid of Fitzgerald that he thought he might be the next victim."

Gary Fitzgerald's lawyer, a sleek, worldly defence counsel from Toronto named Clay Ruby, had a more complex, less appealing personality to deal with. Fitzgerald had been born the fourth illegitimate child of a twenty-one-year-old woman. He was adopted at fifteen months, but his adoptive parents, after a short period of lavishing Gary with affection, turned sour on him. They strapped and beat him, and in reaction, Gary, a loner, began to lie and steal and set fires. A school for emotionally disturbed adolescents diagnosed him as suffering from "a fear of being lost and abandoned." But he was a clever kid, manipulative, and he found a special satisfaction when he joined the Royal Canadian Service Corps. "Fitzgerald," an army report said, "is a credit to his unit." Gary liked guns. He handled them expertly, and he developed into a crack shot.

"My guy's a psychopath," Ruby said after Fitzgerald had undergone a lengthy examination at the Clarke Institute of Psychiatry in Toronto. "The times he's truly happy are when he's killing somebody. His big regret in life, this eighteen-year-old kid, is that he missed fighting in the Vietnam War. He's ill, and he ought to be found not guilty by reason of insanity. But I don't know if we've got enough to meet the Criminal Code definition of insanity. He's not schizophrenic and he's not paranoid, which would meet the definition. He's a plain psychopath, which probably won't."

The trial of Fitzgerald and Schoenberger was held in Barrie, a small city sixty miles north of Toronto and the principal centre for the County of Simcoe, where the killings had taken place. Barrie's courthouse is a new building in gaudy red brick and has an abrupt and graceless look as if it had been put together from a Meccano set. Another building, ancient and grey, a miniature fortress, squats at the rear of the courthouse. It's the county jail, and from the time of the killings, it made a stern and forbidding home for Fitzgerald and Schoenberger, especially for Fitzgerald.

"Don't let that boy escape," Fitzgerald's adoptive mother had said, making a nervous joke to the guards on a day when she visited Gary.

The guards, all too aware that they had possibly the most notorious killer in Simcoe County history on their hands, took Mrs. Fitzgerald at her word. They locked Gary away from the other prisoners in solitary confinement, and he lived there, in "the hole," for several weeks until the end of his trial.

On the Tuesday after Labour Day, 1981, OPP officers patrolled the doors of Courtroom Number Four in the courthouse, checking everyone who entered with metal detectors, and inside, Mr. Justice MacLeod Craig of the Supreme Court of Ontario ordered the trial to begin. Craig, a brisk, balding, no-nonsense man in his late fifties, was a stickler for order and punctuality. ("When he says court will start at ten o'clock," Hechter said, "that means he'll be on the bench and impatient for us to get going at five *to* ten.") The judge came from Owen Sound, several miles northwest of Barrie, and in his youth he had been one of the town's finest hockey players. That gave him two points in common with the crown attorney, who was brought in from outside Simcoe County to handle the prosecution. He was David Watt, a sandy-haired, deceptively nonchalant man in his early thirties. Watt, who made his reputation in the mid-1970s when he successfully argued the crown's side before the Ontario Court of Appeal and the Supreme Court of Canada in the sensational Peter Demeter murder case, was also a native son of Owen Sound and had been so accomplished at hockey that he played in the professional Central League during his years at law school. Watt and Craig spoke the same language.

In their company, the two defence counsel, Hechter and Ruby, seemed the outsiders, both from Toronto, both dark and Jewish, both clever and fast-talking. Hechter had misgivings about Craig's

103

presiding at the trial because Craig had heard the defence's applications for bail and for a change of venue and had rejected them both. The two hearings meant that Craig was already aware of many details in the crown's case, possibly prejudicing him against the defence. Hechter considered a motion to ask that another judge be assigned to the case. But he abandoned the idea, and now, on the first Tuesday in September, he and Ruby sat in court ready to proceed. Hechter was flanked by his junior, Lindberg, and Ruby by his, an engagingly open young man named Michael Kamen. Schoenberger and Fitzgerald sat in the prisoner's box to the right of the defence table and behind a bullet-proof shield. Both were short and brown-haired and neatly dressed in shirt, tie, and suit. Schoenberger had small, pinched features. He wore glasses and a worried expression. Fitzgerald seemed relaxed, on the edges of boredom. He had baby-faced good looks and a pouty upper lip. When he grinned, his mouth glinted with the silver of the braces on his upper teeth. Neither boy's appearance suggested he was a killer.

Jury selection came first in the order of the trial's business, and from the start, it was a slow, painstaking process, mostly because the defence was wary of the wide-ranging publicity that the murders had received in Simcoe County. Would they find twelve local jurors, good and true, who could react impartially to Fitzgerald and Schoenberger? Hechter and Lindberg drew up a list of twenty test questions that they put to the prospective jurors. Had they contributed to the fund for Chester Blackmore's family? Did they or their relatives attend the dance held in support of Constable Hurtubise? The questions also tried to pin down the prospective jurors' biases. Would they find a police officer's evidence more credible than that of other witnesses? As the defence worried along the selection process, Watt was at the same time indicating the sort of jury that the crown aimed at. He rejected for jury service a psychiatric social worker, another woman who counselled mentally retarded adults, even a chef who was retired from the kitchens at a mental institution. Watt, it was clear, wanted no one on the jury who might be versed in psychological concepts. The selection ground through two and a half days, and 103 members of the jury panel were examined by the counsel before seven women and five men were finally agreed on late Friday morning.

"In some ways the jury stuff was my favourite part of the trial," Lindberg said later. "Will let me take some of the questioning of the jurors, and it was the first time I'd stood up in my gown in a courtroom before a Supreme Court justice."

The rest of Lindberg's duties took place more behind the scenes. She had worked on research from the Monday three weeks before the beginning of the trial when Hechter hired her, digging out the relevant case law on the issues that Hechter expected to come up during the trial — the use of character evidence, areas of duress, the relationship between parties to an offence, crown disclosures. Lindberg prepared long memos of law for Hechter on all the points. And when the jury selection ended and the crown began calling its witnesses, she took up another part of a junior counsel's slogging work — making notes of the witnesses' testimony.

"Damn near verbatim," Hechter says. "If she hadn't written down the testimony in such amazing detail, I don't think I'd have been as successful as I was in cross-examination. That turned out to be crucial."

Watt summoned a parade of witnesses to the stand — arresting officers, experts in forensic medicine, fingerprint experts, pathologists, George Richards and his Mattawa friends, teenagers from Windsor who had heard Fitzgerald's talk of shooting policemen who got in his way. "The crown's calling everybody except Max the tracking dog," Hechter said during a recess one day in the second week of the trial. Watt needed the witnesses. Since no one had been an on-the-scene observer of the two shootings, his evidence was entirely circumstantial, but by patching together a mediculously detailed account of the events of those late December and early January days, by drawing from many witnesses details that blended into a complete picture, he intended to demonstrate for the jury that Fitzgerald, with Schoenberger's knowing aid, had coolly and rationally gunned down Chester Blackmore and Richard Verdecchia.

Watt marshalled his witnesses, and as they testified, Hechter, on cross-examination, began to push his own interpretation of events. He would put space between Schoenberger and Fitzgerald. Fitzgerald was the killer — no one, not even Fitzgerald's own counsel, would dispute that fact — and Schoenberger was the unfortunate bystander, the unwilling sidekick, a captive, even a potential victim. The two, Fitzgerald and Schoenberger, were as different as night and day, as black and white, as guilty and innocent.

"What sort of person is Joe Schoenberger?" Hechter asked one of the crown's witnesses, a teenager named John Alp, who was one of the Schoenberger-Fitzgerald crowd back in Windsor.

"A great guy."

"Well, what about this talk of stealing guns up north?"

"That was Fitzgerald blowing off his mouth," Alp answered. "Fitzgerald was the only one who talked about robbery."

Hechter pulled similar testimony in his cross-examination of Kathy Renaud, another Windsor teenager, but it was Clay Ruby's cross-examination of Renaud that, paradoxically, gave Hechter much stronger material. Ruby was upset at Renaud because she had refused to discuss her evidence with him in advance outside the courtroom.

"Why wouldn't you talk to me?" Ruby asked her as she stood in the witness-box.

"I don't think I should defend a person who would kill anybody," Renaud answered. "I don't think Joe would kill anybody, but Gary would have."

Hechter could hardly keep the smile off his face.

The crown's witnesses gave Hechter the chance, too, to remind the jury that it was Fitzgerald who was the crack shot with guns, that it was Fitzgerald who loved to shoot rifles, that it was Fitzgerald who had acted so murderously on the night of January 2. Always Fitzgerald. Not Schoenberger. Put the space between them. Who was it, Hechter asked one of the arresting OPP officers, who led police to Verdecchia's body? The answer came: Fitzgerald. It was Fitzgerald, not Schoenberger, who knew where Verdecchia's body had been hidden — in a snow bank — after Fitzgerald had pumped the bullets into it.

Sometimes Hechter's small, but telling, victories on cross-examination came through pieces of instant good fortune. When Watt was leading a young woman from Mattawa through her examination-in-chief — a woman who owned one of the guns stolen from George Richards' house — Michael Kamen leaned across the defence counsel's table to Hechter and told him that Fitzgerald had once gone hunting with the woman. "Was Fitzgerald a good marksman?" Hechter asked her on cross-examination. "Out with me," the woman answered, "he shot a rabbit through the head from fifty yards." Hechter glanced at the jury as if to check that they had grasped the point, and later, with another witness, he brought out testimony that Schoenberger, by contrast, was just a city boy who'd never fired a gun in his life. The point had been made — and underlined.

As the trial proceeded, as Watt built his case of circumstantial evidence and as Hechter countered with his cross-examination, life in Barrie for the Toronto lawyers settled into a rhythm. The trial lasted from ten each morning until late in the afternoon. Afterwards the lawyers retreated to their hotel rooms to review the day's evidence and plan cross-examinations for the next day. Dinner tended to be late and leisurely. Ruby, a gourmet who maintains a lovingly selected wine cellar at his home in Toronto, invariably ate at the Lafayette, Barrie's single claim to elegant dining, while the others usually scattered to the city's more humble restaurants. Sometimes all of them would take in a movie, sometimes they'd go to the trotting races, and sometimes Lindberg and Kamen would finish the evening over drinks with the Ontario Provincial Police officers, who were, they agreed, a friendlier bunch than either the Toronto cops or the RCMP.

"Good case like this," an OPP investigator on the Chester Blackmore case said in a bar one night, "it gets you lots of overtime. Me and the wife are gonna take a trip to Acapulco in February on what I'm makin' here."

Everybody at the table laughed.

"What happens at a big murder trial," Kamen said later, "is that everybody develops a kind of macabre streak. It's better that way, better than thinking about all the dead people."

Fitzgerald stories yielded many of the dark laughs in Barrie. There were a couple of new tales each day, sometimes ghoulish, sometimes merely amazing.

"When Fitzgerald was in the Clarke seeing the psychiatrists," Ruby said at lunch one day, "he phoned an old girlfriend in Windsor. The girl's mother answered and said the girl couldn't come to the phone. 'She's sick,' the mother said. 'Things aren't that good with me either,' Fitzgerald said to her. Now is *that* a blasé kid?"

"Listen to this, it's unbelievable," Kamen said. "That time when the police pathologist was testifying and he said that Blackmore was shot twice in the face, Gary called me over to the prisoner's box, and he said, 'Not twice in the face. I got him *three* times.' He was so pissed off because he thought the pathologist wasn't giving him enough credit as a good shot."

The woman whom the lawyers nicknamed the "Religious Lady" was another source of black humour. She was a handsome, middle-aged woman from the nearby village of Severn Falls, and she'd developed a strange fascination with Fitzgerald. She attended every day of the trial, holding her Bible and occasionally dragging along her husband, a gent whose obvious lack of comfort in the alien courtroom suggested he'd rather be in Severn Falls. The woman dispatched notes to Fitzgerald, notes of affection and faith and hope. "I love you," she wrote in several of her missives. A couple of times during court recesses she dropped to her knees in prayer, and whenever Fitzgerald entered the

109

prisoner's box, she offered him tiny waves and reassuring smiles.

"She isn't the only one," Kamen said. "At the Clarke, there was a nurse who fell in love with Gary. She wrote him letters after he was sent back here to the Barrie jail. She told him he should escape and run off to Australia with her. The Clarke finally let her go."

"Every big trial gets its own groupies," Lindberg said. "I always see little old ladies at rape cases in Toronto, and any time a bunch of bikers are on trial, that's when you get the adolescent girls. They go crazy."

Lindberg was beginning to feel borderline crazy herself. She couldn't shake a discouraging cold she caught not long after the trial got under way, and she had mixed emotions about leaving behind clients in Toronto. One boy whom she'd previously defended on a break-and-enter charge in the city had left a message at her office; he was charged with two more break-and-enters and wanted Lindberg to defend him. "Hey," she said, pleased at the recognition of her skills, "I'm starting to get repeaters." She was anxious to return to her own clients, but she appreciated the value of the Barrie experience. And she also saw her role as Hechter's junior beginning to shift and change.

"Support seems to be a lot of my job now," she said. "Making things tolerable for the senior counsel. In Will's case, that means reassuring him at the end of the day that his cross-examination made the right points or that his objection to something Craig said would set up the basis for a possible appeal later on. Maybe I'm not the ideal person for that job. I'd prefer just to discuss the issues, but with

Will, when I bring up a point, to me it'll be the beginning of the discussion, whereas he'll take it as my conclusion."

Back in court, after Watt had put in the case for the crown, Ruby called witnesses in Fitzgerald's defence. Ruby wasn't challenging the evidence that his client had fired the death shots. His point was that Fitzgerald was insane at the time of the murders, that he was so mentally ill that he could not, in the language of the Criminal Code, "appreciate the nature and quality of his acts." To establish the point, Ruby relied on three witnesses: two psychiatrists and a psychologist who had independently examined Fitzgerald over a period of several weeks. The first psychiatrist told the court that the shootings were no more than "a technical exercise" to the boy. The second psychiatrist testified that Fitzgerald had told him, "I enjoy shooting faces off." He labelled Fitzgerald "unpredictably dangerous." And the psychologist said that "Fitzgerald gave the killings no more thought than brushing his teeth." The boy, he concluded, "has one of the most severe personality disorders I've ever seen."

Watt chose to attack one of the psychiatrists on cross-examination, belittling the tests he'd given to Fitzgerald. He picked up one of the psychiatrist's Rorschach tests and suggested it was of value only as a kind of parlour game.

Ruby got to his feet.

"Perhaps Mr. Watt could tell us what he sees in the test," he said, "and then we'll know if it works."

"I see ink blots, Mr. Ruby," Watt said.

"Well, that says a good deal about you, Mr. Watt," Ruby said and sat down, smiling.

Watt was not amused. Neither was Craig.

At the end of the first psychiatrist's testimony-in-chief, Hechter stood up to question him.

"Mr. Hechter," Craig asked, "are you requesting the right to cross-examine this witness?"

Hechter looked stunned.

"M'lord," he said, "in cases where there are two accused, counsel for one accused has an *absolute* right to cross-examine witnesses called by the co-accused."

Craig hesitated, and Watt came to everyone's aid.

"I'm satisfied that the authorities support Mr. Hechter, m'lord," he said.

"Go ahead, Mr. Hechter," Craig said.

Hechter sent Watt a glance of gratitude and proceeded to score value points for Schoenberger in his cross-examination of the psychiatrist.

"Is Mr. Fitzgerald a person who's capable of acting suddenly and impulsively?" he asked the psychiatrist.

The answer came easily. Yes, the psychiatrist said, Fitzgerald would go off on his own tangent. He'd follow whatever impulse seized him. Hechter pushed forward another step. Would the presence of another person, someone like Schoenberger, make any difference in Fitzgerald's actions? Hardly, the psychiatrist answered. Well, could someone in Schoenberger's position *anticipate* what Fitzgerald's next act might be? No, the psychiatrist answered again, and his responses were echoed when Hechter put the same questions to the second psychiatrist and the psychologist. Hechter felt confident that he'd set the picture for the jury: Schoenberger could have had no advance warning that this crazy, unpredictable Fitzgerald was going to shoot Blackmore and Verdecchia.

Hechter called his own witnesses, all of them character witnesses who spoke to Schoenberger's past and the promise he showed for the future. "Joey's always been a good boy," his mother testified. Would Mrs. Schoenberger take her son back into the family home, Hechter asked. "Any time," the mother answered and burst into tears. Three of Schoenberger's schoolteachers and an old family friend took their turns in the witness-box and spelled out Schoenberger's history as an above-average student, a religious kid who attended church with his parents, a diligent worker, a responsible boy. They were baffled, they said, by his involvement in these killings. It wasn't in character for the boy they knew.

Hechter and Lindberg had been debating all through the trial over the wisdom and necessity of using one more defence witness — Schoenberger himself. In the early days they leaned in favour of calling him, but as Watt put in his case, as Hechter winkled favourable testimony out of the crown's witnesses and Ruby's psychiatrists, opinion on the value of Schoenberger's testimony began to switch. "I look at the evidence," Hechter said as the deadline for a decision on Schoenberger's testimony approached, "and I don't think the crown has proved anything that Joe needs to answer." There was another consideration in keeping Schoenberger out of the box — if he testified, Watt might upset him on cross-examination. "Joe's got a lot of explaining to do," Lindberg said. "How well will he stand up to Watt's questions? Watt can get very biting and sarcastic." Hechter made a choice. "It isn't a close enough case," he said. "We don't need him as a witness." He and Lindberg put the option to Schoenberger. To testify or not to testify — the ultimate decision had to be his. Schoenberger made up his mind quickly. He opted out of facing the jury, the courtroom, and Watt's inevitable questions. He elected to remain silent, and late on Friday morning, September 25, with the last of his character witnesses, Hechter closed the case for the defence.

Craig adjourned over the weekend, and on Monday morning, at a few minutes past ten o'clock, counsel made their final addresses to the jury. Ruby went first. "This is a dangerous boy," he began, speaking of Fitzgerald, and for almost thirty minutes, sounding more passionate than he had in all the days of the trial, Ruby argued that, of the two places to which the jury's verdict could ultimately send Fitzgerald, he belonged, not in a penitentiary, but in a hospital for the criminally insane. To place him in a hospital, he said, was "the humane verdict of the two and such a little thing to ask." He reviewed the facts of the killings and described the person who had done them as "a broken item. He needs to be mended. Common sense says a man who kills this way can't be sane. These are insane crimes." He acknowledged that public pressure leaned toward conviction of murder and a life sentence in prison. But the jurors, he said, "should abandon vengeance and intolerance." Besides, Ruby finished, pointing to the braces that Fitzgerald wore on his teeth, this was a very young person whose fate the jury held. "He is," Ruby said, "a boy." Next day, one of the newspaper accounts of his address would describe it as "compelling."

Hechter launched into his address as soon as Ruby sat down. "By the time my turn at the jury came," he said later, "I felt pumped up. Usually I'm nervous, but this time I had the nerves two days earlier. In court, I was feeling so psyched. Almost high." He spoke for forty-five minutes and didn't miss a detail or a nuance. He hit his theme early in the address: "Joe Schoenberger may be naive, but he is not a killer." He dissected the crown's case and concluded that it established just one fact — that Schoenberger was present when the killings took place. It proved no involvement on Schoenberger's part, no complicity, no acquiescence. Schoenberger was "guilty of something — bad judgment." But that failure exhausted his guilt. There was no evidence, Hechter emphasized, that Schoenberger aided or abetted or assisted or encouraged the crimes, nor was there evidence that he knew or ought to have known that Fitzgerald would shoot the two victims. He asked for an acquittal on both charges that Schoenberger faced. "Please," Hechter said, "send this boy back to his family."

Hechter felt confident when he sat down. "I was exhausted," he said later. "I'd lost eight pounds during the trial. But I sensed a strong rapport with the jury all the time I was talking. I got good facial expressions from them." Lindberg agreed. "Juror number six, the youngest woman, did you see her?" she asked Hechter. "Number six had tears in her eyes when you were speaking. If somebody's looking for signs, tears are positive."

Watt, speaking last, concentrated on tearing down the defence counsel's two main arguments — that Fitzgerald was insane and that Schoenberger was an unwitting passenger in the adventure. Fitzgerald, he told the jury, was "crazy like a fox." He was using insanity as a means of escaping justice. "Don't be fooled by such a manipulator," Watt said. And don't treat the trial as "a morality play that should decide whether Fitzgerald would be better off in a mental hospital." As for Schoenberger, Watt pointed out that he knew of Fitzgerald's plans to steal guns and commit robberies and that he supplied the car which made Fitzgerald's plans possible. Schoenberger, he said, "wasn't just along for the ride. . . . He was a helpful and willing tool." Watt wanted convictions on both counts for both boys.

Craig set aside the next day, Tuesday, for his instructions to the jury. "Now he's going to give it to you and me," Ruby said to Hechter that morning. "We haven't been humble enough in this trial." Craig's wife was in court for her husband's performance and so were thirty-nine students from an Orillia high school. "Don't be moved by sympathy for the accused," Craig told the jury as he began the address shortly after ten o'clock. "And don't consider what institution is proper for Fitzgerald." Then he commenced a lengthy recapitulation and analysis of the evidence. He was thorough to a fault, and for some in the courtroom, the fault appeared to be boredom. "I've never seen such a restless jury," Hechter said during a morning recess. The Orillia high school teacher took advantage of the recess to lead his students out of the courtroom and back to class. Craig pressed on. His instructions lasted for almost five hours, the only break in the monologue coming in a testy confrontation that Ruby precipitated before the jury returned to the courtroom after a recess in the afternoon.

"M'lord," Ruby said, speaking in his lickety-split style, "I must point out that in your instructions when you talked of the psychiatric evidence in the crown's favour, your voice was bright and lively, but when you talked about the defence of Fitzgerald's insanity, your voice fell off."

"I don't go for that stuff," Craig answered, clearly angered at Ruby's criticism.

He resumed his charge. "A jury," he said, "stands between the public and people who commit crimes." And finally he was finished. The clock showed a few minutes after four, and the jury was excused to begin their decision-making.

Life over the next few days turned into a grind for the jury. Craig ordered them sequestered in a hotel until they reached a verdict, but the International Ploughing Matches had begun in Barrie that week, and the city didn't have an empty hotel room to spare, let alone twelve of them. The jurors had to spend their nights forty miles away in Collingwood, and each morning, sheriff's officers bussed them back to Barrie to continue their deliberations in the courthouse. "Maybe the idea of all that travelling will make them come in with a fast verdict," Lindberg said. It didn't. The jury deliberated through Tuesday afternoon, all day Wednesday, and into Thursday morning. Their agony was reflected in the number of times — seven — that they returned to the courtroom for further instructions from Craig on specific points. The speculation among defence counsel was that the jury had arrived at an early decision on Fitzgerald and was puzzling over Schoenberger's fate. But no one could know for a certainty.

"The jury's got a verdict."

It was the sheriff's officer on duty outside Courtroom Number Four who broke the news at five minutes past two o'clock on Thursday afternoon to Hechter, Lindberg, and Kamen as the three were returning from lunch. Ruby was in Toronto arguing a case before the Court of Appeal. Hechter and Lindberg took their seats in the courtroom while Kamen hurried to the holding cells on the floor below the courtroom. Fitzgerald and Schoenberger were in separate cells several feet apart but facing one another. Both knew that the jury was ready for them. Fitzgerald reached a hand through the bars of his cell in Schoenberger's direction. "Hey Joe," he said, "good luck."

Craig took his place on the bench at 2:20 and the jury filed in. The court clerk asked the foreman of the jury, a dapper, solemn man named Stewart Christie, for the verdicts on Fitzgerald.

On the first count, second-degree murder of Chester Blackmore.

"Guilty," said Christie.

The only sound in the courtroom came from the "Religious Lady" of Severn Falls, who let out a small groan.

On the second count, first-degree murder of Richard Verdecchia.

"Guilty."

The clerk asked for the jury's verdicts in Schoenberger's cases.

On the first count.

"Not guilty," Christie said.

"The moment between Christie's words on the first count and the second count," Lindberg said later, "were the most tense of the whole trial. Joe could walk. He could go free. There was hope after the first count. But maybe the jury was going to make a saw-off — acquit him on the first count and find him guilty of something on the second. The tension stretched. Really tight."

On the second count, the first-degree murder of Constable Richard Verdecchia.

"Not guilty," Stewart Christie said.

A rush of wind seemed to fill the courtroom, as if everyone in it had simultaneously gasped in air. Schoenberger leaned over the rail of the prisoner's box and hugged Hechter. He took off his glasses, rubbed his eyes, and grinned in the direction of his parents. The Schoenbergers, with tears and laughs, were hugging one another.

Craig called for order — "That's enough," he said — and when Hechter asked that his client be discharged from custody, the judge fixed a stern look on Schoenberger.

"All I can say to you, Schoenberger," he said, "is that you are a very fortunate young man, and you are free to go."

In the corridor outside the courtroom, the crush of reporters, TV cameramen, and radio interviewers waving microphones was so dense that the Simcoe County sheriff talked of invoking the Riot Act. "I was naive," Schoenberger said over and over to reporters. "I guess I'll have to be a better judge of friends." He had lost his worried look. He was free and ecstatic. But neither his freedom nor his ecstasy would last. Hechter knew there was more grief ahead for Schoenberger.

"David Watt had told me a couple of days earlier," Hechter says, "that if by some miracle Schoenberger was acquitted, there'd be new charges laid against him. Watt was opposed to it, but the Simcoe crown attorney, John Murphy, wanted to get Schoenberger. To me, it was bad taste and sour grapes."

Back in the courtroom, while the press conference raged outside, Craig asked Fitzgerald if he wished to speak before sentence was passed on him.

"I view my conviction as a small obstacle in being helped and possibly changing," Fitzgerald said in the silence of the courtroom. "All I can do now is move forward."

It was the first time most of the people in the room — judge, jury, and spectators — had heard Fitzgerald speak. His voice came as a shock. It made a small, high-pitched sound. Ruby had been right — Fitzgerald was, after all, just a boy. Craig sentenced him to life in prison without possibility of parole for twenty-five years, and the guards took him from the courtroom.

"I don't feel anything," Fitzgerald said a few minutes later when Michael Kamen visited him briefly in the cells. "I should feel something, but I don't."

"That's the same thing Gary told me months ago," Kamen said later. "Right after the killings, back in January when I first talked to him, he said, 'I don't feel anything.' He knew he was supposed to. He knew something was wrong. But he couldn't find it inside himself."

Upstairs in the courthouse, Murphy, the Simcoe crown, led Schoenberger into his office and laid a fresh charge against him for the attempted murder of Neil Hurtubise, the OPP constable who survived Fitzgerald's shooting spree. Schoenberger was taken back to the county jail while Hechter, furious and raising his voice as he never had in the courtroom, railed at Murphy.

"This is goddamned cruel," he said.

"We'll give your man bail in a couple of days," Murphy said, a cool, unmovable customer.

"A couple of *days*?" Hechter shouted. "I want him out now!"

Hechter, Lindberg, and Kamen walked the two blocks to their hotel, where they gathered in Hechter's room and drank champagne and beer.

"What are we celebrating?" Kamen said at one point. "Joe's still in jail."

"Listen," Hechter said, "just don't leave me. I don't feel like being alone right now."

Hechter put in a few calls to Murphy's office, and by late afternoon the two men arrived at an agreement on bail. Schoenberger would be released immediately to his parents on a $25,000 bond.

"That's it," Hechter said to the others. "We can leave Barrie behind."

Among the three of them, the Toronto lawyers had only one car. It was Lindberg's Volkswagen, the infamous Beetle with the quirky brakes.

"Oh my god," Hechter said. "I can see the newspaper headlines now: 'Client Acquitted. Defence Team Wiped Out in Car Accident.' "

The brakes held up, and the three, feeling giddy, whooped and hollered and shouted their way back to Toronto.

"You know what?" Kamen said in a brief sombre moment on the ride. "The jury made a trade-off. They convicted Gary and then they could give themselves a pat on the back for letting Joe go free."

Lindberg delivered the two men to their homes. Kamen made a sandwich and watched film reports of the trial on three different television networks. At Hechter's apartment, his wife had baked a welcome-home cake, and he, too, watched the TV reports. Lindberg went out to dinner with a friend. She didn't bother with television.

"Why should I see it on TV?" she said. "I was right there when it all happened."

The Monday after the end of the Barrie trial began too early for Lindberg.

"I learned something," she said later. "Which is that if someone comes to your door at eight in the morning, don't answer, because who else could it be except the police. This cop served me with a summons for the time my car went through the garage door out by Highway 427. It's crazy. They've charged me with careless driving."

Later in the morning she went to Family Court to look after a case for one of the lawyers in Hechter's office. A mother had taken her thirteen-year-old son on a shop-lifting expedition at a Woolco store. The mother had been convicted in Provincial Court. Now it was the son's turn.

"He's a good kid," Lindberg said to the crown before the case was called. "He really is. Goes to school and has no previous record. The mother's already got a conviction. The best thing is to let the kid go and you'll probably never have him back here again."

Her sweet good sense persuaded the crown, and the thirteen-year-old left the court still without a record. Lindberg left with the feeling that she, too, would never return to the Family Court building.

"Anything to do with family law doesn't interest me," she said. "I'm a defence counsel."

That night, Lindberg and Michael Kamen went to *True Confessions,* a film that gives a gritty, funny, insider's view of relations between cops and hoods and lawyers. Kamen came out of the movie feeling exuberant.

"The movie is exactly the way it is in that kind of environment," he said. "Like, the most exciting part of the Barrie trial for me was when we smuggled the eggrolls in to Joe Schoenberger. This happened on the last Wednesday night. Caroline and I were out for a Chinese meal, and I remembered something Joe once said about the two things he missed most in jail were sex and Chinese food. I was thinking he's up there eating a lousy prison dinner and maybe tomorrow he's going to hear a verdict that'll send him away for twenty-five years. He ought to have his Chinese. So we got the eggrolls in to him, and I had this funny thrill about pulling a stunt like that."

"The part of the Barrie experience that was the best for me," Lindberg said, "was understanding the personal pressures that trial lawyers have to handle. For starters, we had this eighteen-year-old client who could go down for life or he could walk. Then you add a bunch of other pressures."

She ticked them off.

"The fact that it was a policeman who was killed. The fact that the press was constantly looking over our shoulders. And the fact that we were working in Barrie, away from our normal Toronto situation. All those things, they could destroy you."

Lindberg thought it over.

"What I learned," she said, "is I have to develop a resistance to the stresses of this business. I don't want to be one of those counsel who gets an ulcer and dies young."

Later in the autumn, the Barrie crown attorney laid more charges against Joe Schoenberger: accessory after the fact in murder of Chester Blackmore, accessory after the fact in the murder of Richard Verdecchia, and breaking and entering and theft in connection with the removal of the weapons from George Richards' house in Mattawa.

"We may be in court for a long time," Will Hechter said.

On December 23, 1981, Lindberg appeared in Etobicoke's East Mall Courthouse to stand trial on the careless-driving charge. Her lawyer was Mark Kerbel, an associate of Hechter's, and Lindberg was her own star witness. She was uneasy as she gave testimony, and afterwards she said, "It's so much more natural for me to be a counsel than a witness."

The judge dismissed the charge.

Late in January 1982, a leading Toronto defence lawyer named Harry Doan hired Lindberg to act as his junior in a murder case. The crown was alleging that the accused man, Doan's client, had killed a fifty-year-old prostitute, stuffed her body in a blue steamer trunk, sold her collection of Royal Doulton figurines, and fled to Scranton, Pennsylvania.

"I like this case," Lindberg said. "In the Barrie trial, all I got to do in court was examine the prospective jurors. In this one, Harry says I'll be taking some of the witnesses through their testimony. That's good. I'm getting closer to a real criminal counsel's work."

* * *

"Some cases, a counsel can laugh out of court," Dave Humphrey, criminal lawyer, was saying. "In some cases, even a smile is out of order. Some cases call for a display of righteous indignation. And a hell of a lot of cases require a plea of guilty. If your client is guilty and is clearly going to be proved guilty, the last thing he wants is a trial. The crown's got him by the short hairs, and what he needs is a hell of a good plea-bargainer."

It was a bright morning in late winter, and Humphrey was holding forth in his office in a handsome renovated brownstone on Sultan Street in midtown Toronto. Humphrey, in his mid-fifties, is a raconteur of the flamboyant school. Tales and opinions, epigrams and sermonettes rattle from his mouth like bullets from a Gatling gun. Off duty — and sometimes on duty — he's the Great Entertainer among lawyers of the criminal defence bar. And he looks the part, a husky man with a broad, expressive face and eyes that can nail a witness or an audience at thirty paces. With his sharp suits and his repertoire of gestures that underline punchlines, he's the sort of natural comedian — an upbeat Rodney Dangerfield — who could work one of the high-roller rooms on the Strip at Vegas.

"I had a rape case," he said in his office. "There wasn't much evidence against my man, and the crown's case looked pretty weak. But sometimes it's the weak cases that slip out of your hands if you're not careful. All the witnesses had testified, and it was the night before the crown and I were to present our arguments to the jury. I was sitting at home, getting ready to write out my address, and I thought to myself, instead of a long harangue, I'll keep this thing tight. So next day in court I got up, walked over to the jury box and I said, 'Members of the jury, if this case is rape, then I'm a monkey's uncle, and though the resemblance may be amazing, I ain't.' Then I went back and sat down.

"Herb Langdon was the crown, and he had such a hard time to keep from falling down laughing that he didn't address the jury for longer than fifteen minutes. The judge was just about as brief. The jury went out, and we barely had time to light a cigarette when they were back with a verdict of not guilty.

"Now, suppose I hadn't used that one-line address. Suppose I'd given a long, impassioned speech. That might've made the jury stop and think, hey, if Humphrey's so serious about this thing, maybe there really is a case against this guy. As it was, this was one of those times to laugh a charge out of court.''

Humphrey abruptly switched topics. He was in a mood to scattershoot his views on the courtroom process, and his next subject was entitled How Clients Perceive Lawyers.

''I had a guy charged with murder. He'd escaped from the reformatory and whacked his girlfriend over the head with a brick. Killed her dead. So it's first-degree murder. The guy and the girlfriend had a little nine-month-old baby, and the crown tipped me off not to mention the baby when we got to court. It seems the police had found a note from the guy when he was in reformatory telling the girlfriend to throw the baby in the Don River. That wouldn't have sounded nice in court. Anyway, I huddle with the crown and negotiate the charge from murder to manslaughter, and I take the news to my guy.

'' 'No way,' he said.

'' 'If you don't take it,' I said, 'you'll go down for murder one.'

'' 'I wanta fight the charge,' he said. 'I'll get off.'

'' 'Goodbye,' I said.

''The guy got himself another lawyer who was glad to fight the murder charge. This lawyer shouted at the judge, shook the crown attorney by the neck, and made all kinds of noise. He may even have mentioned the nine-month-old baby. The result was the guy got convicted of murder and was sentenced to life. But all the time he's sitting in jail, he's gonna be saying what a terrific lawyer he had, somebody who stood up and told those bastards in court where they could get off, not like that Humphrey who only wanted to *negotiate*.''

Humphrey lit a cigarette and blew a ribbon of smoke. ''A legal-aid case I had, a French Canadian charged with manslaughter. This guy had already done four bits for armed robbery. His girlfriend was cheating on him, and one night he beat her up in a drunken fight and killed her. The guy phoned the cops to tell them about it. He was crying on the phone, the whole remorse thing. It was genuine, and I got the crown to reduce the charge from manslaughter to assault with bodily harm.

'' 'No,' the guy said when I told him. 'I won't go for it. I can get off. I was drunk when I hit her.'

'' 'If you were drunk,' I said, 'then the law says that's manslaughter.'

'' 'All right,' he said. 'She was cheating on me. I was provoked into hitting her.'

'' 'That's manslaughter, too,' I said.

'' 'Look,' I told him. 'You're a toothless Frenchman who killed an Ontario girl. You got a record stretching your whole adult life. Any jury's going to put you away.'

'' 'No,' he said, and he hired himself another lawyer who ranted and raved on his behalf. The guy got eight years for manslaughter, but he figured the other lawyer, not me, was the hero.''

Humphrey let out another smoke stream. ''The point is, you can go into court and say very little and be more effective. Arthur Martin — now there was a *great* criminal lawyer — he's speak very quietly and be very polite to everyone. He'd ask a few questions and make a couple of soft-spoken arguments to the judge. First thing anybody knew, he'd have his client's confession ruled inadmissible or he'd impugn a key crown witness's testimony or he'd accomplish something else just as crucial, and the case against the client would collapse. It was all so simple and low-key that the client would say, 'Hey, why'd I hire an expensive counsel like Arthur Martin? Any lawyer could've done that.' The hell *any* lawyer could have."

Humphrey's phone rang.

"Seymour!" Humphrey said, hunching forward as he talked into the receiver. "How nice to hear from you. . . . You've been *arrested*? What for? . . . Book-making. Is a police officer there? Let me talk to him. . . . Good day, officer. It's too nice a morning to be out arresting people. What plans do you have for Seymour? . . . I see. Just booking him. Well then, he'll be out by the time night falls. That's fine. Thank you, officer, most kind of you. . . . Do I have any message for Seymour? Tell him to save his money for the lawyer's fee. Good morning, officer."

Humphrey had a case in the Supreme Court of Ontario that took up most of the first week of March 1981, and each day he wore the same tie, a dark four-in-hand decorated with little pigs and the repeated letters "MCP," which stood for Male Chauvinist Pig. Humphrey was defending a muscular extrovert named Gord Knowlton who had played linebacker for nine years in a Canadian Football League. The charge was rape. But Humphrey figured that the complainant, the woman who claimed that Knowlton had raped her, was being less than straightforward in her accusations, and the necktie with the little pigs and the MCPs struck him as entirely appropriate to the occasion.

Nobody disputed the hard facts, neither Knowlton nor the complainant, whose name was banned from publication by court order. Knowlton had met the woman, a twenty-five-year-old airline stewardess, almost four years earlier when she was a cheerleader for the Toronto Argonauts and he was an Argo linebacker. Their relationship was instant and, in Knowlton's word, "lustful." Once, on a short boat cruise, they kept score of the number of times they had sexual intercourse. The score was entered on a piece of paper tacked to the wall of their cabin, and it had reached fifty-five before the boat returned to port. Knowlton's burden was that he wanted to marry the stewardess, but she had doubts about long-range commitments. She preferred to cast around for a broader spectrum of male companions, and it was on a night when she was engaged in a little casting that events leading to the alleged rape occurred.

The stewardess arrived home at two a.m. after a night of drink and dance at a disco. Knowlton showed up at the door of her apartment. She was in pyjamas, he was in a Tarzan mood. He carried her in his arms to his car, drove to his apartment, and ripped off her pyjamas, tops and bottoms. She hurled abuse and a punch at him, and he aimed a slap at her. It landed. For the next twenty minutes there followed what Knowlton described as a "quiet period," which gradually gave way to a round of familiar love-making.

"She enjoyed it," Knowlton said. "As she always did."

"Gordy," she said after the sex, "that's the last time."

"But I want to spend the rest of my life with you."

The stewardess put on her pyjamas, and Knowlton drove her home, where, after reflecting on the evening's events, she decided to lay the rape charge.

Humphrey took a shot at plea bargaining. He'd plead Knowlton guilty to a lesser charge, assault causing bodily harm. "The appropriate charge," said the crown attorney on the case, Margaret Browne, after reviewing the evidence, "is rape." Humphrey wasn't surprised. "That woman," he said of Browne, "is dying to nail Knowlton."

The trial began before Mr. Justice Thomas Callon of the Supreme Court sitting without a jury, and when Humphrey's turn came to cross-examine the stewardess, he weighed in with a heavy but skilful hand. In examination-in-chief the woman had testified of her reluctance to have sex with Knowlton on the night in question. She hadn't consented to the act. It was rape. Humphrey moved to establish the highly sexual nature of her previous relationship with Knowlton. How about the boat cruise? How many times did she and Knowlton make love? Fifty-five? Could she check the score sheet? Humphrey's cross-examination wasn't intended to blacken the stewardess's reputation. Its aim was to emphasize her fondness for the act of love and the length and variety of her sexual history with Knowlton.

As a witness in his own defence, Knowlton followed Humphrey's deft questioning, and his testimony was at once canny and emotional, a wondrous mix of the sincere and the self-serving. He appeared to be in agony as he testified, perspiration staining his suit jacket, and when he finished, he gave way to tears. But he was candid and effective. "I know I'm not an intelligent person," he said from the box, "but there's no way you rape someone you're going to marry." Under Humphrey's lead, Knowlton relived his three-and-a-half-year affair with the stewardess, underlining most significantly its stormy nature. The couple often argued, Knowlton testified, but the bitterness invariably dissolved in bed, where the sex was frequently "rough." What happened on the night of the alleged rape — apart from the slap, which Knowlton said was a regrettable reflex action — was all of a piece with the couple's previous relationship.

In his address to Mr. Justice Callon, Humphrey didn't kid around with one-liners. His buttery summing-up projected a flow of logic and common sense. Knowlton was a man obsessed by the complainant. "Obviously he is terribly immature and so totally and hopelessly in love with her. She was truly his queen and he was her devoted subject." But Knowlton made a terrible mistake. "The accused for the first time in their unusual relationship of three and a half years slapped the complainant. That's why he is here. It's not because they had sexual intercourse. That, indeed, is old hat." The slap coloured the interpretation of events that the complainant offered in her testimony. "She was dramatically distorting the facts in her favour. She was presenting facts of the case deliberately to get revenge on the man she hates." What does the law say about this bizarre set of circumstances, Humphrey asked. "The accused believed she was consenting to have sexual intercourse with him, even though she may have been pretending to consent. In law, Knowlton cannot be convicted of rape if he believed she was consenting unless it can be established that the consent was brought about by violence."

As far as Mr. Justice Callon was concerned, Humphrey had rung the right bells. His judgment squared with Humphrey's reasoning. Knowlton, Callon said, made "the credible witness," while the stewardess's testimony was "inconsistent with her conduct and inconsistent with any reasonable understanding and assessment of the circumstances." As to the key matter of the complainant's consent — did she or did she not give it? — Callon pursued a winding line. "There was no general reluctance on her part to accompany the accused to his apartment." Once inside the apartment, she may have been "somewhat at odds with her feelings," but there was "no attempt to escape the situation." In fact, Callon said, "she still retained her desire for sexual gratification from the accused." Hence, consent existed and rape did not. Knowlton was acquitted.

"In my thirty years of being a lawyer," Humphrey said after Callon announced his decision, "I've never heard a judgment where the complainant is in effect called a liar."

"*He* lied," the stewardess said of Knowlton as she left the courtroom.

Humphrey accompanied Knowlton and his friends to a small victory party at a table in the bar of a nearby Holiday Inn. He had a gift for Knowlton, something that Humphrey said would aid Knowlton in remembering the difference between good women and evil women. It was Humphrey's tie, the one with the little pigs and the MCPs.

A couple of weeks later, Knowlton dropped in to Humphrey's office. He was ebullient. The Montreal Alouettes had offered him a fat contract. His boss at the executive-management recruiting firm where he worked had a better idea. He wanted Knowlton to forget about football and concentrate on the firm. The boss would reward him with a piece of the business. Everything was coming up roses for Knowlton. Down in Florida on a holiday after the rape trial, he'd picked up a piece of paper from the floor of a bar. It was a hundred-dollar bill. In the office, Humphrey passed the time of day with Knowlton, who soon left on his happy way to have a few celebratory drinks with friends from a radio station.

Much later that night, an attendant at a waterfront parking lot called the police. Someone, he complained, had beaten him up. The attendant, a thirty-year-old named Salahudin Khawaja, said that a customer had objected to paying a one-dollar parking ticket. This customer had punched Khawaja in the face, kicked him in the groin, and thrown him over a parked car. Then the man jumped in his own car and accelerated out of the lot. Another customer caught a glimpse of the fleeing automobile's licence. He memorized the letters and numbers and passed them on to the police, who checked the car's ownership.

It belonged to Gord Knowlton. The police charged him with assault causing bodily harm.

At first, Humphrey said he'd have nothing to do with Knowlton's fresh round of trouble. "Discretion, they tell me, is the better part of valour," he said, "and discretion says I should give Gordy a pass this time round." A young criminal specialist named David McCombs took over the case, a sensible second choice for Knowlton. Almost immediately, however, Knowlton discovered that he needed a second lawyer, a civil-litigation man, because the parking-lot attendant announced that he was launching a civil suit against Knowlton for damages suffered in the assault. Knowlton consulted a lawyer named Ron Dash, who entered into negotiations with Khawaja's lawyer. A deal was struck. Khawaja would accept $5,000 for punitive damages and for assorted other complaints including loss of income while he recuperated from his hurts. In return, Khawaja agreed not to pursue the assault charge. The various lawyers contacted the crown attorney who was handling the case, Norm Matusiak, and he, too, gave his blessing to the plan. All seemed to be in order for a swift resolution of the affair except for clearing a final hurdle. Since an assault charge had been laid and since it was listed for hearing on a court docket, a judge's approval was necessary for the formal withdrawal of the charge. The case was scheduled before Judge Charles Cannon in Etobicoke Provincial Court on August 18, 1981, and Knowlton's lawyers thought the presence of a senior counsel by their client's side would be at least helpful to their cause.

Which senior counsel?

Dave Humphrey, of course.

Humphrey agreed to re-enter the case. "You have to feel a little sorry for Gordy," he said. "After he pays the five grand, he'll have nothing left in the bank." Humphrey's services were on the house.

The appearance in Judge Cannon's Provincial Court lasted all of five minutes. Matusiak, the crown attorney, explained the circumstances, and the judge nodded his head. "I commend all participants and counsel concerned for the view they have taken in this matter," he said. "Justice has been served." Humphrey smiled. His job, mostly a matter of lending his silence and his weight to the proceedings, was done.

Six days later, the *Toronto Star* raised the Knowlton case for fresh examination. "Was justice cheated this week," the paper's story began, "when an assault charge against an ex-football player, Gordon Knowlton, 31, was dropped when he paid $5,000 in damages in an out-of-court settlement of a related civil suit?" After several hundred words of looking at the matter from all sides, quoting lawyers with varying views, the *Star* arrived at no particular answer to its question.

"Maybe an arrangement like that smacks the wrong way," Humphrey said in his office, speaking of the Knowlton settlement, "but it's not illegal or immoral."

Then Humphrey told a story. It was all about the lawyer's son who got himself so stoned on drugs and liquor that he tore through a friend's house, wreaking havoc to the tune of $15,000. Police charged the boy with the offence of causing wilful damage. But when the boy's father, the lawyer, anted up $15,000 to cover the cost of repairs to the ravaged house, the wilful-damage charge was dropped.

"This kind of thing," Humphrey said, "is unusual but not unheard of."

He paused to light a cigarette.

"All the same," he said, "I trust Gordy'll keep himself out of any more trouble. *I* can't stand the excitement."

Dave Humphrey laughed.

At the 1957 Grey Cup game between the Hamilton Tigercats and the Winnipeg Blue Bombers at Varsity Stadium in Toronto, a Hamilton defensive back with the onomatopoetic name of Bibbles Bawel intercepted a pass and was hotfooting down the sidelines toward a certain touchdown when a man lingering on the edges of the field impetuously stretched out a leg and tripped Bibbles. The man with the outstretched leg was Humphrey. When Maria Callas, on her farewell world tour, concluded a concert at Toronto's Massey Hall on the night of February 21, 1974, the sell-out audience hailed her with a host of bravos — and one boo. Humphrey was responsible for the jeer.

"Her performance," he said later, "was a disappointment." No one would mistake Humphrey for a shrinking violet. As a young man, he drove a taxi to pay his room and board and joined the U.S. Navy to see the world. He once flew planes, he used to sail a racing Albacore, and he still takes to the road on one of his motorcycles. Humphrey is a man to touch all bases. He's a knowledgeable opera buff, and an ardent golfer, and his understanding of the Bible is long-standing and intimate. For years he taught Sunday school at a Presbyterian church.

In the late 1970s he was elected to serve on the Discipline Committee of the Law Society of Upper Canada, the august body that oversees the profession in Ontario. The appointment meant that Humphrey qualified as probably the only lawyer in the province's history who has both served on the Discipline Committee and been reprimanded by it. The reprimand came in March 1964 when the Law Society penalized Humphrey $1,500 for "unbecoming conduct." What was unbecoming in Humphrey's conduct, according to the Law Society, was his fraternization with a couple of gents named Vincent Feeley and Joseph McDermott. The two happened to be leaders among Ontario's gambling community, and Humphrey's reason for associating with them seemed to him to be perfectly natural. They were occasional clients whose company he enjoyed. The Law Society was not amused.

But, utterly consistent with Humphrey's free-form ways, and his philosophy of live and let live, the companionship with Feeley and McDermott led him to good works as well as temporary trouble. It came about that in the summer of 1963 Feeley and McDermott were serving time in Toronto's Don Jail while they waited an appeal on their convictions for bribing a police officer. In prison, they struck up an acquaintance with a little man named Donald Coston, who was facing trial for murder. Coston's story was grim. He and his wife and a younger, bigger man had been drinking together. Coston passed out. When he came to, his wife and the young man lay on a couch. They were making love. When Coston objected, the young man began beating him with his fists. Coston looked for protection. His hand fell on a kitchen knife, and he stabbed the young man, who died.

Murder, said the police.

"What you need," McDermott and Feeley said to Coston, "is a good lawyer."

"I've got no money," Coston said.

"No sweat," said McDermott and Feeley.

The gamblers' pal, Humphrey, took the case, argued self-defence, and won an acquittal.

"I'm free," Coston said after he walked out of the courtroom, "because of a fair trial — and three good men."

From the rough and tumble of Humphrey's life, driving cabs, sailing the seven seas, and hanging out with gamblers, from the four years he put in the beginning of his legal career as a crown counsel matching wits with the giants of the defence bar, and from his own long experience as a defence giant, he has evolved a few maxims that he follows in his conduct of court cases. Humphrey's maxims, it's not surprising, aren't the sort of principles that law schools normally embrace.

"The cabs and the navy were the best preparation I could've had for the legal profession," Humphrey says. "Doing that kind of thing, you get to meet pimps, prostitutes, cops, thieves, and drunken lawyers, and you get an insight into what's going on with people who aren't part of the grey middle classes.

You learn about the kinds of individuals who are likely to get themselves into trouble. You figure out their strengths and weaknesses. You get a feel for these men and women, and without the feel, it'd be difficult, probably impossible, to take the measure of a court case. It's a matter of atmosphere, that's what a trial is, and unless you can assess the atmosphere, your client can kiss his chances goodbye."

Another Humphrey maxim centres on simplicity. "I see counsel going into court, and they've got twenty defences they're arguing for their clients. They wrap themselves up in these twenty defences, a bunch of legalisms and textbook stuff, and they're thrashing around, talking their heads off. All right, somewhere in the twenty defences there's one good defence, one possible winner, but when a counsel's arguing twenty defences, what's going to happen is that the good one's bound to merge with the other nineteen and head straight down the drain. The smart route is to arrive at the one winning defence out front and concentrate on it. I mean, people make a big deal out of me reading a motorcycle magazine while a trial's going on. That's nothing to get excited about. All I'm doing is waiting for the useless technical arguments to pass by until I can get down to business with my one solid defence.

"Besides, I like motorcycle magazines."

"A cold-blooded murderer," John Hamilton said.

Humphrey, imperturbable, didn't move an eyeball.

"The police had the right man," Hamilton said a moment later.

Humphrey sat rock-steady in his chair.

"A cold-blooded murderer," Hamilton said a second time.

That made Humphrey react, calling Gordon Allen a killer *twice*. He raised his head in Hamilton's direction and gave him a long, fishy look.

"Hell, John," he thought, "you're *really* shooting from the hip."

This was on an astonishingly warm afternoon in April 1981, and it was John Hamilton, not Humphrey, who was generating the controversy. The two men — Hamilton is a criminal lawyer with a fast-talking style — were appearing side by side before Metro Toronto's executive committee with their hands out. They were asking Metro to pay the legal bills they'd racked up in defending two Toronto policemen. Humphrey had acted for Staff-Sergeant Gerald Stevenson, Hamilton for Sergeant Robert McLean, and both cops, alas, had been found guilty of using a false affidavit.

The circumstances were curious. A woman named Lauralee Lorenz and her lover, Gordon Allen, were suspected of having bumped off the woman's husband in March 1978. Stevenson and McLean, two members of the homicide squad, took on the case, and as an aid in pushing toward a conviction they had confronted Allen with an affidavit apparently signed by Lorenz in which she implicated Allen in the murder. As Stevenson and McLean hoped, the affidavit drew a response from Allen that they believed to be incriminating. That came as good news for the two cops. The bad news was that the affidavit was a phony, concocted by Stevenson and McLean, who forged Lorenz's signature, and when their ruse was discovered they were charged and convicted of a criminal offence, while Allen and Lorenz, with Allen's statement ruled inadmissible as evidence at their trial, were acquitted of murder.

Humphrey's bill for his services to Stevenson amounted to $9,903, Hamilton's for McLean to $8,906, and payment of the bills out of public funds hinged on approval of Metro's twelve-member executive committee. The committee was sitting in session on this warm April afternoon in the large, sumptuous council chamber at Toronto's city hall, and it parcelled out five minutes each to Humphrey and Hamilton to make their pitches. Humphrey, looking spruce in a medium-grey suit, light-grey shirt, and deep-red tie, exuded reasonableness in his address to the committee.

"The officers committed a technical breach of the law," he said, "and I'm not suggesting that council should support the police in disobeying the law. But in this case, Stevenson and McLean were employing an imaginative investigative technique. I'd remind you that the offence was so technical that neither officer was aware he was committing it. I'd also point out that at the officers' trial, even though they were found guilty, the judge gave them an absolute discharge, and they have no criminal record.

"Look," Humphrey went on, "I took the case because I approve of Gerry Stevenson and what he did to try and solve this particular murder. If I'd won for him, then I'd automatically be paid by the city. That's the policy — to pay police officers' legal bills when they're acquitted. But since Stevenson wasn't acquitted, if you people decide not to pay me out of the public purse, I won't charge him a penny."

Hamilton came out firing during his allotted five minutes. McLean and Stevenson, he said, "had the right man. The court that acquitted Allen didn't have all the evidence before it. It didn't have Allen's statement to McLean and Stevenson or the police wiretaps of calls between Allen and Lorenz. All that evidence was ruled inadmissible.''

The committee members seemed uneasy and baffled under the blizzard of information — and accusations — that Hamilton and Humphrey served up to them. ''Do you mean,'' one puzzled alderman from the Borough of North York asked Humphrey, ''that the policeman signed his *own* name to this affidavit?'' ''No, Lorenz's name,'' Humphrey said as he ran down the facts once again in primary-school fashion. The committee chairman, growing impatient, called for a vote. Hands flashed in the air, six in favour and six against paying the lawyers' bills. The tie meant a loss for Humphrey and Hamilton, since they needed a majority vote to win approval of cash from Metro's funds. The two lawyers picked up their briefcases and left the council chamber, radiating mild disgust.

Next day, trouble dropped on John Hamilton. Gordon Allen made noises about suing for libel over Hamilton's characterization of him as a ''cold-blooded murderer.'' Allen's counsel at his murder trial, a high-profile criminal lawyer named Eddie Greenspan, got into the act by dumping on Hamilton's statement as ''the kind of comment I would expect from someone without any knowledge of the law.'' Hamilton appeared to laugh off the attacks. ''The next time Mr. Allen drives down from his home in Orillia,'' he told one reporter, his tongue stuck deep in his cheek, ''I'd like him to come by my house and babysit my children.'' But he was sufficiently concerned to consult a lawyer friend who specialized in libel matters, and the friend devoted two weeks to planning a defence against Allen's threatened suit. Other criminal lawyers rallied to Hamilton's cause, criticizing Greenspan among themselves for breaking an unwritten rule of the inner circle of criminal counsel by going public with a knock at one of their own. Then, swiftly, the fuss evaporated. Greenspan voiced no further criticism of Hamilton's remarks, and Allen decided against raising the old murder issue in a libel action. Hamilton was off the hook.

"It's very satisfying to defend cops against criminal prosecutions," he said in his office one day a few weeks later, "which is why guys like Humphrey and me handle any cop cases that come along. And lately, believe me, a lot are coming along."

Hamilton is a lean, stripped-down man in his mid-forties with the ascetic look of a long-distance runner. From the beginning of his career as a defence counsel in 1963, he's carried a reputation as a bright, brash, aggressive battler. Within five years of his call to the bar, he had taken two cases to the Supreme Court of Canada that established leading decisions on their subjects, one setting limits on police entrapment, the other defining a common bawdy-house. Hamilton has known a share of rounders in his time — and a share of cops.

"A police officer's whole career is in the balance when he's tried," Hamilton said. "If he's guilty, he can never again be an effective cop. Look at McLean and Stevenson. Both of those guys are working desk jobs now. They couldn't handle a homicide investigation, no matter how good they are at it, because they'd have to go to court to testify, and the first question a defence counsel would ask them is, 'Aren't you one of the officers who was convicted of faking an affidavit?' Their credibility would be shot. But with a bandit, if he's in the break-and-enter business and he gets convicted, the conviction doesn't interfere with his profession, apart from the temporary nuisance of serving a jail sentence."

Hamilton, restless and in perpetual motion, paced around his office. "It's a nice change of direction to defend cops," he said. "You know that, with them, you're on the side of the good guys for a change."

Humphrey, meanwhile, was fed up with the business of Stevenson and McLean.

"I've had it with the case," he said in his office. "I'm never going to appear before another civic body for the rest of my life. The six people on that committee who voted for us were right and the other six didn't understand what the hell John and I were talking about."

Humphrey let out a sardonic laugh.

"It's easy to figure out why the six turned us down," he said. "Number one, it isn't popular to do anything nice for lawyers. Pay a lawyer's bill? Are you crazy? Number two reason is just as plain. It's not a good idea these days for a politician to appear too enthusiastic about the police. Which is ridiculous."

"The reason the Bencardino and de Carlo case was so interesting," Humphrey reminisced one afternoon, "was that nobody could figure out at first whether they were really guilty or not guilty."

The case began late on a March night in the early 1970s when four young men — Moretti, Quaranta, Presta, and LaGamba — let themselves into a supermarket in the sprawling northwest section of Toronto known as Little Italy. The four young men came equipped with two large cans of gasoline. They had arson in mind. Presta and LaGamba left the store before the fireworks began, assigning the other two to carry out the mechanics of the job. Moretti applied himself to his chores zealously, sprinkling gasoline over a large area of the store. He was, as it turned out to his misfortune, over-zealous. When he lit a match to the gas, the supermarket went off like a bomb. Moretti was killed, and Quaranta, standing by the door to the street, suffered cuts and burns and broken bones. One other person was an unexpected victim of the blast, a cleaning lady named Maria Simone, who, unknown to the arsonists, was working on the second floor of the building next door to the supermarket. Maria Simone died almost immediately, and her death made the crime not merely arson but murder.

When Presta and LaGamba heard of the plot gone wrong, they caught a plane for their old home town in Italy. They expected to find sanctuary, but what they received instead was a jail cell. Italian police learned of the crime in Toronto from their Canadian counterparts, and they arrested Presta and LaGamba under an Italian law which gives the country's courts jurisdiction over any Italian-born citizen who commits a crime anywhere in the world against another Italian-born citizen. Unfortunately for Presta and LaGamba, Maria Simone was a daughter of Italy.

Paolo Quaranta, the wounded arsonist, stood trial for murder in Toronto and, despite an enterprising defence by his counsel, Eddie Greenspan, was convicted. The sentencing judge came down hard on Quaranta, putting him away for life with no parole for twenty-five years. But Quaranta, even as a jailbird, was a talkative fellow, and he had an intriguing story to tell anyone who would listen. The police listened, because Quaranta's tale was that the four arsonists had been put up to the job by Raffaele Bencardino and Giuseppe de Carlo, who happened to be the owners of the supermarket and who wanted the place burned for its insurance money. Bencardino and de Carlo were accordingly charged with Maria Simone's murder, and in February 1973 they stood trial, Arthur Maloney acting for Bencardino and Dave Humphrey for de Carlo.

"Weird case," Humphrey mused. "Quaranta came down from the Don Jail and testified for the crown that Bencardino and de Carlo had hired the four guys to burn the supermarket. Even worse, he said that he saw the owners at the store around the time of the fire and he heard one of them say something like, 'Do a good job, boys.' It looked bad for our people. Well, the night after Quaranta testified, I got a phone call at home from the wife of a former client of mine named Bruno Pisani who was currently residing in the Don. The word from Pisani was that he'd been talking to Quaranta, and Quaranta wanted to change his testimony. With that news, Maloney and I tried to get the crown, Frank Armstrong, to recall Quaranta to the stand. That failed. We tried to get the judge to call Quaranta as *his* witness. That failed. So we ended up calling Quaranta as *our* witness, which was a mistake for a couple of reasons."

First reason: "The only part of Quaranta's testimony that he changed was the part about seeing Bencardino and de Carlo at the supermarket the night of the fire. It was nice he said he lied about that little item, but the fact was that we could already place our guys with their wives at a steak-house miles away from the supermarket throughout the entire evening. It happened to be the Feast of St. Joseph that day, and the two couples were out celebrating Joe de Carlo's feast day. We had witnesses. Quaranta changed that part of his story, but he didn't change another part, the part where he said he heard the two owners talking to Moretti about burning down the place. Thanks a lot.''

Second reason: "Since we called Quaranta as our witness, that gave Frank Armstrong the opportunity to cross-examine Quaranta on the reasons for his sudden change of testimony. I mean, here was Quaranta on the stand, tears in his eyes, scared silly, and looking clearly like he'd been recently beaten up. Armstrong wanted to know what Bruno Pisani had to do with the situation, Bruno Pisani who was Dave Humphrey's old client. Armstrong went to town on the guy.''

So he did, as the trial transcript indicates.

ARMSTRONG: "Did Bruno tell you he had been convicted of possession of counterfeit money?''

QUARANTA: "Well, I believe he did say that, but he had about ten dollars false money. That is all, and that was the end of it.''

ARMSTRONG: "Mr. Humphrey had acted for him in that matter?''

QUARANTA: "What do I know?''

ARMSTRONG: "Didn't he tell you that Mr. Humphrey acted for him?''

QUARANTA: "I don't believe so.''

ARMSTRONG: "Never had any discussion about the fact that Mr. Humphrey had defended him on this charge of possession of counterfeit money?''

QUARANTA: "No, sir.''

ARMSTRONG: "Because if he had, it would be pretty surprising to you, would it not, that Bruno was befriending you, a major witness against one of Mr. Humphrey's other clients?''

QUARANTA: "What do I know?''

ARMSTRONG: "What did Bruno Pisani say to you that prompted you to tell him that you lied about this matter?''

QUARANTA: "That is not the way it went. That talk did not happen."

ARMSTRONG: "Didn't he say anything to you?"

QUARANTA: "I just said those two words to him, and that's all."

ARMSTRONG: "What words?"

QUARANTA: "I said I lied at certain points."

ARMSTRONG: "Without him asking you?"

QUARANTA: "Was he a judge to ask me questions?"

ARMSTRONG: "I put it to you, Paolo, that Bruno Pisani told you that you had to change your evidence on that one material point, and that was that you did not see the owners in the store on the night of the fire, and as long as you tell that story they will let you live to at least rot in jail. Isn't that true?"

QUARANTA: "Not true."

"Armstrong's argument," Humphrey went on, "was that Pisani had beaten up Quaranta and made him change his story. We said that, hell, everybody in the jail knew Quaranta was a rat who was testifying for the crown and, ergo, he was fair game for a beating from any of his fellow inmates. The judge got excited and ordered Quaranta to be held in a safe place, which turned out to be the women's section of the jail in the town of Whitby forty miles east of Toronto. It was supposed to be a tremendous secret, but there wasn't a lawyer or a convict or a guy on the street who wasn't aware within five minutes that Paolo Quaranta was the only prisoner in the women's section of the jail in the town of Whitby. Not that it mattered any more. Quaranta had done his damage to us."

But, as the trial unfolded, it was not the twisting testimony and eccentric adventures of Quaranta that proved to be a pivotal element in the ultimate fate of

Bencardino and de Carlo. It was another issue, a point of pure law.

"There was evidence," Humphrey went on, "that our two guys had bought six thousand dollars' worth of stolen goods on a previous occasion from some or all of the arsonists. These goods, mostly cigarettes, were in a garage out back of the supermarket. Well, when the judge came to charge the jury, he said that the evidence of the purchase of the goods, *stolen* goods, was capable of corroborating the evidence of Quaranta on the arson and murder. Maloney and I said that was wrong, that the evidence of the stolen goods didn't connect our guys with the arson. Maloney objected to the charge like crazy. After a while I told him not to bother. My reasoning was that, ethically, we were obliged as defence counsel to bring errors in the judge's jury charge to his attention. We'd done that. Why press it further? Suppose we got the judge to change his mind on the corroboration point and he redirected the jury, but then the jury went out and still found our guys guilty. If that happened, we wouldn't have an error in the judge's charge that we could use as a basis for asking the Court of Appeal to give us a new trial."

Which was precisely the sequence of events that followed. The jury convicted Bencardino and de Carlo, not of murder but of manslaughter, and the judge sentenced them to fifteen years in prison. Maloney and Humphrey proceeded to the Court of Appeal and succeeded in obtaining an order for a new trial. On what grounds? On the grounds, the Court of Appeal held, that the trial judge had erred in telling the jury that the mere existence of the stolen goods offered enough corroboration of Quaranta's testimony against Bencardino and de Carlo.

Two more trials followed. The first, before a judge who was cautious and painstaking, was washed out in mid-trial when the judge grew so cautious and painstaking that he made himself ill and was unable to continue. The third trial finally resolved the fortunes of Bencardino and de Carlo, but not before other strange and comic episodes intervened. For example, the trip to Italy.

"Frank Armstrong," Humphrey said, "decided to take commission evidence from the other two arsonists, Presta and LaGamba, which meant we packed off to Italy, the whole cast of us: Armstrong, Maloney, me, Leybourne, who was the cop on the case, the court interpreter, a shorthand reporter, and an Italian-speaking professor from the University of Windsor Law School. All that crowd, *plus* our spouses. This entourage arrived at the courthouse in a little town south of Rome where Presta and LaGamba were being held, and it was bedlam. The judge, Garoffolo by name, wore shades in court and ran the place like a dictator. He had a guy sitting in front of him, a strange person — sleeveless sweater, long, dirty fingernails, a 1935 Corona typewriter. That was the court reporter, and he'd only start typing when Garoffolo dictated something to him. Maloney asked what the hell was going on, and Garoffolo told him to shut up or he'd throw him in the cells for contempt. That's the Italian system.

"The prisoners were brought in, Presta and LaGamba. They were wearing ancient handcuffs made of wood and iron, and they had the worst case of jailhouse pallor I've ever seen. Those guys were so pale you could practically see through them. By then, they'd been in the can a couple of years without being tried. Italian courts are permitted to hold prisoners for five years before somebody makes up his mind whether to put them on trial or not, and in Italy nobody appears to have heard of bail.

"Anyway, these guys came into court and Frank Armstrong put some statements and questions to them. They clammed up. Silent. Mute. They'd decided their best strategy was not to get involved in any Canadian trial. Armstrong was so mad he was blowing smoke out his ears, and Garoffolo threatened to bury Presta and LaGamba in prison for the rest of their lives. But the two guys stuck to their silence. *Omerta* was the order of the day. That meant there was no new evidence against our guys, and the last I saw or heard of Presta and LaGamba, they were being led to their cells in that old courthouse. Maybe they're still locked up. Who knows?"

Back in Toronto, at the third trial for Bencardino and de Carlo, Humphrey and Maloney called a witness who turned out to be crucial — Mrs. Bencardino, the wife of one of the two supermarket owners.

"She had a story," Humphrey remembered. "She said one day she went down the basement of the supermarket where her husband and the other owner were talking to a guy. This guy was two things. He was one of the arsonists and he was one of the people that the supermarket owners had bought the stolen goods from. He wanted to peddle more stolen goods, and according to the wife, the owners were saying, 'No more stolen goods. Forget them. They're more trouble than they're worth.' The guy got mad. He flashed a gun, and he said, 'You don't buy any more stolen goods from us and we're going to get you for it.'

"And that was the story we emphasized for the jury. We said that the motive for the fire was revenge. It had nothing to do with insurance money. It had nothing to do with personal gain of our guys.

The four arsonists set the fire because they wanted to get even with the two owners for not buying any more stolen goods.''

When the jury at the third trial retired to consider the Humphrey-Maloney version of the crime and to arrive at its verdict, Humphrey telephoned his mother.

"She's not Catholic, my mother," he said, "but she was educated in a convent and to this day she says her beads. Can't break the habit. I phoned her and said, 'Mother, we got a tough case here, and I think you better do something about it. Get on those beads. Give those things a workout.' Then I sat around with the Bencardinos and the de Carlos waiting for the verdict."

The jury members deliberated for several excruciating hours. But when they returned to the courtroom, it was clear that they'd gone for the revenge theory as the motive for the crime. Bencardino and de Carlo, they announced, were innocent.

"So what happens?" Humphrey said. "The families go crazy with joy. Laughing. Weeping. Hugging. Mrs. de Carlo comes up to me and says, 'Oh, Mr. Humphrey, there's one person we owe this to.' 'Who?' I ask. 'Your mother,' she says. My *mother*? 'It was the beads,' she says.''

Bencardino and de Carlo — "two hard-working guys who'd never had a record of any kind" — returned to the grocery business in Toronto. Moretti was dead. Presta and LaGamba, for all anyone knows, languished in an ancient Italian jail. But Paolo Quaranta and his saga were scheduled for a longer run.

"The prison people shipped Quaranta to a penitentiary in British Columbia to serve his sentence," Humphrey said. "They figured he'd be safer out there. That's where Quaranta foxed them. He put in a couple of years. Then he escaped. He made his way to New York City, and after a while everybody knew he was there. The police knew, the RCMP knew, the jail people knew. But nobody cared, because they felt sorry for him. Under all the circumstances of the crime, he should never have been convicted of murder. Anyway, a couple of years went by, and I got a phone call from a lawyer in New York. He said he was acting for Quaranta, and Quaranta wanted to come back to Toronto. What did I think?

" 'Well,' I said to this New York lawyer. 'I'm sure nobody is excited about your client. Out of sight, you know, is out of mind. But if Quaranta returns to Toronto, somebody from the police is going to have to remind him that he hasn't finished his sentence. However distasteful it may be to all concerned, they're gonna lock him up.'

"Quaranta's New York lawyer thanked me and hung up. That was the last word I heard on the case of Bencardino and de Carlo."

Though Humphrey couldn't have guessed it, when John Papalia sent a Scotch and water over to Max Bluestein's table at the Town Tavern one night in March 1961, the stage was being set for one of Humphrey's small classics in criminal defence. Papalia, aka Johnny Pops, was a Mafia enforcer. Bluestein was a gambler who ran a string of floating crap games around Toronto. The Mafia wanted a slice of Bluestein's action as a replacement for its own gambling clubs which were being phased out of operation by diligent police work. Bluestein had so far refused the mob's overtures, and on this March evening at the Town — a now-defunct nightclub near the corner of Yonge and Queen streets in downtown

Toronto favoured by jazz musicians, assorted villains, and diners who recognized a culinary bargain, $1.20 for a delicious repast of roast beef and mashed — he was receiving his last chance to co-operate. If he accepted Papalia's offer of a drink, he was signalling that the mob was in. Turn it down, and he was keeping the crap games to himself.

A waitress approached Bluestein's table and began to set the Papalia drink in front of him. Bluestein's action was unequivocal. He waved away the waitress and Johnny Pops' Scotch. Bluestein rose from the table and made his way to the Town's lobby. Papalia followed, motioning four or five mob cohorts to accompany him. In the lobby, they fell on Bluestein with fists and various blunt instruments. Bluestein lashed back with a stiletto he carried for just such occasions and managed to sink six stab wounds into one attacker, a hood named Frank Marchildon. But sheer numbers — five or six to one — made Bluestein a certain loser, and he was left bleeding, battered, and barely conscious on the floor of the Town lobby while Papalia, Marchildon, and company scattered down Queen Street.

The police eventually pieced together the facts of the case and obtained convictions against three of the attackers, including Papalia, who was sentenced to eighteen months, and Marchildon, who got four months. But the case was difficult to prosecute, mainly because the habitués of the Town, under-standably nervous about getting in the bad books of the mob guys, made reluctant witnesses. Most reluctant of all was the Town hat-check girl, Eva Anderson, whose post in the cloakroom off the lobby gave her a clear and shocking view of the bloody events. Shortly after the attack, Miss Anderson was heard in a nervous conversation on the cloakroom telephone.

"No, Johnny," she said. "No, no, I can't do that. No. *No!*" Presumably her caller was Johnny Pops, the Mafia enforcer, advising her to forget about his presence in the club that night, and by the time Eva Anderson arrived in court as a witness for the crown against Papaliá and the others, she had been struck dumb.

"Miss Anderson," Joseph Addison, the magistrate presiding at the trial, said in some anger, "could have given complete identity of the attackers because the assault took place in front of her desk." Addison ordered the poor hat-check girl charged with perjury.

At which point, enter Dave Humphrey as the Anderson defence counsel.

"Ah, Little Eva," he remembers. "I liked her. I liked the Town, I liked its roast beef. What I didn't care for was the case against her. It looked tight."

But Humphrey, for all his talk of feel and intuition in handling court cases, had acquired a fairly sophisticated understanding of psychiatric concepts, and he elected to apply some of his knowledge on behalf of Little Eva.

"Hysterical amnesia," he says. "Nobody talked much about that sort of thing twenty years ago, but I figured that maybe something so traumatic could happen to somebody that they'd forget all about the event. Erase it from their memory so that it no longer existed for them."

Humphrey contacted a psychiatrist by telephone and put the thesis to him, hysterical amnesia as it applied to Eva Anderson's situation.

"Yes," the psychiatrist said, "it's perfectly possible. But I'd like to speak to Miss Anderson myself."

"Oh no," Humphrey said, not anxious for the psychiatrist to get too close to his client. "She's so upset that she can't deal with anybody before the perjury trial.''

"Well, all right," the psychiatrist said. "I guess I could testify for her about the likelihood of hysterical amnesia."

"When it came to the day of the trial," Humphrey remembers, "I couldn't keep the psychiatrist from talking to Eva while we were waiting out in the courtroom corridor. But that turned out to be a benefit for us because the psychiatrist really warmed to Eva and her predicament, and when he got in the witness-box, he came on like the world's greatest authority on hysterical amnesia. The crown was sceptical as hell. *Hysterical amnesia?* But the tougher he got in crossexamining my psychiatrist, the more positive the psychiatrist became. He was so convincing that the judge said, well, sure, Little Eva simply couldn't remember what happened at the Town that night. She was acquitted."

Eva Anderson returned, secure, to a normal existence, which was more than Max Bluestein and John Papalia were able to claim. Bluestein, left slightly paranoid by his beating, became convinced that grief was hounding his tail. His paranoia deepened in October 1973 when he parked his car in a suburban Toronto shopping plaza and returned to find sticks of dynamite wired to its ignition. Two months later, in December 1973, he shot and killed a man whom he suspected of plotting against him. The man, entirely innocent of evil intent, was Bluestein's best friend. The court found Bluestein to have been legally insane at the time of the shooting.

As for Papalia, he served seven months on his sentence in the Bluestein case, then was whisked to New York City, where he pleaded guilty to a Mafia drug conspiracy charge. He spent four years in the

Lewisburg, Pennsylvania, prison before returning to his home base in Hamilton, Ontario, where he kept a low profile. That lasted until 1973, when he was sentenced to six years for a $300,000 extortion scam. One of Papalia's co-accused in the extortion was a Montrealer of dubious repute named Paolo Viola. Along with Papalia and a couple of others, Viola was convicted at the trial, but his conviction, unlike Papalia's, was overturned by the Ontario Court of Appeal. Viola's counsel, both at the trial and at the successful appeal, was none other than Dave Humphrey.

There seems to be something else about Humphrey — he inspires affection. That's not an altogether common quality among criminal lawyers, people who by the very nature of their profession are essentially hit-and-run operators. But Humphrey, relaxed and funny and good company, generates loyalty and friendship among his peers. And so it was that in the late spring of 1980, Mike DeRubeis, a former articling student of Humphrey's, and now busy in his own litigation practice, got together with a few other grads of the Humphrey office and organized a night of tribute, a celebration of thirty years at the bar for Humphrey. They carried it off in style. Seventy lawyers and judges gathered in black tie at Toronto's Royal York Hotel. There were cocktails in a Royal Suite. Vintage wines and witty speeches with dinner in a private banquet room. Presentation to Humphrey of a Karsh portrait of himself. But from the evening, with all its glitter and distinction, Mike DeRubeis prizes most the memory of a conversation he had over dinner.

"I was talking to John Robinette," he says. "I mean, this was John Robinette, the greatest of all the counsel, and he said, well, the way Dave had performed in court over the years, he had probably turned out to be the smartest and most effective criminal lawyer at the bar today.''

* * *

On the night of March 4, 1983, John Arnup put the matter in immediate and unequivocal perspective. Arnup has been a justice on the Ontario Court of Appeal since 1970 and before that practised as a civil litigation specialist of the first rank, and on this March night in 1983, he was addressing a dinner gathering of six hundred lawyers and their spouses in the Concert Hall of Toronto's Royal York Hotel. His subject was John Robinette.

"In my own years as counsel," Arnup told the dinner, "I appeared against John Robinette in twenty-five or thirty cases, including one in the Privy Council and one that is still the longest civil case ever tried in Canada. I have seen all the great counsel who practised in the last fifty years, and in my opinion John Robinette is the greatest all-round advocate of them all."

It's Robinette's versatility that causes men like Arnup to praise him so highly. It's his longevity. And it's his scholarship. When Robinette was called to the Ontario bar in 1929, he emerged with the gold medal and with such high marks that the student who won the silver medal, Fred Catzman, says, "I was *pro forma* the runner-up, but John was so far in front of everybody else that it didn't count." When Robinette spent his early years as a lawyer teaching at the Osgoode Hall Law School, he developed such a smooth, clear, instructive lecturing style that, as one of his students, Senator David Walker, puts it, "what with Robinette being as young as us fellas he was teaching, what with him being so much smarter than us, and what with him handling the tough technical subjects like mortgages, he just bowled everybody over." Clearly Robinette, the son of an acclaimed Toronto criminal lawyer, was cut out for the law, and when he moved from the classroom to the courtroom in the mid-1930s, his gifts shone even more brightly.

He made his initial reputation through the 1930s and early 1940s as a sound technical counsel, noted mainly for his care and precision in arguing briefs before the Ontario Court of Appeal. The legal profession's insiders cottoned on to his special skills, and in 1947 so did the rest of Canada. That was the year when he defended Evelyn Dick, a woman from Hamilton, Ontario, in a trial that became the sensation of the decade. It was a steamy and internationally publicized murder case, and Robinette won an acquittal for his client in a dazzling display of courtroom pyrotechnics. He took another fifteen murder cases after Dick, losing only one, and his name, frequently blazoned in the headlines, seemed forever locked in the public imagination as "John Robinette, the great criminal lawyer."

But Robinette, not satisfied with the intellectual challenge of murder cases, which he says "run too much to type," moved on. Through the 1960s and 1970s, he acted in a spectacularly wide range of civil actions including a succession of complicated and multi-million-dollar combines cases. He appeared before the Supreme Court of Canada more often than any other counsel in the court's history. And he made himself the wisest lawyer in the land on constitutional issues, so learned that the federal government retained him to argue in a string of key cases leading up to the crucial 1981 hearing that eventually resulted in the repatriation of Canada's constitution and the enactment of its Charter of Rights. Robinette was approaching his late seventies at the time of the case, but he had no intention of gearing down. There were more trials ahead of him, more appeals, more intricate legal puzzles to sort through.

In the catalogue of Robinette's courtroom appearances, there is nothing typical about the Steve Suchan trial. It was a murder case, and Robinette lost it. His client died on the gallows of Don Jail in Toronto. For a rare occasion in his career, Robinette was devastated by the results of his advocacy. And yet it was the Suchan case that, without any hesitation at all, Robinette was pleased to recall and analyse during a conversation in his office on a bright late-autumn afternoon in 1981. As ever, ego wasn't something that intruded on a good legal discussion.

Robinette's office is on the forty-seventh floor of the Toronto-Dominion Bank Tower, one of the three floors occupied by McCarthy & McCarthy, the firm with which Robinette has been associated as counsel for more than thirty years. The office is medium-sized and neutral. It speaks of a man whose life is orderly, consistent, and compartmentalized, three attributes that, as it happens, nicely sum up Robinette. He has lived in the same large stone house in the Forest Hill section of Toronto since 1943 and has spent his summers in Southampton on Lake Huron since 1928. He has a couple of diversions that he single-mindedly devotes himself to, travel and reading. He embarks with his wife on frequent and regular journeys outside Canada, and his reading takes him far beyond the law. "He has an amazing broadness of mind," Bernie Chernos, a fellow counsel, says of Robinette. "You want to talk about the stories of Willa Cather, okay, he's read her. He's the most civilized man I've ever met."

Steve Suchan would seem at first impression a client that the civilized Robinette wouldn't relate to except as the bearer of an intriguing legal problem. Suchan was a bank robber by profession and a murderer by happenstance, but, large as his failings were, Robinette liked him. "He was a kindly sort of fellow," Robinette said, remembering Suchan during the conversation in his office. "At the trial, when it was his life that was at stake, he worried more about the way I was taking things than he did about himself. He had some culture to him. He was a good violinist and played in some orchestras around Toronto. There was a lot that recommended him to me." But Suchan had another side. "His basic trouble was his laziness. He got in with these other fellows, hold-up people, and he thought, gee, this looks like an easy way to make money. It was too bad he didn't stick to the violin."

The "other fellows" whom Suchan hooked up with were known around Toronto in the early 1950s as the Boyd Gang, perhaps the slickest bunch of villains in the city's history. Edwin Alonzo Boyd was the brains of the outfit, and from time to time he'd recruit assistants for his meticulously planned and executed bank stick-ups. Hence, "the Boyd Gang." Boyd was so cool and ingenious that when the police at last nabbed him and locked him and two of his occasional henchmen, Leonard Jackson and Willie "The Clown" Jackson (no relation), in the Don Jail under close surveillance pending trial on a long list of hold-up charges, he engineered a successful escape. The breakout wasn't a matter of guns and violence but of a hacksaw smuggled into the jail and a rope fashioned out of prison bed-sheets. The three patiently hacked through a barred window, lowered themselves forty feet into an exercise yard, and scaled a sixteen-foot outer wall. They scurried to a nearby apartment where, by pre-arrangement, Suchan arrived in a car and drove them deeper into hiding into the Toronto underworld. It was Sunday, November 4, 1951, and the Boyd Gang was back in business.

Suchan, in his mid-twenties, was the youngest member of the operation. But he was eager, daring, and skilled at the risky game of robbing banks. He took extra assurance, and a measure of pride, from his constant companion, a .455 Smith and Wesson revolver. He acquired the gun in a trade for his violin. Suchan carried it when he teamed up with Boyd and the two Jacksons in a hold-up shortly after the Don Jail escape. The take was $46,207.13, the largest amount robbed from a Toronto bank to that date. Citizens were outraged at the gang's audacity, the police were embarrassed, and the robbers were laughing.

By late winter of 1952, however, a pair of Toronto policemen thought they had sniffed out two of the gang. The officers were Sergeant of Detectives Edmund Tong and Sergeant Roy Perry, and partly through diligent sleuthing, partly through a piece of good fortune, they came into possession of the description and licence number of a car that they suspected Suchan and Leonard Jackson were using to get around the city. At midday on Thursday, March 6, they spotted the car on a busy west-end street.

Suchan was at the wheel and Jackson in the front passenger seat, though at first Tong and Perry weren't certain of their identity. The two policemen tailed the car for a few blocks until it stopped for a traffic light. "Pull over to the curb, boys," Tong called to the pair from the passenger side of the policeman's car. Suchan did as he was instructed. The police car stopped to the rear and the right of the Suchan-Jackson car, and Tong stepped out, his hand empty of any weapon. He had approached to within three or four feet of Suchan's door when Suchan rolled down his window, turned in the seat, and fired his Smith and Wesson. He caught Tong in the left chest. He continued to shoot, hitting Perry, who had begun to move from behind the steering-wheel, in the right arm. Jackson, a pistol in his hand, stepped from his side of the car. "Christ, it's a cruiser!" he shouted at Suchan. "Get out of here!" The two roared away in their car and spent the day and night travelling by car, taxi, and bus to Montreal, where each kept an apartment under a fake name. Their freedom was brief. Montreal police arrested both men within a few days in two separate raids, each accompanied by a hail of bullets, and returned them, wounded, to Toronto. When Edmund Tong died in hospital on March 23, Suchan and Jackson were charged jointly with murder.

Robinette's interest in the adventure was no more intimate than the average newspaper reader's until one night a few weeks after the murder charge was laid when he was labouring over a brief late in his office at McCarthy & McCarthy. "There was a cleaning lady on the floor," he remembers. "She was a hard-working, decent, quiet woman, and she came to me, just the two of us alone at night in the empty offices, and she said her son was in trouble. Would I help him? 'What's his name?' I asked. 'Steve Suchan,' she said. 'Isn't he charged with murder?' She nodded. Well, she was such a nice woman that I couldn't say anything except that I'd help her.''

Leonard Jackson had his own lawyer. He was Arthur Maloney, in only his ninth year of practice but a man destined to blossom into a brilliant defence counsel. Maloney is sweet-talking and loquacious, as Irish as a glass of Bushmill's Whiskey (a drink he wouldn't turn away). He's a fervent Catholic, and his sense of religion, a mix of hard-line righteousness and genial kindliness, suggests he'd have made a swell priest, part thundering Jesuit and part Bing Crosby in *Going My Way*. He channelled his drive to serve into other areas besides the law; he sat as a Conservative M.P. for five years, helped to found the Canadian Society for the Abolition of the Death Penalty, and acted as Ontario's first ombudsman from 1975 to 1978. When the call came to represent such an apparent loser as Leonard Jackson, he accepted. The call came from an unexpected direction.

''I was on my way into the Great Hall at Osgoode for my lunch one day,'' he remembers, ''and Chief Justice James McRuer stopped me. 'I've just come from court over in City Hall,' he said. 'This fellow Jackson was before me and he doesn't have a lawyer. May I appoint you to act?' Well, it was the last thing I wanted. I'd never handled a major murder trial. But you don't say no to a chief justice, especially McRuer. And besides it was my chance to sit beside John Robinette.''

Maloney had already experienced a strange brush with the case. On the night of March 5 that year, he was taking a late dinner in the dining-room of the Metropole Hotel, a comfortably down-at-the-heel

Toronto landmark of the day, and as he was eating, two policemen whom he knew from his courtroom appearances wandered in for a beverage.

"What are you boys up to?" Maloney asked.

"Plenty," one of the officers said. "Some time in the next twenty-four hours we're gonna pick up a couple of thugs."

The two policemen were Tong and Perry.

The case against Suchan and Jackson was in the hands of a tough, veteran crown counsel named Bill Gibson. "He wasn't much in the administration line of things," Robinette says of Gibson. "But in court ability he was one of the best two or three crowns we've had in Ontario during all of my years."

It was clear to Gibson and everyone else in the case that only one man could have fired the single bullet that killed Tong. Suchan seemed almost certainly the correct candidate for that role, though there might be some lingering possibility that Jackson, too, had fired his gun. Whoever pulled the trigger on the fatal shot, Gibson intended to establish that both men were guilty of murder because they had conspired together to use violence in resisting the arrest of Jackson, who was at the time a fugitive from justice. Or perhaps he could prove another conspiracy — one to carry out *any* unlawful purpose by violence and to assist each other in the purpose. If a conspiracy had been formed, then the Criminal Code said that both men were parties to the actions that one or the other carried out in furtherance of the conspiracy. If one man killed Tong, in short, both men in the conspiracy were equally guilty of murder.

The defence to Gibson's case had to be, by necessity, narrow and legalistic. "The best we could hope for," Robinette says, "was manslaughter. After all, someone was dead." Suchan's story, which

Robinette would use as the basis of his case, was that, shortly before Tong and Perry pulled him over, his car and another had nearly collided. He thought it was the men from this car who were shouting at him to park at the curb, and he wanted to avoid any confrontation which might lead to the discovery that he was driving Jackson, a fugitive. He didn't recognize Tong as a policeman or Tong's car as a police cruiser, and he fired his gun only to disable the other car's engine and help him make his own getaway. His intention wasn't to shoot Tong. He didn't *see* Tong when he turned in his seat to fire. The facts, as Suchan declared them, made him guilty of manslaughter at worst. Jackson's defence was more direct. He hadn't fired his own pistol and he wasn't aware that Suchan was carrying a gun. He hadn't made a pact with Suchan to resist arrest by violence; he was himself prepared to take violent action to avoid his own apprehension — he would even have shot at the police — but he didn't expect or intend to get assistance from Suchan. Hence, there was no conspiracy to resist arrest, and the event that followed, Tong's death, couldn't be tied in to a joint act by the two men.

"What we wanted the jury to do," Maloney says, "was come to the conclusion that Jackson hadn't shot his gun and Suchan didn't mean to kill Tong, and then give them both manslaughter."

But before Robinette and Maloney had their day in court, they temporarily lost their clients. So did the police. Suchan and Jackson had been locked away with their old associates in crime, Edwin Boyd and Willie Jackson, who had also been recaptured. The four occupied the Don Jail's death row, a group of cells isolated from the rest of the prison population. Escape-proof, the Don's officials figured. Not escape-proof, however, to Boyd, whose devious mind concocted another break-out scheme. This time, his agencies were a key modelled from a scrap of metal and a hacksaw once again smuggled in from the outside. On September 8, the four lit out, over the wall and through the wilderness that filled a valley running north from the jail.

The daring escape sent a shiver of memory through Robinette. "In 1918, my father acted for a man named Frank McCullough," he says. "This fellow was convicted of murder and sentenced to hang. While he was waiting for his execution, McCullough escaped. It was from the same cell that my client Suchan was occupying in 1952. McCullough's escape was the great sensation of 1918, just the way Suchan and the others became the great sensation of 1952. Eventually, McCullough was caught."

So were the Boyd Gang, nabbed in a farmer's barn after a massive manhunt several miles north of the jail on September 16, eight days from the date of their escape. The murder trial had already been scheduled to start on September 22, a mere week away, and Robinette, arguing that he'd had too little time to prepare his defence, applied for an adjournment to Chief Justice McRuer, who had designated himself to hear the case.

"You should have asked for an adjournment earlier than this," McRuer said. "Back on September 8."

"At that time," Robinette said, "I wasn't sure there would be a trial."

McRuer turned him down.

"The Chief Justice was a stern man," Robinette says. "He could make things hot for defence counsel."'

On September 22, Bill Gibson began marshalling for McRuer and the jury the crown's case against Suchan and Jackson in swift and orderly fashion. The parade of witnesses, forty-three in all, included the wounded Sergeant Perry, the shopkeeper who exchanged Suchan's violin for the Smith and Wesson, and an expert from the RCMP's Crime Detection Laboratory who swore that the fatal bullet came from the Suchan gun, and their testimony shaped an argument for the accused men's guilt that seemed relentless and inevitable. Two pieces of evidence struck Robinette as especially damning. One established that two of Suchan's bullets went through the police cruiser's windshield. "If you're trying to put a car's engine out of commission," Robinette says, "you don't shoot into the windshield. Bill Gibson kept hammering that point to the jury." The other critical piece of evidence was physical — a dressmaker's dummy from the basement of the house where Suchan and Jackson had been hiding out. The two used the dummy for target practice on the day before Tong was killed. "We argued with McRuer that the dummy should be kept from the jury," Robinette says. "If they got a look at it, we knew they'd form the unmistakable impression that Suchan and Jackson were pretty deadly shots and weren't likely to miss anything they aimed at. The dummy has bullet holes in it — through the heart and through the head." Robinette and Maloney took the position that the dummy was, as evidence, irrelevant and inflammatory. McRuer rejected this arguments, and the dummy was carried into the courtroom. "That just about finished us," Robinette remembers. "The jury looked at the dummy and went into a kind of stunned state. I was pretty shocked myself."

When Gibson finished the crown's case, Robinette and Maloney called one witness each, Suchan for Robinette and Jackson for Maloney. Suchan's testimony was consistent and credible, and following Robinette's deft examination-in-chief, he stuck to his story that he hadn't intended to shoot Tong and that his purpose in firing was to protect his own position, not Jackson's. The latter piece of testimony paved the way for Robinette to counter the crown's contention that Suchan and Jackson had entered into a common purpose to resist arrest. No joint act, Robinette would argue, no conspiracy, and therefore no double conviction for murder. Towards the end of Suchan's testimony, Robinette led him to tell the jury that in Montreal when the local police fired at him and wounded him during the shoot-out capture at his apartment, he hadn't shot back. The point Robinette hoped to demonstrate was that Suchan wasn't normally given to shooting policemen, that his gunning of Tong was a single, unplanned, accidental fluke.

"In fact I think there was another reason why Suchan didn't shoot at the Montreal police," Robinette says. "He was one of those fellows who may have been weak in spirit. When he got into the shooting in Toronto, it was because Jackson was beside him. He wanted to impress Jackson. But he would never have shot at the Montreal police. He was alone at the time, and there was no one to impress."

Suchan stepped from the witness-box, and Jackson took his place. He responded to Maloney's examination-in-chief with the story that Maloney expected, telling the court that Suchan's shooting of Tong came to him as a terrible surprise, an event that had been neither planned nor expected. But when Bill Gibson began to cross-examine Jackson, his story developed holes. He conceded that, by riding with

Suchan in the car, he was, as a fugitive, looking to Suchan for protection. He knew he could count on Suchan in a show-down with the police. When McRuer got into the act, following up Gibson's cross-examination of Jackson with his own clarifying questions, Jackson grew belligerent. He abandoned most of the story that Maloney had led him through.

"I was shattered," Maloney remembers. "I listened to Jackson and I knew he'd thrown in the sponge. He virtually admitted that he knew Suchan was carrying a gun, that it was loaded, and that he knew Suchan would use it to shoot anybody who tried to stop the pair of them."

Jackson finished his self-damning testimony.

"I asked later what made him say the things he had on the stand," Maloney says. "He looked at me and he said, 'If those bastards, that judge and that prosecutor, want me this bad, hell, I'm gonna give myself to them.' Then he thought it over, and he said to me, 'I let you down, didn't I?' I answered him back. 'You didn't let me down,' I said. 'You let yourself down.' "

It was time for counsel's address to the jury. Robinette went first. He offered the jury his theory in Suchan's defence, that the shooting was accidental and that Suchan was guilty of no more than manslaughter. Robinette spoke for thirty-five minutes in his measured, steady manner, and then, toward the end of the address, referring to the shooting in the Montreal capture, to the wounds that Suchan received from the police bullets, Robinette conjured up the image of Suchan lying in his own blood on the apartment floor. "Something intervened," he said. "He could have died there, but he didn't." It was a rare excursion into melodramatics for Robinette, a suggestion that a greater force had somehow saved

Suchan, and it was a line that, to Robinette's chagrin, Bill Gibson wouldn't let him forget.

Maloney followed with his address — "Leonard Jackson will not walk from this courtroom a free man," he said, "but he does not deserve to die" — and then it was Gibson's turn. "I've been working on this case for months and months and months," he began. "Today for the first time, I've heard it said that the case involved divine intervention. . . ."

"That was a spectacular opening," Robinette says today. "I've never forgotten those words of Bill's. They just got the jury riveted and they made a kind of mock of the reference I'd put in about a higher power. Bill followed that same blunt approach all the way through his address, and the jury seemed to go for it. Bill was bound he'd get a murder conviction."

He got it. McRuer briefly instructed the jury after Gibson's address, and the jury left the courtroom to arrive at a decision. They were out for a mere one hour and forty-five minutes and returned with the same verdict for both Suchan and Jackson.

"Guilty of murder as charged."

For the first time in the trial, McRuer's emotions surfaced. His voice grew soft and trembling.

"You shall be taken to the place from where you came," he said in turn to both Suchan and Jackson, "and there kept in close detention until the sixteenth of December, 1952, and thence you shall be taken to the place of execution, and there be hanged by the neck until you are dead. May God have mercy on your soul."

Robinette turned to Maloney as the two men sat side by side at the defence table.

"My God," he said, "I've never heard those words before."

Robinette and Maloney rushed to appeal the case, asking for a new trial on the grounds that the evidence had not shown there was a common intention on the part of Suchan and Jackson to resist arrest and that McRuer had erred in allowing the dressmaker's dummy to be entered as evidence. On November 12 they presented their arguments before five justices of the Ontario Court of Appeal. The judges listened, retired to consult together, and returned in fifteen minutes. Appeal dismissed.

Robinette and Maloney travelled to Ottawa on December 5 and applied to a justice of the Supreme Court of Canada sitting alone for leave to appeal the case to the whole court.

"It was Mr. Justice James Estey who heard us," Robinette says, "and he gave us all the time in the world. I think what bothered him about the case was that McRuer had made us go on with the trial so quickly after the jail escape without an adjournment. We played this point up with Estey, and I'm sure he was disturbed enough to take our arguments more seriously than he might have."

Estey announced that he'd reserve his judgment for a few days.

"That was unusual," Robinette says. "On applications for leave, the judges normally come ahead with a fast answer, and they never bother with written reasons."

Estey took a week to ponder the case, and he produced fourteen pages of judgment. It added up to a close analysis of all that law that Robinette and Maloney had cited to him, but its conclusion was the same as the two lawyers had heard from the Ontario Appeal Court. Leave to appeal, Estey held, was denied. The date was December 12, four days to execution date.

Suchan and Jackson, alone on the Don's death row (Boyd and Willie Jackson, convicted of bank robbery, were serving time in a penitentiary), found religion. It was Arthur Maloney's doing. Suchan's mother, a Catholic, had approached him as a co-religionist, regretful that her son had left the Church and asking if Maloney could coax him back. Maloney recruited Father John Kelly, a Catholic priest who later became president of St. Michael's College in Toronto, and in daily visits to Suchan, Kelly brought him around to his old Catholicism. Jackson followed. He was Jewish, but the conversations between Father Kelly and Suchan so intrigued him that he asked the priest to baptize him into the Catholic faith. Jackson took to his new religion with such zeal that, as his final meal before the execution, he demanded to be served the same food that Christ ate at the Last Supper. Father Kelly pointed out that the communion which Suchan and Jackson would take on the morning of the execution was a re-enactment of the Last Supper. That satisfied Jackson, and he switched his order to the same meal that Suchan had chosen — fried chicken, apple pie with ice cream, and a fat cigar.

Robinette visited Suchan for the last time at five o'clock on the afternoon of December 15. Suchan had written a letter to his mother. It was in Slovak, but Suchan translated it for Robinette, reading aloud to him in the cell on death row.

"Straight from my heart, I love you, Momma," the letter ended. "And my small brother, a million times. Please forgive me, Momma, for bringing you so much sorrow."

Robinette left the jail.

"When he read the letter to me," Robinette says, "it tore me apart."

A few hours later, shortly after midnight on December 15 and early on the morning of December 16, Suchan and Jackson were hanged.

"Arthur said something to me about the hanging," Robinette remembered almost twenty-nine years after the execution, sitting on the late-autumn day in 1981 in his office at McCarthy & McCarthy, smoking his pipe and thinking back. "Arthur said, 'Y'know, John, you never had a man executed. Well, you'll be a better person for it.'"

Robinette tapped the ashes out of his pipe.

"I guess Arthur was right," he said. "You lose a case like that, lose the man, and you probably learn to have more sympathy with people. Maybe it all makes you a little more human.

* * *

As he'll let you know himself, Harry Walsh has a tendency to dominate his surroundings. At a party, over the dinner table, or in a courtroom, it's Walsh who catches the eye and the ear. He has the looks appropriate to a Roman senator: he's short, but his figure is upright with just a hint of stately paunch, and his head is noble, with long silver sideburns sweeping majestically over his ears. His voice tone is soothing, his delivery insistent, his choice of language correct in a deliciously traditional style, and those attributes equip him ideally for two roles: litigation lawyer — he is, in his late sixties, the dean of Winnipeg's counsel — and raconteur. He doesn't shirk either.

"Dorothy Christie's case seemed at first glance to be hopeless," he begins a recollection one autumn

173

morning as he sits in his office in a building at the corner of Portage and Main. "She was a petite and comely woman of some twenty-four years of age, and she was married to a big, husky, handsome fellow who was a year or two older than she. The marriage was only of about six months' duration, but it was already going badly for Dorothy. Indeed, her husband, who was nicknamed Bunny, had bragged to her that he had recently slept with two other women. Nevertheless they continued to live together in a boarding-house in one room that served the function of living-room, kitchen, and bedroom. They were of modest means, and their one extravagance was Bunny's motorcycle. He belonged to a club of fellow motorcycle addicts — nothing evil or illegal about them, nothing that suggested Satan's Choice or the Hell's Angels — and on many occasions husbands and wives of the club would ride into the country to enjoy the fresh air. That was what Mr. and Mrs. Christie were doing on the Friday in June 1957 that ended in Mr. Christie's death and a charge of murder against Dorothy Christie.

"Now, during the weeks prior to the tragedy, Dorothy was bothered by headaches and insomnia. She had a prescription for pills from her doctor to alleviate the dual complaint, and on the evening when she and her husband returned from this particular Friday outing, she took one pill before she retired for the night in the same bed with her husband in the room that was bolted shut from the inside. Dorothy awoke at about seven o'clock the following morning and snuggled up to her husband. He didn't move. She sat up and looked at him. There was a small hole in his temple from which blood was trickling. Even to Dorothy's untutored eye, it was clear that he was dead, and lying beside him, in between the body and Dorothy, was the husband's twenty-two calibre rifle.

"Dorothy looked around the room. The door remained bolted, the windows were down, and there was no evidence of an intruder. In the agony of the moment, Dorothy realized that it could only have been she who shot her husband, and yet she had no memory of the act. She telephoned to her husband's brother. 'I have shot Bunny,' she told him, 'and I'm going to shoot myself.' Then she picked up the rifle, and though she hadn't any knowledge of firearms, though she had never before in her life so much as fired a gun, she somehow managed to manoeuvre the rifle into position and shoot herself in the abdomen.

"Christie's brother had meanwhile called the police and directed them to the boarding-house, and when they arrived, they broke down the door and rushed Dorothy to the hospital. Eventually she recovered and gave the police a simple statement in which she said that she must be the killer but that she loved her husband despite their differences and could never do harm to him. She was charged with murder, and when her family retained me to act on her behalf, I recognized that in all the curious and damning facts of the case there was only one possible defence. That was a defence of automatism. I would argue that Dorothy was in such a state of mind, a sleepwalker's state if you will, that she could form no intent to commit murder. Intent in those days, back in 1957 before amendment to the Criminal Code, was an integral part of the definition of murder under the Code, and without the presence of intent to kill, there could be no murder.

"The trouble with such a defence, automatism, is that it is one which engenders suspicions in the minds of a jury. It sounds like something a lawyer might put up in desperation to save a hopeless case. And indeed there was virtually no precedent that I could find of automatism being raised as a defence in earlier capital cases. There were no Canadian cases on the subject and not much solace in the few English cases. But I was determined, and I had facts on which to base my argument. There were the sleeping pills. It turned out that Dorothy Christie had renewed her prescription on the day before the killing. It was for twelve sleeping pills, but on the morning after the crime, police found the pill vial on the floor of the room, and it was empty. Although the only pill that Dorothy remembered having taken from the vial was the one on the fatal Friday evening, it seemed that she must have ingested eleven more pills at some point during the late-night or early-morning hours. She could not remember, but she must have done so. And when I interviewed her doctor and her pharmacist and a chemist who analysed the type of pill that Dorothy took, I became convinced that the consumption of so many pills would have reduced her to a legitimate state of automatism.

"The matter came on for trial, and the crown attorney put his case to the jury based on the very cut-and-dried events that seemed so persuasively to point to Dorothy's guilt. Then it was my turn. I called the doctor and the pharmacist and the chemist to the witness-stand, and then I called Dorothy. As a general rule, defence counsel are reluctant in a murder case to use the accused person as a witness even when he or she is perfectly innocent. One never knows whether the poor accused, out of sheer nervousness, might blunder into an injudicious answer. But with Dorothy I had no choice. She was the only person who could testify as to certain facts in her favour. She was the only person who could swear, for instance, that she did not flush the sleeping pills down the toilet or otherwise dispose of them. So I called her, and she made an excellent witness.

"The courtroom in the Winnipeg Courthouse in which the trial was behind held was then and is now a formidable place. The ceiling is high and of stained glass, the walls and prisoner's dock and witness-stand are of marble, the well of the courtroom is very large, and the judge's bench towers over everything. Behind the judge, on the wall, are three words in giant type, 'Truth. Justice. Mercy.' I imagine an accused person looks at the words and wonders, 'Why mercy? I'd just like to be acquitted.' In those surroundings, Dorothy Christie, so tiny and pretty and distressed, struck a very appealing figure for the jury, which was all male. And when she answered my questions on examination-in-chief, she spoke honestly and forthrightly and said that, yes, it must have been she who shot her husband. As she talked, her voice had a monotonous quality, as if, even there in court, she remained in a kind of trance, and I trusted that the jury took note of her strange and distraught condition.

"I finished my questioning, and the crown rose to cross-examine Dorothy. He took her through a few unimportant preliminary points. Then he reached the obvious and expected highlight of his cross-examination, namely the rifle. What about the rifle? Hadn't it been around the Christie living-quarters for some months? Didn't she see her husband handle it? Had she really not ever held the gun herself? The crown began to press Dorothy for answers, and he was most insistent.

"As he talked, the crown walked around from behind his table, which was about seventy feet from the witness-stand in this large and imposing court-room. He picked up from the table exhibit number six in the case, the rifle itself, and he made his way very deliberately on the long route that took him behind the counsel tables and past the jury-box toward the witness-stand. He had reached a point directly opposite the middle of the jury-box when Dorothy, seeing him with the rifle in his hands, the terrible murder weapon, and knowing that he was going to press more questions about it, broke into a shuddering shriek and began to sob in a most pitiful manner. The crown counsel stopped in his tracks, holding the rifle, and at that moment one of the jury-men looked at him and said something that was quite audible over the sound of poor Dorothy's sobbing.

" 'You son of a bitch,' he said to the crown counsel. 'You son of a bitch.'

"It was an electrifying moment. There had been a question on the crown counsel's lips, but it went unasked. He looked up at the judge in a silent inquiry. The judge said nothing, and the crown turned and walked quickly back to his table. Dorothy had by then recovered, and the crown continued with a few more questions. He was, however, clearly shaken by the events, and his line of cross-examination had lost much of its thrust. Soon he finished and sat down.

"A little later, when I made my address to the jury, I found them most receptive to my argument of auto-matism. 'If the mind does not know what the hands do,' I said to them, 'there is no crime,' and I could almost feel them reaching out to me in agreement. Indeed, when they retired to consider their verdict, they were back in the courtroom within a mere thirty minutes. Not guilty, they said, and at that announce-ment the courtroom, which was packed, broke into applause and cheers as if the spectators were at a sporting event. Dorothy Christie walked away not to the gallows but to freedom. And I felt very content. It was the first time that a defence of automatism had succeeded in a British Commonwealth court.

"And" — Walsh pauses to let the drama sink a notch deeper — "I was, of course, most grateful to the jury member who spoke so frankly to the crown counsel."

Violence in the family. Wife shoots husband, son guns down father, husband kills wife's lover. Walsh has defended in dozens of such grim trials. "Killing is rarely an instance of planning and deliberation," he says in his courtly way. "Rather, it is usually the result of emotions running amuck, and so often that occurs within the family unit." Perhaps Walsh's own background opens him to a special relationship with cases that begin in family grief. He grew up in Winnipeg's rough North End, and when he was fifteen his father died, leaving the widow and mother to raise six children on a small income. To pay his way through the University of Manitoba, Walsh sold newspapers at the corner of Portage and Main, outside the very building that now houses his office. His first wife, the mother of his two children, lived in sickness for a dozen years and died a young woman. Walsh survived, and throughout his practice, over forty years at the bar and over one hundred murder cases, he has identified with families and their distress.

"A case in the summer of 1962 up in the town of Selkirk, about twenty-five miles north of Winnipeg," he launches another reminiscence. "A fellow named Thomas Baty was accused of murdering another chap of the town, Rudy Bendl. Both men were in their early thirties, both worked at the Selkirk Mental

Institution, and both owned small spreads of farming land. Baty was married and had three young children. Bendl, on the other hand, was a bachelor and had something of a reputation as a Lothario in the community. He was alleged to have had relations with many local women, some of them married, and among his married partners was Baty's wife, Zelda. That, according to the crown's case, was the motive for Thomas Baty's killing of Rudy Bendl.

"The affair between Bendl and Zelda Baty dated back several months before the night of the crime, but as so frequently happens in these matters, Thomas Baty was the last person in town to learn of his wife's trysts. It was the wife herself who told him about her relationship with Bendl one night in the middle of July after she had drunk several glasses of wine. Her tongue was loosened and she said that Bendl wished to marry her and to take her and the three children to live in Australia. Baty was devastated. In the two weeks that followed, he was unable to eat or sleep and he grew weak and gaunt. To make the situation more painful, he was compelled to work at the Mental Institution alongside Rudy Bendl, and now that the affair was out in the open, now that Zelda Baty had moved from her husband's house to live with her mother, Bendl felt free to taunt Baty, bragging about his escapades with Zelda. On a couple of occasions, the two men fell into fisticuffs, and each time, Bendl knocked Baty to the ground. Baty was clearly being driven to the very brink of emotion.

"On the day of the killing, the first Saturday in August, Baty wept in front of his brother and complained bitterly that he could not stand the idea of Bendl taking his children to a place as far off as Australia. This was what was upsetting him, the fear of loss of his children, and that Saturday, after midnight, he decided to act in the manner he thought any red-blooded Canadian would in the circumstances. He would confront Bendl and warn him off. He drove to the Mental Institution, parked his stationwagon, and went up to Bendl's room. He carried with him a double-barrelled shotgun which he kept in the stationwagon to shoot badgers on his farm property. He pounded on Bendl's door, waking him up and also waking the man in the next room, and there followed a short, loud discussion between Baty and Bendl. The next sound that the man in the neighbouring room heard was the blast of a shotgun. When he made his way into the hall, Thomas Baty was emerging from Rudy Bendl's room, and inside Bendl lay dead.

"At the trial, I elected to base my defence of Baty on a contention that the killing was accidental. I set the stage by eliciting testimony from the police ballistics expert that Bendl's body showed powder marks and signs of gases from the barrel of the shotgun. This established that the gun had been fired from very close range and in circumstances, I would argue, that indicated a struggle had taken place. Then I summoned Baty to the witness-stand. As in the Dorothy Christie case, he was the only witness who could testify to certain crucial events. I led him through the preliminary matters, establishing his feelings over the revelation of his wife's affair with Bendl, the threatened loss of his children, and finally I brought him to the night of the shooting.

" 'Why,' I asked, 'did you carry a gun when you called on Rudy Bendl?'

" 'Well,' Baty answered, 'he'd already given me a couple of beatings. I needed it to frighten him away from me.'

"That was a good, sensible explanation, so I moved on the to the next logical question.

" 'Did you,' I asked, 'have any intention of shooting Bendl?'

" 'No,' he answered, 'I just didn't want any trouble. I just wanted my kids. I told him Zelda was a young woman and could have many more children and why did he have to have *my* children?'

"Baty was a most passionate witness. He wept on the stand, and there were several people in the courtroom, friends and relatives of his, who were also weeping.

" 'What happened in Rudy Bendl's room?' I asked.

" 'He tried to grab the gun,' Baty said, 'and it went off.'

" 'Did you intend to shoot him?' I asked again.

" 'I didn't mean to shoot Rudy Bendl,' Baty said from the witness-box. 'What good would it do me? I've lost my kids, my wife, my job. Now I'm sitting in prison next to that execution room.'

"Well, this was very powerful testimony, but everything depended on the way in which the jury reacted to it. Would they accept Baty's version of the shooting? It was my feeling in the Selkirk courtroom that they would. A jury doesn't apply the principles of law with surgical precision, not the way a judge sitting alone on a case is more likely to. People on a jury understand life as it is lived in the community more acutely than a judge does. That has been my experience of juries. They are composed of people who are out in the world, and they accept the emotions that affect a man like Thomas Baty. At least, that was how I was reading the jury in Selkirk.

"The jury was out of the courtroom not more than forty minutes and returned with a verdict of not guilty. It was an extremely popular decision in Selkirk. Everybody in the community seemed to think that Baty had acted properly in challenging Bendl, the interloper in his family, and if there was an accident that ended in death, it was too bad for Bendl, but Baty should not have to suffer more than he already had.

"And he did not" — Walsh smiles and shakes his head in mild disbelief — "because, as I understand it, after all the turmoil, Thomas Baty's wife Zelda rejoined him with their children in the family household. It is strange what passions these cases let loose."

Walsh leads the way out of his office building. It's the Childs Building, ancient and endearing, and the only stone structure left among the glass and steel towers at Winnipeg's principal intersection. Walsh's firm — Walsh, Micay and Company — has occupied the seventh floor of Childs ever since Harry Walsh and Archie Micay were called to the bar in 1937 in a class of eleven men and one woman (she, Walsh proudly points out, was Ruth Vogel, who served as executive assistant to Stuart Garson when he was Premier of Manitoba and Minister of Justice in Ottawa under Lester Pearson). Walsh and Micay articled with Edward James McMurray, Solicitor General in a Mackenzie King government and for decades Winnipeg's wizard of the criminal courts. Walsh caught some of his relish for litigation from McMurray, and in the long years since McMurray's retirement and death, he has assumed his old mentor's starring role in the courts.

Now Walsh is steering through the noon-hour crowds to lunch in the Winnipeg Inn cross the intersection from the Childs Building. This is Walsh territory. The maître d' in the plush Velvet Glove Room bows him to his favourite table, the one directly opposite the fireplace, and Walsh orders without consulting the menu. Over the mushroom soup and grilled pickerel, he recalls the Zimmerman case. Another family in distress.

"They lived on a farm outside the town of Ashern, seventy miles from Winnipeg up near Lake Manitoba," Walsh begins. "The father, John Zimmerman, was a man in his middle forties and he was an autocrat around the house. More than that, he was cruel. He used to beat his wife. Mabel was her name, and drunk or sober, he would beat her and abuse their three children. It later came out at the trial that on one occasion when the younger daughter, Barbara, was two years old, John Zimmerman seized her and shook her and threw her to the floor, all the while screaming at her, 'Talk, talk!' It seemed that poor little Barbara had not yet spoken a word and was so traumatized by her father that she did not begin to talk until she was four years old. That was the father's pattern of behaviour, one of violence and irrationality, and in retrospect, it was small wonder that one of the members of the family finally killed him.

"On the day of the killing in January 1968, the father arose at four in the morning. That was his custom. He was unable to sleep more than a very few hours each night, and when he was awake, he demanded that the others also be out of their beds. This particular morning, matters seemed to be coming to a head. The father was as usual angry at his wife for no apparent reason. He was dissatisfied with a job he had at the creamery in Ashern. And he was venting rage at his son, Keith, a lad of twenty-two. The father blamed Keith for the death of some of the farm's calves earlier in the winter, and he argued with the boy over Keith's expressed feelings that it was time he left the farm and made his own way in the world. By eight o'clock when John Zimmerman departed for the creamery, some four hours after the family had risen, he had worked himself into a towering temper.

" 'I'll see that you suffer,' he said to his wife as he went out, according to the later word of the wife and son. 'I'll make you suffer if I have to kill you. You better think fast because you don't have much time to think any more.'

"Mabel Zimmerman and Keith Zimmerman fretted over the father's parting statement all through the rest of the day.

" 'If you leave home,' the mother said to her son, 'I know he'll kill me tonight.'

"Late afternoon came. It was dark, in the deep of Manitoba winter, and the family was in a terrible state of fear as they awaited the father's return. They heard his car, a little Volkswagen, coming down the driveway to the farmhouse. Suddenly Keith must have decided to act. He told his mother to lock herself and Barbara in a room — the third child, another daughter, was away from home that night — and he rushed down to the basement and came back with a rifle. He ran out the back door, not pausing to put on a coat against the bitter cold. His father had pulled the car into the garage about fifty feet from the house. The garage doors were open, and John Zimmerman hadn't yet moved out from behind the steering wheel. Keith fired through the back window of the car and hit his father in the shoulder. John Zimmerman got out of the car. Keith fired again and caught the father in the chest. The father pitched to the ground, and Keith rushed over to him and shot once again into his body as the father lay fallen.

"Keith returned immediately to the house. 'Mum,' he said. 'I had to shoot Dad.' Then he said something strange but significant. 'You'll sleep tonight, Mum,' he said.

"Mabel Zimmerman telephoned to the local RCMP detachment, and the officers arrived immediately. Keith sat at the kitchen table in a shattered state. His mother poured him cups of coffee, which seemed to bring him around, and a little later when the RCMP officers took him and the murder weapons to the station, he gave them a statement that was frank and open and forthright. Indeed, the statement later contributed in an instrumental way to my case for Keith.

" 'All I could think of,' he said to the RCMP, 'was just to stop Dad from coming in the house.'

"The defence I mounted at Keith's trial for the murder of his father was an extension of the principle of self-defence, which is rarely resorted to in a capital case. Usually, of course, self-defence arises when you yourself are attacked. The law says you may resist and defend your person provided you do not use more force than is necessary under the circumstances. In the Zimmerman case, Keith was acting not in his own defence but in the defence of a third party, his mother. That is a quite different matter. Still, I had many of the elements for my argument — the long history of the dead man's brutality to his wife, the threats that he had uttered on the morning of his death, the fear that young Keith felt for his mother's life. What I lacked was a weapon that I could place in or near the father's hands. It was all very well for him to have threatened the wife's life, but how was he going to act on the threat? What weapon, apart possibly from his bare hands, would he employ? If there was such a weapon, then I could be more persuasive and convincing in arguing that

Keith felt an immediate danger to his mother's safety, so immediate that he was compelled to act as drastically as he did in order to save her life. But there appeared to be no weapon.

"Then I made an extraordinary and fortuitous discovery. I was looking through the photographs that the police had taken at the scene of the crime within an hour or two of the killing. One photo showed a view into the garage. The car was parked, and the door on the driver's side stood open. Through the window of the open door, I could make out the top of an object that was leaning against the back wall of the garage. I looked at the object more closely. Was it what I thought it was? I got a magnifying glass and studied the object in the photo for several minutes before I was completely satisfied. It *was* what I suspected. It was the barrel of a rifle, and that rifle, leaning against the garage door, would have stood within easy reach of the father as he stepped from his car. I had my weapon.

"It was very curious about the rifle. By the time I discovered it in the photograph — this was several weeks after the killing — it had gone missing from the garage. I questioned Mrs. Zimmerman, and she said the garage had been cleared out and she could recall no rifle. I believed her. She was an honest person, as was Keith. What was even more curious was that the RCMP had absolutely no notion of the rifle's existence. They had apparently missed it at the scene of the crime, and they hadn't spotted it in the photograph. The first news they had of the rifle came at the trial when I cross-examined the chief investigating officer. I showed him the photograph. Could he identify the object against the garage wall? No, he said, he couldn't be certain. Would he look at it through a magnifying glass? He would, and when he looked, he registered complete astonishment. He was forced to admit that the object was certainly a rifle, that he had entirely missed it in the investigation, and that the rifle must have been standing in its place when John Zimmerman parked his car a few feet away from the weapon on the night of the killing. I thanked the officer most sincerely.

"Well, the jury sat up and took deep interest in that piece of testimony, and when I addressed them, reminding them of the sense of terror that prevailed in the Zimmerman household, of Keith's statement to the RCMP in which he expressed the necessity he felt to act on his mother's behalf, and of the presence of the rifle so close to the father's hand, I was certain that I had them with me. They felt compassion for the Zimmerman boy's predicament, and they were searching for a means to express those feelings. I believe the rifle showed them the way. It must have been difficult for them — they were at their deliberations for five hours — but ultimately they came back with a verdict that acknowledged my argument of self-defence.

"They acquitted Keith Zimmerman."

Walsh finishes his meal and orders coffee.

"A year or two later," he continues, "I received a letter post-marked in the Ashern area. It was from young Keith. He wrote that he was working at a good job, and he enclosed something he wanted me to have — an invitation to his wedding."

Walsh sips his coffee.

"In my profession," he says, "a man learns to appreciate a happy ending."

CHAPTER FIVE

The Human Comedy:
Family Law

Mal Kronby, short, dark, and looking like a better-groomed Al Pacino, strolled in straight from court, still wearing his gown, and sat down for lunch.

"Family law is the human comedy," he said, all very naturally, "and the case I got on today is something from the Marx Brothers."

This was in the lawyers' dining-room on the second floor of Osgoode Hall. It's a room that makes the law inescapable. The walls are lined with shelves of case reports. The vaulted ceiling suggests a Dickensian courtroom, and the stern portraits of nineteenth-century judges that ring the room might be characters from *Bleak House*. All of them, that is, except the dashing fellow in the painting at the north end of the chamber, William Osgoode himself, a mere thirty-seven years old when he was named first Chief Justice of Upper Canada in 1792.

"Kraft and Kraft," Kronby went on. "Nobody's over five feet and everybody delivers lines out of *A Day at the Races*. The issue is actually very simple. Mrs. Kraft obtained an interim judgment in 1973 for alimony from my client, Mr. Kraft, $100 a week. He didn't get a penny. He went to Honduras and got mixed up in the fruit-juice business. Six years later the wife brought another action, this present one, to collect everything Kraft owed her and more. Kraft's answer is he has no money. He lives on a pension from his son. Simple issue — what can Kraft pay today? But Mrs. Kraft's lawyer insists on parading through witnesses — I see Chico, Harpo, Groucho, even Margaret Dumont — and they all talk about big money deals that may or may not have taken place in Honduras in 1975.''

Kronby raised his hand to signal for a menu, and the waitress placed it in front of him before he'd bothered to finish the gesture.

"By my count, we already have two witnesses who are skating at the edges of perjury, one who's making the noises of a double agent, and Mrs. Kraft's lawyer has taken the distinctly unusual step of impeaching a prime witness for his own client. This fellow — he's the suspected double agent — just will not give the answers from the stand that the lawyer has been led to expect, something about the witness standing guard in a Honduras hotel room over a pair of Mr. Kraft's pants from which he was temporarily absent and which were alleged to contain $20,000 cash. Is *that* the Marx Brothers or isn't it?''

Kronby unreeled a few more episodes. "Mrs. Kraft demands a Yiddish interpreter when she testifies, but she's answering in English before the interpreter starts translating. And her witnesses, the businessmen from Honduras, these are men with single-track minds. I can only get one answer out of them on cross-examination.

" 'What time of day is it?' I could ask.

" 'Kraft is the most evil bastard in the whole entire world,' they'd answer.

"It could only happen in a matrimonial case. The human comedy.''

Kronby consulted the menu. It conspicuously omitted any mention of beer, wine, or spirits. Once, briefly, in the 1960s, the Osgoode dining-room offered alcoholic beverages at noon, but sales stuck at a figure far below the profit level. A few lawyers braved one dry sherry per meal, but the great majority were reluctant to be observed imbibing at midday by their peers or, more risky, by the judges who traditionally took lunch at a select table near the back entrance. The exception was an Irish professor from Osgoode Law School, a dazzling raconteur named Desmond Morton. He regularly washed down his lunch with three or four ales. Morton was the secret envy of the lawyers' dining-room.

"Cheese omelette and coffee, regular," Kronby ordered.

Mal Kronby grew up lower-middle-class, the only Jewish kid in the Beaches section of east-end Toronto. The rest of his life has been spent putting distance between himself and the old neighbourhood. He's managed it effortlessly. Class clings to the man. He's articulate, a lawyer who speaks in paragraphs. He dresses in combination of tweed jackets, Cacharel shirts, and figured ties, a look of sophisticated *sportif* that would make Fred Astaire sigh in appreciation. He's a nice player of racquet games and cooks a fine Chinese meal in a wok. Consider his wife, Mimi, vivacious and bright, she puts in a full and admirable day as a social worker. Their two teen-aged sons go to schools for smart kids. Kronby is a flutist and every second Sunday afternoon sits in on a two-hour jazz workshop. Once, in some spare time, he took a solo flight in a single-engine plane.

"It was a hell of a rush, very exciting," he says. "But after that moment of glory I didn't see much point in continuing the exercise."

Kronby was called to the Ontario bar in 1959, and not much later, when he was working in a small

general firm in downtown Toronto, an annulment
case walked through the door that changed forever
the direction of his practice.

"To call it an annulment case is to call Château
Lafitte Rothschild a wine," he said. "Husband and
wife were married in Canada. Husband at the time
was ostensibly divorced, wife was indisputably
widowed. Eventually they separated, and husband
sued, alleging adultery on the wife's part. Wife — my
client — denied the adultery. More to the point, she
said, was that husband had a prior subsisting marriage from 1941 in Lithuania, that wife number one
was still alive, and that husband and wife number
one had never been divorced under Lithuanian law.

"We therefore counter-claimed for annulment on
the grounds there had been no valid marriage in
Canada, asked damages because the husband's
allegations of adultery had tainted my client's reputation in the small Toronto Lithuanian community,
and claimed more damages for assault on the basis
that my client only consented to have sexual relations
with him in the belief, which we could now show to
be erroneous, that she was legally married to him.

"I looked at the facts and said to myself, 'This
isn't a real case, this is a question from the Family
Law exam at school.' And there was *more*. The husband admitted his 1941 Lithuanian marriage, but he
raised a marvellous defence. He said the marriage
wasn't valid because wife number one, at the time he
married her, was still bound by a marriage she'd
entered into in *Siberia*. Therefore he was free to
marry wife number two in Canada. It was a gorgeous
crossword puzzle.

"I had to make myself into an expert on marriage
and divorce in Lithuania, *circa* 1941, and in the end I
satisfied the court that the husband's Lithuanian

marriage was still valid. The husband couldn't prove the Siberian marriage. We won.

"Years later, by a coincidence I relished, another case involving a marriage in Lithuania came into my office.

" 'Ah yes,' I said to the client as I reached very suavely for these old documents on my shelf, 'the Lithuanian situation. Very unique.'

"He was impressed."

Not long after the case had taken hold of Kronby's imagination, he and another lawyer opened their own firm with an eye to building a family-law practice. "Matrimonial law is like crabgrass," Kronby says. "Once it flourishes, it pushes everything else out." By the late 1960s Kronby's reputation as one of the three or four most accomplished lawyers in the Toronto divorce business was secure.

"The majority of lawyers avoid matrimonial law," he said, testing the texture of his cheese omelette. "Compared to it, commercial litigation is a picnic. Maybe a matrimonial case isn't always as complex in law, but that doesn't make it easy to deal with. It's the blood and hormones of the practice that most lawyers can't stand."

Kronby amplified.

"I handled a separation agreement for a woman. Reasonably routine. I sent her a modest account. She returned a cheque for half the amount along with a letter that said she was happy with the result and the service and the fee. She had nothing to complain about except that I wasn't — her words — *supportive enough*. Where did I fail her? I couldn't imagine. All I'm certain of is that more than in any other kind of law, clients look to you to be accessible. Pats on the back. Sometimes they call you at home for a pat on the back at three o'clock in the morning, which, all things considered, is a fairly likely hour for matrimonial emotions to run rampant."

Worst grief of all for a lawyer, Kronby went on, are divorce actions where custody of the children emerges as a raging issue.

"Higher authority," Kronby said, happy enough with the omelette. "That's who to turn to. In a custody action, naturally you have to protect your client's interest. Why else has he retained you? But you try to steer the client in a direction that will most help the kids, and that's the point at which you look to higher authority."

Such as?

"Here's a typical scenario. Husband and wife split. Wife wants to take the kids. Husband is ninety-nine per cent agreed. But husband's mother is screaming in his ear, 'What, Eddie? You're crazy! Leaving the children with that bitch? You're a better parent. Eddie, get the kids. For your mama, Eddie.' All right, the lawyer on the other side and I convince our clients to let a psychiatrist assess everyone, and he comes down with a definitive analysis, the wife should have the children. Eddie heaves a sigh of relief. He's off the hook. He goes to his mother and says, 'It's for the best, ma. Higher authority.' "

As Kronby talked, another gowned lawyer passing by on the way to pay his lunch bill patted him on the shoulder, and smiled.

"Jim MacDonald of MacDonald and Ferrier," Kronby said when the man was out of hearing range. "He's one of the reasons why matrimonial practice is respectable and respected these days."

True enough, divorce lawyers of a couple of decades back carried an image of sleaze. Rigged adultery. Shady ladies. Private detectives breaking into hotel rooms with flash bulbs blinking at the evidence in the bed. The Archbishop of Canterbury, of all people, helped ease divorce out of the shadows with his 1966 pronouncement that irretrievable marriage breakdown was "an appropriate ground of divorce". The Divorce Act, largely the work of Senator Arthur Roebuck, followed in Canada a couple of years later, making it no longer necessary to base divorce on one party's fault. Grounds other than adultery — indeed, "irretrievable marriage breakdown" — put the private eyes and shady ladies out of business. And for Kronby and other Ontario matrimonial lawyers, the province's Family Law Reform Act, a 1978 statute, brought another measure of civility to their practice. Designed to avoid endless litigation, the Act declared that, at the break-up of a marriage, family assets must be equally divided and non-family assets might be divided at the court's discretion in shares between the former spouses.

"Then there was Jim MacDonald," Kronby said. "He made matrimonial law a specialty. It was principally through his pioneering that now we've got an excellent matrimonial bar in this city. It works to the advantage of both sides in a divorce action to hire lawyers who know the territory. Good matrimonial lawyers, specialists, identify the issues and move toward a settlement in a hurry. Get some general practitioner on a case, in over his head, and there's trouble."

Kronby loaded his coffee with cream and sugar. "A guy phoned me the other day, lawyer I know. He's acting for a husband and he says he doesn't think the wife's lawyer has read the Family Law Reform Act. 'The wife is settling for half the family assets,' he says, 'but she helped the husband set up his business, kept the books for a few years, and

195

she's probably entitled to a share of the non-family assets. What do I do?' I told him he was under a duty to his client. If the case gets to court, the judge'll spot the discrepancy. It isn't the responsibility of the guy who phoned me to make the wife's case. Too bad she retained the wrong lawyer.''

Kronby made the point that matrimonial lawyers routinely settle cases involving a couple of hundred thousand dollars. "It's easy to accumulate that much in family assets. But suppose that sum, $200,000, was the subject of dispute in a commercial case. The lawyers'd be overwhelmed by such a staggering amount and they'd fiddle for years over motions and pleadings and delays. In a matrimonial case, $200,000 is everyday money.''

Seven hundred and seventy-four thousand dollars, on the other hand, is a figure that raises even Mal Kronby's cool a degree or two. It was the package amount, $774,000, he won for Mildred Bregman in a 1978 action against Sidney Bregman. "A very interesting little case,'' Kronby says, using his understated smile.

Sidney Bregman is a partner in Bregman and Hamann, a Toronto architectural and engineering firm that, among other lucrative jobs, served as project consultants on the Toronto-Dominion Centre and First Canadian Place and handled the engineering work for the Eaton Centre. By the time of the divorce action, Mr. Bregman had accumulated net assets of $2.8 million and enjoyed a gross annual income of $500,000. Mrs. Bregman, as the marriage disintegrated, wanted her share of the loot. Just before the contest went to trial, Kronby offered to settle at $900,000, a figure that included a division of the family assets, maintenance payments for the wife, support for the one child still at home, and a share of the business assets. Sidney Bregman's lawyer wouldn't move above $650,000. The parties went to court for five days in June 1978, and in the end Mr. Justice David Henry struck the bargain at $774,000.

"Maybe what the case is most illustrative of is the discretionary component the judge has under the Family Law Reform Act," Kronby said over his coffee. "This was a situation where the wife had worked while the husband finished his last couple of years at university, then stayed at home and looked after the kids while the husband went out and became a rich and famous architect. Beyond half the family assets, what's the wife's compensation?"

In Mr. Justice Henry's discretion, it was $300,000. "In my opinion," he was at pains to write in his careful forty-four-page judgment, "it would be inequitable in this case to limit Mrs. Bregman's share of the total assets to her share of the family assets. Taking Mr. Bregman's worth at $2.8 millions, I consider it fair to say that Mrs. Bregman's contribution to his ability to achieve it (and) her assumption of responsibilities (leaving) him free physically, intellectually and mentally to work at his profession and to manage his personal investments which are considerable entitles her to a share of the non-family assets accumulated by him to the extent of $300,000."

"As well," Kronby said, "we engaged in those intriguing wrangles over assets that might or might not have been considered part of the family property and therefore equally divisible between the two parties." The Oriental rugs, for example, and the Picasso and the forty-two-foot racing boat. Once again, after all of counsel's arguments were tallied up, it remained to Mr. Justice Henry's discretion to divvy the spoils.

Bregman got the boat. Value: $160,000. "I find," the judge wrote, "that this boat has been used almost exclusively by Mr. Bregman for sailing and entertaining. He is a serious sailor who participates in racing during the season from May 1 to mid-October. He uses it also as a means for entertaining business clients." But Kronby's arguments on behalf of Mrs. Bregman prevailed when it came to the Picasso, a $24,000 gouache. It had hung in Bregman's office for two years after its purchase in 1970, then in the study at the family home in the plush Forest Hill section of Toronto for three years, until, with the marriage disintegrating, Bregman spirited it back to his office. "I infer on all the evidence," Mr. Justice Henry held, "that Mr. Bregman, for whatever reason, decided in 1972 to make the Picasso part of the furnishings of his home, that when he removed it in 1975, that was an attempt, too late in the day, to alter its status again."

On the Oriental rugs, Kronby broke even. Bregman developed a passion for Oriental rugs as his career entered its harvest period. He hunted them down, studied them, coveted them, bought them. He had sixty of the rugs by the time the marriage ended, worth either $160,000, if Bregman's courtroom testimony were accepted, or $200,000, if the testimony of a rug expert called by Kronby were believed. Mr. Justice Henry went for the $200,000. But, his lordship pointed out, there were two categories of Oriental rugs in the collection. Some were on the walls and floors of the family home; others were kept in boxes by Bregman for "occasional inspection and display to guests and collectors". He held that the former were properly family assets and the latter belonged exclusively to Bregman. A saw-off.

"Needless to say," Kronby said, finishing off his coffee, "I found the case a challenge and a delight."

He paid for lunch and made his way to a court-room on the fourth floor of the building across the street from Osgoode Hall. Kraft and Kraft, the version of matrimonial law's human comedy according to the Marx Brothers, was resuming after the noon recess. One of Mrs. Kraft's witnesses, another of the bitter business rivals of Mr. Kraft, was on the stand, a crumpled man with the face of a failed vaudeville performer. Kronby cross-examined him.

Kronby: "You started an action against the Home Juice Company, the Honduras company with which Mr. Kraft was associated, in January 1979. Is that correct?"
Witness: "I did. Yeah."
Kronby: "An affidavit of merits was filed on behalf of the defendant in April 1979, right?"
Witness: "Yeah."
Kronby: "Since then, nothing has proceeded. What has happened to your case in the last six months?"
Witness: "It slept."

Kronby turned slowly and looked at the man in the witness stand.
"It slept," Kronby repeated. "Ah, *le mot juste.*"
He wore a look of deep appreciation.

* * *

It was on the day of the old man's heart attack that life seemed to turn finally hopeless for "Jim Oliver" (not the boy's real name). He was twelve years old when the old man had the attack, on a snowy day in

December 1977, and he'd already seen a share of trouble. Earlier in the year the police caught him with a trail bike that had been stolen from another boy. A Family Court judge heard the police's evidence and decided Jim was guilty of possession of stolen property. The judge declared Jim a juvenile delinquent. His mother and father found him sniffing glue. His father strapped him. At school Jim was placed in a class for slow learners. He couldn't read, not even street signs. Other kids called him a dummy. Life was sour. And then the old man had the attack.

It happened after school. Jim was in a gang of boys who were packing snowballs and hurling them at any handy target, themselves, street lights, houses. They threw at one house and the old man who owned it came out of his door and chased the boys down the street. "Get away, you little buggers," he yelled. The boys ran out of his range and the old man turned back home. He climbed the stairs to his front door, grabbed his chest, and fell down. He was dead.

Someone told the police that Jim was in the gang, and a constable from the Youth Bureau was in the Oliver house by dinner-time. "Why do you pick on Jim?" Mrs. Oliver said to the constable. "He's told me what happened. There were other boys in on it. Why are you here? At this house? Why *Jim*?" The constable took Jim to the police station and asked him questions. He didn't lay a charge, but the police kept an eye on Jim in the following months, and on February 9, 1978, he was back in the same Family Court, accused of stealing a package of Export A cigarettes from an A & P store.

It was Judge Warren Durham's Family Court in Brampton, Ontario. Brampton is the judicial centre for the Regional Municipality of Peel in southern Ontario. Much of Peel is made up of Mississauga, a sprawling, densely populated community next door to Toronto on the west. Many of its residents commute from Mississauga to jobs in Toronto. Jim Oliver's father is one of them. He works as a mechanic. He and Jim's mother moved up from Nova Scotia in 1964 with their children, all ten of them. Two of the older kids had run into grief with the law. Michael, in his twenties now and settled down to a job in a warehouse, spent two months in training-school for stealing a car when he was younger. Paul, three years older than Jim, was put on probation for stealing a motorcycle. Jim was the youngest and the most troubled.

Judge Warren Durham thought so. He's a soft-spoken, gentle man in his early fifties. He wears a neatly trimmed beard that gives him a dashing look, and in the summertime he likes to push off in his sailboat, the *Jennie*, and cruise down Lake Ontario. He practised law in the town of Oakville, just west of Mississauga, specializing in family litigation, and he was appointed to the Family Court in Brampton in the spring of 1974. His manner is leisurely, as if nothing — no senior judge, no overloaded court docket, no anxious lawyer, no disturbed kid — could push him to an unconsidered decision.

In Jim Oliver, he recognized, he says, "a boy who was suffering, the kind of thing I'm too familiar with in this job." Jim appeared in his court four times from winter to early summer of 1978 as Judge Durham searched to find help for him. Jim was locked into the system. Once a boy has been declared a juvenile delinquent under the provincial Juvenile Delinquents Act, a step that a Family Court judge may take when he's convinced the child has committed a criminal offence, then the judge can shuffle him into all sorts of slots. He can place the kid in a foster home, commit him to an industrial school, leave the child at home on condition that he report to a probation officer, or improvise some other solution.

"The potential power I have over a kid is enormous," Judge Durham says. "I can keep jerking him back into my court till he's eighteen years old."

When the judge first saw Jim on the charge of the stolen trail bike and declared him a juvenile delinquent, he merely adjourned the case *sine die*, to a future indefinite date that might never arrive. He was giving Jim another chance. Jim couldn't handle it, and when he came back to court, pleading guilty to stealing the Export As, Judge Durham ransacked his options for another answer.

Nothing worked.

A new school didn't work. For the last few months of the school year, April to June 1978, Jim was switched to a school that ran a special class for kids with learning disabilities. He was baffled. He reacted against the class. He'd chew gum and blow bubbles. He'd pretend to faint and crash from his seat to the floor. The other kids laughed, and the teacher of the special class threw up his hands.

The Clarke Institute of Psychiatry in Toronto didn't work. A psychiatrist talked to Jim and the rest of the Olivers and wasn't optimistic. "The relationship between the Oliver children," the psychiatrist wrote in his report, "tended to be superficial. Each seemed to go his own way. Weak members are not carried and in the case of Jim are allowed to go it alone." But, the psychiatrist wrote, "the snowball incident had a profound effect on them all, particularly Mrs. Oliver. They suddenly became very aware of Jim's problems and very guilty because of their earlier lack of concern. They are dealing with this guilt now by becoming very protective of him and projecting their anger at outside agencies, particularly at school. At present, they feel hopeless."

Judge Durham adjourned Jim's case from February 9 to April 6 to June 16 to July 27, each time hearing reports on Jim's stumbling life, each time postponing his final decision, each time looking for help in finding a solution.

"All right," he said in court on July 27, "if ever a child needs a child's advocate, someone who acts for him in court and for no other individual or agency or bureaucracy, then that child is Jim."

He adjourned the case once again until Jim had a lawyer of his own. The lawyer turned out to be Jeffery Wilson, and it was Jeffery Wilson more than anyone else who directed the rescuing of Jim Oliver.

Wilson looks like a kid himself. He's in his late twenties, and he has a slight build, a heart-shaped face, and a big puff of dark hair. His words rush when he talks, and what comes out is a jumble of eagerness and expertise. He's smart and he's competitive. Another lawyer, a slightly older man who, years ago, was Wilson's counsellor at summer camp, remembers this of him as a camper: "Jeffery went all out in everything, every sport, every activity, but you couldn't call him an over-achiever because he achieved anything he set out to do."

Wilson practises alone in a bright, airy set of offices in the ancient and refurbished Gooderham Building in downtown Toronto, built in 1892 and nicknamed the Flatiron Building for its curious wedge shape. The décor in Wilson's own office reflects his passion. On the walls there are framed black-and-white photographs of kids playing games, kids hugging adults, kids laughing so loud you can almost hear their voices in the room. A copy of Lewis

Carroll's *The Annotated Alice* lies on a shelf behind Wilson's chair, and Mordecai Richler's *Jacob Two-Two Meets The Hooded Fang* cozies up to it. Wilson earns his money by handling divorce actions and drawing separation agreements, but he puts his emotions — along with his brains — on the line when he acts for kids like Jim Oliver.

"People come in here with a big alimony case," he says, "and I tell them, 'The fee you pay me will help some kid.' I lose money on the children and pay the freight with the adults."

Wilson is a founding member of Justice For Children, an outfit that, in the Ralph Nader style, takes on causes and cases on behalf of kids. He wrote a textbook for lawyers, *Children And The Law*, nine chapters, 367 pages, eighteen pages of indexes and eighteen of cited cases, all the law there is that touches on children and on, as Wilson writes in the book's preface, their "powerless and repressed status". That's Wilson. With no prompting he'll make statements like this, the words tumbling over one another: "Everybody has his agent in society. The worker has his union, the manager has his corporation. But who's the child's agent? He's got none. At the very least, when he comes before a court, *any* court, Family Court, the Supreme Court, when his parents are arguing over his custody, he should have representation. If he isn't part of the decision-making process, then whatever decision is arrived at isn't going to work."

All of which leaves a question. Why? Why does Wilson say such sensible and unexpected things? Why Justice For Children? Why *Alice* and *Jacob Two-Two*? Why? Wilson's a bachelor. Why the kids?

Maybe part of the answer surfaces from his past. When Jeffery Wilson was a boy, not yet a teenager, one of his parents died. Some months later, the surviving parent died. At the second funeral, as the service was about to begin, young Jeffery ran down the aisle.

"You promised me," he cried. "You promised me it'd never happen again."

"That cry," someone who was at the funeral remembers, a friend of Jeffery's older brother, Steve, "that cry was the most heart-rending sound I've ever heard."

An uncle looked after Steve and Jeffery. He was a social worker and the director of a summer camp, and the two brothers turned out just fine.

Wilson got his call to the Ontario bar in March 1978, and from the start he geared himself to represent kids in court. He acted for thirty of them during his first year of practice. Most arrived in his office through referrals from other lawyers. A few came because they'd seen him on television championing Justice For Children. In Wilson they recognized someone dramatically different from their notion of a lawyer.

"The use of the child's advocate is still very limited," Judge Durham says. "In my court there are exactly twelve lawyers, busy practitioners, who'll give their time to act for kids. That's because it takes a special breed of cat to do the job. Family Court isn't a place for the adversary system. You don't want to waste a lot of ammunition trying to prove the kid isn't technically guilty. Ninety-five per cent of them plead guilty anyway. The reason the child's advocate is in court is to come up with ideas that'll help the kid after he leaves here."

When Judge Durham asked in court for a lawyer to represent Jim Oliver, his words were more a suggestion than an order, since he had no power to compel a child to be represented. But a student from Osgoode Hall Law School was in court that day. Judge Durham encourages law students to hang around his Family Court on the premise that maybe they can help a kid who needs a steer in the right legal direction. The student at Jim's hearing left the courtroom and phoned Jeffery Wilson, whose reputation he knew. A meeting was set up with the Oliver family, and, since they couldn't afford to pay a lawyer's fee, the Ontario Legal Aid was rung in. By September 13 Wilson had a certificate from Legal Aid to take on the case.

He interviewed the Olivers in their home. He spent time with Jim. And he came away convinced of a couple of things.

"Jim's problem has everything to do with learning," he said. "I saw that right away. He's one of those sad kids who can't make connections in his head. He can be taught to do it by people who really give a damn about teaching him. But he isn't getting it right now. That's his trouble. All the other stuff, stealing the cigarettes and fooling around with the trail bike, they're just a reflection of his frustration with an educational system that can't even teach him to read."

Maybe, Wilson figured, the Toronto Learning Centre had an answer to Jim's problem. The Centre makes a specialty of reclaiming kids, usually kids with learning disabilities, whom public schools have failed to reach. "Most of our youngsters,' said Ray Carlaw, TLC principal at the time Wilson approached it on behalf of Jim, "come to us in a rather demoralized state. They're the losers of the world. They've been dumped off in basements or they've been given the back room of some place because, you know, we really don't want to expose learning-disabled youngsters to the normal kids in the world." The TLC isn't a back room. It operates out of tidy and tranquil quarters in an office building in North Toronto. It gets results through patient, upbeat, and concentrated teaching methods. It has a staff of forty for 154 students. It exudes optimism. It is very expensive — $6,800 per student per year.

Wilson inspected the Centre and persuaded it to inspect Jim. Inspecting Jim wasn't easy. "When you talk to him," Carlaw said, "you must refocus him in to you constantly in order to get him to look at you and talk to you, snap him back into what you're doing because he tends to wander." Still, Carlaw was confident that, sure, the Centre had a program that would equip Jim to deal with words and numbers and street signs. One problem, though, Carlaw told Wilson. He'd better move fast or two things might happen — there wouldn't be room for Jim at the Centre and, besides, it could be too late for Jim.

And the money? The Centre's $6,800 tuition fee? Who was to come up with the cash for Jim?

"That's where things may hit the fan," Wilson said. He had a brainstorm. It was to ask Judge Durham for an order making the Region of Peel responsible for paying Jim's way at the TLC. He'd rely on Section 20(2) of the Juvenile Delinquents Act, which says that "In every case it is within the power of the Court to make an Order upon the parent or parents, or *upon the municipality to which the child belongs* (italics mine), to contribute to the child's support such sum as the Court may determine. . . ." The potential flaw in Wilson's scheme lay in the word "support". Did the definition of "support" include education? Wilson thought the answer ought to be in the affirmative. But would Judge Durham agree with him? Wilson set to work preparing his argument. There were, alas, no cases that defined "support", and no other lawyers, it seemed, had tried to use Section 20(2) of the Juvenile Delinquents Act to manoeuvre a municipality into paying for a child's education. Wilson was starting from scratch. He needed Scotch tape and paper-clips to hold his argument together. There was only one element that was certain — the Regional Municipality of Peel would oppose the role of paymaster that Wilson was about to assign it. When it got notice of the Jim Oliver case, things would heat up.

The Brampton Courthouse, where the case was heard on November 7, 1978, is a smart new two-storey brick building that sits in strange isolation in fields far south of Brampton's business and residential areas. Inside, Judge Durham's Family Court is small and functional and hints at friendliness. The docket showed eleven cases for the seventh, a busy day, but the judge was prepared to give all the time and attention that was necessary to get through the Oliver case. It began at ten o'clock and continued past the lunch break until 2:20 before Jeffery Wilson had finished calling his witnesses and presenting his arguments.

As Wilson performed, Jim Oliver sat beside him at the counsel table. Jim worked on his nails, not randomly and nervously but with a surgeon's dedication. He'd study one nail for two or three minutes, then bite it sharply with his front teeth. More study, more trimming, then a close inspection to ensure that all nails were retreating toward the quick at the same rate. His face, hunched over the nails, gave away no expression. It kept to a protective blankness. It was a wary teenager's face. It had a light touch of acne. His body showed the same signs of adolescence, of new muscles growing. He was slim, about five feet five, and wore his dark hair in a neat and conservative cut. He was neatly and conservatively dressed, too. A patterned shirt, jeans, white socks, and soft Hush Puppies. He worked on his nails.

Wilson called six witnesses: the principal of the Peel school that Jim attended during the last three months of the previous spring; Ray Carlaw from the Toronto Learning Centre; the executive director of a counselling agency for teenagers in Peel; a social worker from the Peel Board of Education; Jim's mother; and, very briefly, Jim himself. A simple pattern emerged from Wilson's questioning. Peel's public schools, the witnesses told the court, couldn't teach Jim. Jim would benefit from the Toronto Learning Centre's methods. And when he began to learn to do things he'd never managed before, to read, then his hassles with the police would fade away.

"I think Jim's behavioural problem is a manifestation of incorrect educational programming," Ray Carlaw told the court in his testimony, echoing Wilson's own earlier analysis. "I don't believe he really is a behavioural problem. I think he's acting out of frustration, and I think if I was as learning-disabled as he is, I would act out as well."

Carlaw made a strong witness, confident and skilled, occasionally angry, sometimes dramatic. Wilson asked him to outline to the court a program for Jim at the Centre. Carlaw's answer was long and thorough, but at one point it boiled down the Centre's approach to a few powerful words.

"I would set Jim up in a program where first of all we will have optimum success," Carlaw said, his voice rising, the volume stepped up. "Optimum success. We will not allow failure. Failure will *not* occur."

Wilson smiled at the words. Judge Durham quickened his note-taking. Jim's attention switched off his nails and focused on Carlaw. The other witnesses, sitting on the public benches, shifted and stirred, something unmistakable filled the courtroom. It was nothing less than a sense of hope. This kid, this Jim whose life had been so irredeemably lousy, so drenched in defeat, was going to be rescued. Carlaw's words represented a turning-point in the hearing. From the moment he spoke them, the odds began to run in Jim Oliver's favour, and everybody in the courtroom recognized the rising sense of hope.

Policewoman Grant recognized it. She spoke for the crown at the hearing, a correct, no-nonsense woman in her forties who worked for the Peel Youth Bureau. She sat at the crown's table, serving as the Family Court equivalent of the prosecutor, but she called no witnesses, cross-examined Wilson's witnesses perfunctorily, and when it came time to present the crown's argument, told Judge Durham that "I can only say from what I have heard this morning that I really cannot disagree with Mr. Wilson in terms of what is in Jim's best interests." Policewoman Grant wasn't going to quell the sense of hope.

Wilson's argument lasted almost thirty minutes. His job was to provide Judge Durham with precedents in earlier and accepted law that he could rely on to make an order directing Peel to pay for Jim's tuition at the Learning Centre. Wilson talked first of a "necessary". The word came from an 1891 English decision by the Court of Queen's Bench. It held that, for an infant, education was like food and clothing, a "necessary". Aha, Wilson was saying to Judge Durham, you *see*. The Ontario Juvenile Delinquents Act says you can order a municipality to pay for a delinquent kid's "support". And how is "support" to be construed? Very broadly, broadly enough to include education, as broadly as the way in which the old Court of Queen's Bench construed "necessary".

Wilson, standing at the counsel table, making sudden hand gestures at the stack of papers in front of him, bending over quickly to check a reference in a case-book, his body in constant, tense movement, cited more old decisions. And more. Sometimes he'd disappear into a thicket of case law, out of the sight and comprehension of everyone in the courtroom except Judge Durham. Then he'd reappear with a few sentences that would unmistakably link Jim Oliver's immediate situation to the musty concepts left over from century-old English judgments.

"In Jim's circumstances," he said, still hammering at the union of "necessary" and "support", "he will not be able to learn a trade without the special education he needs. I asked the question specifically of Mr. Carlaw, who gave me a very blunt response that if Jim does not get the education he needs, then his chances of succeeding in society — and I'm just recollecting this — it was something like nil."

"Support," Wilson was saying in short, equals "necessary", and both embrace education.

Judge Durham nodded.

Wilson took on Section 20 of the Juvenile Delinquents Act, the section under which the judge would make his order. He had more cases. He had Ontario Supreme Court decisions to show that when a Family Court judge makes a support order against a municipality, thereby compelling the municipality to spend taxpayers' money, he should balance "the child's own good and he best interests of the community".

"Well, I argue most respectfully," Wilson said to the judge, "that this is a case where these two things — child's own good and best interests of the community — absolutely coincide. This community will suffer if the interests of this child are not satisfied with a proper education."

Wilson sat down.

"This is indeed a sad court," Judge Durham said. "It's a place where the community regularly brings their frustrations."

The two sentences began his judgment. He could have adjourned the hearing for a couple of weeks and mulled over the judgment in his chambers. Instead, he chose to wing it, to dictate his decision off the top of his head for all in the courtroom to hear and for the court reporter to record. It took more than half an hour. Judge Durham liked to ramble and to touch all bases. He reviewed each witness's testimony in detail. He unloaded a blast at the Peel Board of Education. "I don't know that Jim has failed school," he said. "I think the school system has failed Jim." He offered his own definition of education and praised the Toronto Learning Centre. He began to wind towards the nitty-gritty of his decision. Wilson moved restlessly in his chair. Judge Durham said he liked the 1891 case from the Court of Queen's Bench that Wilson brought him. "I notice one of the judges was talking about the circumstances of being 'in this working-class England where it's so necessary to learn a trade', and I was impressed in thinking how strongly those words carry on almost ninety years later."

Yes, Judge Durham went on, education is a "necessary" for Jim. Yes, he needs this support. I will order it, and, yes, Peel must pay. He moved swiftly to the end of his judgment. He was using Section 20 of the Juvenile Delinquents Act to direct Jim to attend the Toronto Learning Centre for the balance of the school year beginning the very next day. He ordered the Regional Municipality of Peel to send a cheque to the Centre for $5,780 covering tuition for the balance of the year. And he adjourned the case until June 28, 1979, when all parties would once again appear before him for another assessment of Jim's situation.

Judge Durham smiled at Jim and banged his gavel.

"His judgments," Wilson said in the corridor outside the courtroom, "they're like the *Whole Earth Catalogue*. You read through a lot of philosophy and sociology before you finally get to the law. But, hell, he's on the same wavelength as me. Thank God."

Jim stood in the corridor with his mother. He was wearing his blank expression. Ray Carlaw walked up to him. He shook Jim's hand and said he looked forward to seeing him in school the next day. Jim smiled. His face revealed something no one in the courtroom had seen. Two deep dimples.

Back in his office, Wilson waited for trouble. "Quite frankly," he wrote later in the week to one of Jim's teachers at the TLC, "when I cynically consider the worthwhile and beneficial implications of this decision for the purpose of ensuring all children an education, I would not be surprised if this bureaucracy, as with others, strains the success of the decision by various appeals to higher court."

Within a few days, Wilson's mail turned up a letter from Osler, Hoskin and Harcourt. It ranks among the two or three most high-powered law firms in

Toronto. It boasts seventy-three lawyers and two floors of slick offices in First Canadian Place on King Street. One of its clients is the Regional Municipality of Peel. The letter let Wilson know that Peel had instructed Osler, Hoskin to launch an appeal of Judge Durham's decision. But, the letter went on, the appeal would be delayed because the member of the firm's litigation department who tended to Peel's business, J. Edgar Sexton by name, was tied up for several weeks running a complicated prosecution on behalf of the federal government under the Combines Investigation Act.

"Those guys, they're wheeling out the heavy artillery," Wilson said, and he set to work moving paper in and out of his office. Letters, legal memos, notes for his argument on the appeal. He exchanged several letters with Osler, Hoskin to arrange for Peel to pay Jim's tuition at the TLC even while the appeal was in the works. He drew his bill for fees and disbursements in Jim's case and mailed it to the Ontario Legal Aid, $1,031.56 — or about thirty-five cents an hour for all of Wilson's time. He wrote letters recruiting witnesses to appear at Jim's June hearing before Judge Durham. He received a note from a woman named Rosemary Underwood of the Ontario Association for Children with Learning Disabilities saying she'd heard about the Oliver case and offering her expertise. Wilson sent back a letter welcoming her aboard. And he enclosed a cheque for fifty dollars, a donation to Mrs. Underwood's association.

Early in March, Osler, Hoskin served Wilson with its Record in *Peel* v. *Oliver*. The firm's first step in the appeal procedure was to bring a motion before a judge of the Ontario Supreme Court requesting leave to appeal. If the judge decided there was merit in

Osler, Hoskin's argument, then he'd send on the case for a full-scale appeal hearing before another Supreme Court justice. The Record set out the argument that Osler, Hoskin would present on the first motion. It came bound in bright blue covers, forty-three pages of submissions and cited cases and quoted law.

Wilson was impressed. "Some of it makes me edgy," he said. "I mean it's strong, especially the stuff about necessaries."

He was referring to paragraphs 39 and 40 of the Record, the crunch in Osler, Hoskin's argument.

> 39. It is submitted that insofar as schooling of the Respondent Oliver may be considered a necessary of life, this schooling is provided by the public education system at no cost. The public education system in the Province of Ontario provides both regular programs and special education programs for children with learning disabilities such as that experienced by the Respondent. It is submitted that education as a necessary of life for the Respondent should be interpreted as restricted to these programs provided in the public education system. Anything more is not educational as a necessary of life, but remedial treatment.

> 40. It is submitted that the parents of the Respondent should pay for any special private schooling of the Respondent over and above that provided by the public education system.

"Maybe they're right," Wilson said. "Right in law. I mean."

He stayed in his office late into the night for most of a week preparing his reply to Osler, Hoskin's arguments, his Respondent's Statement. It ran to thirty-eight pages, enclosed in a tan folder, and it repeated in different phrasing all of the points he'd made to Judge Durham. He read it over several times, made changes, inserted new case situations, had his secretary retype it, and then, struggling against his reluctance to let the Statement out of his hands, released it to be served on Osler, Hoskin.

"Fat's in the fire now," he said, shrugging.

In the meantime, through the winter and spring, Wilson checked in regularly with the Oliver family. The reports on Jim's progress were positive. He'd missed only two days of school at the Learning Centre and he was beginning to find a handle on books and the printed word.

"He likes school, he smiles a lot," Wilson said. "But he thinks the cops are out to get him because he's doing such neat stuff at the Centre."

The cops got him. On April 21, a month after Jim's fourteenth birthday, he walked out of a Canadian Tire store with a tail-light and a generator for a bicycle. He hadn't paid — $5.18 — and a security guard spotted him. The police laid another delinquency charge against Jim. Wilson arranged to have it dealt with during the June appearance before Judge Durham.

And there was another problem. Ritalin. It's a drug that acts as a calming agent on children who might otherwise be restless or hyperactive. The TLC used Ritalin on Jim, 120 milligrams a day in pills that he took at nine in the morning, noon, and three in the afternoon.

"At the Centre," Wilson said, "they prescribe Ritalin like jelly beans. I worry. I'll fight like hell to keep him in the place, but I'll fight like hell to get him off Ritalin. I hate drugs."

Osler, Hoskin's motion for leave to appeal reached court on May 29. It was to be heard at Osgoode Hall in Weekly Court, a forum where lawyers appear before a Supreme Court judge, without clients or witnesses present, to argue issues that have to do more with procedure than with substance. Wilson arrived at Osgoode at 9:15 that morning carrying a fat briefcase and accompanied by a bearded law student who was along to help with the manual labour, running for books and chasing down last-minute references. The two men collected armloads of case-books from the Osgoode library and carried them into the courtroom where Mr. Justice Richard Holland was presiding over Weekly Court. The room was small and elaborately decorated in gilt and in regal colours. The judge, a man with a plummy accent and the face of a basset hound, sat high on his bench at one end of the room, and below him the well of the courtroom was crowded with lawyers in long black gowns, vests, tabs, and winged collars. The Queen's Counsel occupied the front of the court, beyond a low barrier, and the rest of the counsel distributed themselves on benches that sloped upwards toward the back of the courtroom.

J. Edgar Sexton wasn't among the lawyers on either side of the barrier.

"Steve Smart," a brisk young man whispered, sliding onto a bench beside Wilson and holding out his hand. "Osler, Hoskin. Sexton's out of town. Matter of some importance. We're asking to have the motion adjourned."

Wilson looked unperturbed. "Sure," he said. "Okay."

Smart waited his turn on the list of matters scheduled for hearing that day.

"M'lord," he finally began, pausing while an elderly and vague court clerk handed up to the judge the thick stack of documents in *Peel* v. *Oliver*. "M'lord, we are respectfully requesting an adjournment."

Smart's voice took on an even, measured quality, a drone, and the lines came out of his mouth at a practised clip as if he'd mastered them long ago.

"Case of real importance," he told the judge. "Constitutional questions ultimately involved. . . motion will need several hours to argue. . . our Mr. Sexton to take the appellant's brief. . . held up out of town under circumstances of some urgency. . . ."

Mr. Justice Holland seemed relieved. The list of cases was already long enough, and he'd grant the adjournment. Wilson got to his feet and requested protection for Jim during the adjournment. He got what he wanted.

"I'm endorsing the papers," the judge said as he wrote on a document in front of him, "with an order that the Family Court judge's program in respect to the Respondent is to go ahead until this court, the Supreme Court, orders him to stop."

Wilson and Smart bowed in the direction of Mr. Justice Holland's bench and headed quickly out of Osgoode Hall, gowns flying, to the building across the street. They were going to ask the Registrar of the Supreme Court to assign them a special Weekly Court date when the motion could be heard.

"No way I'm gonna do that," the Registrar told them in his office. He had a W.C. Fields air. He'd seen it all and wasn't impressed. "You say it'll take half a day to argue? That means *all* day. I don't believe anything lawyers tell me. I'll put you on the list waiting for cancellations — *Peel* v. *Oliver* is it? — but you're way down the line."

There was a sense of anticlimax to the morning — all that preparation, all that machinery cranked up, for a motion that wasn't heard and now might be heard only in the unpredictable future — but Wilson gave off no sense of exasperation.

"Part of the law business," he said. "You wind yourself up and then nothing happens. Osler was entitled to an adjournment. It was only the first time up for the motion. I expected anything to go on. Or nothing."

Wilson walked back to his office.

On June 27, the day before Jim's case was to return to Judge Durham's court, the Supreme Court of Canada got into the act. That was the date it handed down its oral decision in the case of *Viking Holmes* v. *Peel*. It was another case that originated with Judge Durham. In January 1975 and again in April 1976 he had acted under that handy section of the Juvenile Delinquents Act, Section 20, to commit two delinquent kids to the care of a group home for troubled adolescents run by a private company called Viking Homes. He'd also ordered Peel Region to pay $43 per day for each kid's upkeep. Peel, represented by J. Edgar Sexton, appealed the decision. Mr. Justice John Holland — no relation to Mr. Justice Richard Holland — held that Judge Durham had exceeded his authority. Under Section 20, Mr. Justice Holland ruled, Judge Durham could commit a delinquent child to an industrial school or a foster home or a children's aid society, or to a parent or a probation officer, or to any "other suitable person". But he couldn't commit the child to a group home like Viking because it didn't qualify as "other suitable person". Viking took the case to the Ontario Court of Appeal. The Appeal Court agreed with Mr.

Justice Holland. So, as of June 27, did the Supreme Court of Canada.

Judge Durham had been slapped down by the highest court in the land, but he'd long since made a new legal play under Section 20. Shortly after Mr. Justice Holland's decision in the Viking case in the spring of 1977, Judge Durham ordered a young girl who appeared before him, a suicidal teenager, to be delivered into the care of a former policeman named Tom MacKenzie. By no coincidence, Tom MacKenzie happened to be a supervisor at Viking Homes. More ways than one to skin a cat, Judge Durham said, as he directed MacKenzie, who qualified, in the judge's view, as an "other suitable person" under Section 20, to take the suicidal teenager to live at Viking Homes under his supervision. And who was to pay her expenses, $43 a day? Why, the Region of Peel.

Peel once again appealed Judge Durham's decision, and while the appeal was winding through the judicial system, the judge received an unexpected visitor. Madame Justice Mabel Van Camp of the Supreme Court of Ontario came calling on him in his chambers at the Brampton Courthouse. It was a winter day close to Christmas 1977, and Madame Justice Van Camp had no appointment and had sent no advance notice. Supreme Court justices, according to fixed custom, don't just drop in on lesser members of the bench, announced or unannounced.

"I couldn't figure it out," Judge Durham said afterwards. "She chatted for twenty minutes. She said Supreme Court people didn't get out of their courts enough and see the world. She was interested in the dynamics of my court, how I function, that kind of thing. Strange visit but, you know, *nice*."

During the chat, Judge Durham didn't mention the Viking case. He had no reason to. Madame Justice Van Camp didn't mention it either. She had a reason for her silence. Not long after her visit, a decision came down from the Supreme Court on Peel's appeal of Judge Durham's order placing the young girl in Tom MacKenzie's custody. The decision turned down the appeal, holding that this time Judge Durham had acted within his powers under the Juvenile Delinquents Act. Tom MacKenzie qualified as an "other suitable person" in Section 20's terms and Peel must pay for the girl's upkeep in the Viking home. The decision was written by Madame Justice Van Camp.

"Now that," Judge Durham said, "*that* caught me by surprise."

"What a humane thing to do!" Jeffery Wilson said when he heard the news of Madame Justice Van Camp's visit to Judge Durham. "But, you know, it was a real break that the appeal went to Van Camp. Just mention kids in her court and her eyes water up."

Peel took the Van Camp decision to the Ontario Court of Appeal. But the appeal hadn't yet come on for argument by June of 1979, and, going into Judge Durham's court, Wilson was left to contend with the Supreme Court of Canada's ruling in the first Viking case.

"Sure, it says a Family Court judge can't commit a kid to a group home," he said. "But the Toronto Learning Centre isn't a group home. My situation is different from the Viking case. If it comes up in front of Durham, I can distinguish it. No problem."

He paused.

"I don't *think* there's a problem."

Wilson wasn't bothered either by Jim's fresh trouble with the Peel police, the $5.18 theft from the Canadian Tire store. "It's one of those situations," he explained, "where I say, 'Oh, you naughty boy,' but inside I'm glad because this new charge'll help me argue that Jim ought to be kept at the Centre till his head is really straight."

The hearing on June 29, a serene summer day, got under way in Judge Durham's courtroom at two o'clock in the afternoon. Jim Oliver sat beside Wilson at the counsel's table. He'd grown since the previous November. So had his fingernails. He looked huskier, a little taller, and he'd abandoned the surgeon's approach to his nails. His face, though, still gave away no emotion. His mask was in place, and if he'd grown to trust the people in the courtroom he wasn't letting them know.

Two men took their places at the crown's table. One, bulky, wearing a snappy sports coat and a genial expression, addressed the court only once during the afternoon. "I'm just here about the money," he told Judge Durham, smiling. He was a lawyer from the Peel offices and his job was to report back to his bosses on the sum Judge Durham might order the municipality to pay for Jim's schooling.

The other crown representative was from the Peel Youth Bureau, Sergeant Tom Crossin, a heavy man in his early fifties, deadpan expression, greying hair cut short, the look of an intimidator. But, like Policewoman Grant at the November hearing, Sergeant Crossin took a distant second place to Jeffery Wilson in the proceedings. At one point Sergeant Crossin suggested to Judge Durham that Jim might be better off in a training-school learning a trade, and he raised an objection to the cost of the

Learning Centre, now up to $7,400 a year. Judge Durham brushed him off. Gently.

"Crossin's a nice guy as these people go," Wilson said during a short recess in the hearing. "I've seen cops in that job who'd say, 'Okay, Jim, you got off this time, but wait'll you turn sixteen. We'll be watching for you.'"

Wilson called seven witnesses to the stand.

"Jim was a problem when he came to the Centre," Jim's teacher, a dark, handsome woman in her early thirties, testified. "He was learning at a mid-grade-one level. Now he's at the grade-three level with potential for grade five, and he's one of the most conscientious workers I've come across."

The second witness heaped more praise on Jim. She was the head of the Centre's junior school, a bright-faced, confident woman. "When Jim came, he was a hunched-over, defeated-looking young man," she said. "Later I saw a big smile on his face, and I came to know him as an outspoken, polite, and charming gentleman."

A psychologist from the Family Court Clinic at the Clarke Institute testified about the effects of Ritalin. "It's positive for Jim," he said. "It gets at an organic problem. Jim's mind, you see, jumps around. That's reflected in his physical jitteriness. Without the Ritalin he's mentally ill all over the place. But as a permanent solution, well, research is just starting on whether the need for Ritalin is ever-lasting."

What about the stealing, Wilson asked, the theft from the Canadian Tire store?

"It's remarkable he hasn't done more than just take a bicycle generator," the psychologist answered. "The thing is, he knows there's a chance he may not go back to the Toronto Learning Centre, and that's upsetting him. The stealing was a way of asking for help.''

Rosemary Underwood stepped to the witness stand, an assured woman wearing a frilly dress with a flowered pattern. She told the court she was executive director of the Ontario Association for Children with Learning Disabilities. "A learning disability," she said, "has to do with the neurological or nervous system. With Jim it affects his ability to listen. It's as if there's a part in him missing, and he has trouble just paying attention.''

Is there an answer, Wilson asked, a solution for Jim?

"For children with learning disabilities," Mrs. Underwood answered, "you can't just get at the social and emotional factors. You have to get at education, and group homes and training-schools are no good for that. They just lead to frustration and failure. This $7,400 at the Toronto Learning Centre isn't out of line for helping Jim. If he was taken out of the Centre at this stage, society would end up paying a lot more in welfare and crime and unemployment insurance. Jim'd become a liability on the community. It would be traumatic not to let him stay at the Centre. Most unkind. Most inhumane.''

"See what I'm doing?" Wilson said during the recess. "I'm piling on the evidence that the Centre is in the best interests of the kid and so on, and then whenever Osler, Hoskin gets us into court on appeal, I've got everything in my favour on the record. The crown doesn't like what's happening, though. They're mad at me for taking the whole afternoon.''

Wilson called more witnesses: the principal of the Centre, Mrs. Oliver, and Jim.

For Jim's testimony, Wilson moved out from behind the counsel table where he'd stood to question the other witnesses and took up a position, almost intimately close, beside the witness-box. He leaned in towards Jim. Almost everyone in the courtroom, Jim's teachers and his mother, Mrs. Underwood and the Clarke Institute psychologist, strained in their seats, willing that the boy would perform, that he'd come up with the right answers, *impressive* answers.

Wilson: "Jim, you try and speak up loud enough so that everybody in the room, right down to the back seats there, can hear you. Okay? Now, Jim, what's good about the Toronto Learning Centre?"

Jim: "Get more teaching there."

Wilson: "What about the teachers?"

Jim: "They're nice."

Wilson: "Do you want to go back?"

Jim: "I need an education."

Wilson: "Why is that, Jim?"

Jim: "I want to learn to drive. I want to read good enough so I can drive a truck."

Wilson: "What's that in your hand there, Jim, your report card?"

Jim: "Report card, yeah."

Judge Durham: "May I see it, Jim?"

The judge looked at the report card. Jim let his head hang down, studying the floor of the witness-box. The courtroom fell utterly silent.

Judge Durham: "A very good report, Jim. Good for you."

Wilson: "What about this offence, Jim, the bicycle generator that you took from the store? Do you have any idea why you took it?"

Jim: "No."

Judge Durham: "Why did you do it, Jim?"

Jim: "I don't know. I wanted it."

Judge Durham: "Will you do it again?"
Jim: "No. I know I won't."

For the first time, with his last words, Jim's voice lost the monotone he'd used to answer the other questions. His voice rang clearly. He was almost animated. He was also scared.

Wilson: "No more questions, Your Honour."
Judge Durham: "All right, Jim, you go back to your seat."

The judge held out his hand to stop Jim.

"Jim," he said, "I've always liked and respected you."

The teachers from the Centre, sitting in a group at the back of the courtroom, murmured to one another. They smiled. The kid, they told themselves, had done all right.

Wilson's address to Judge Durham, twenty-five minutes long, covered familiar territory. The Learning Centre, he said, was the place for Jim. "The municipality, Peel, has had plenty of time to come up with another plan," Wilson said. "But it hasn't thought of any real alternative to the Centre." Section 20 of the Juvenile Delinquents Act, he went on, gave the judge enough power to act in Jim's best interests. He cited the cases and authorities. He avoided mention of the Supreme Court of Canada's oral judgment of the day before in the Viking case. "With Jim," Wilson finished, "he's just seeking a fair deal under the Juvenile Delinquents Act."

As before, Judge Durham dictated his judgment. As before, it was thorough and labyrinthine and heavy on digressions. Ritalin took him up one path.

"A lot of thought has gone into the treatment, but in the case of Ritalin, I wish there was another way. Maybe the people at the Centre will find it." He took another detour to slap down the government's tendency to tuck kids with learning disabilities into provincial training-schools. "A training-school costs $93 a day. That's staggering. And the point is that the children go into these places and come out no better than they were before. But if they're properly educated, then they stay in society and turn into productive people."

The judge joined in the silent conspiracy with Wilson to avoid the Supreme Court's Viking decision. Not relevant, he implied, not in Jim's case anyway. But, again as before, he went over each witness's testimony. "There's even more evidence than there was last time, back in November, that the only way Jim's going to get on a good course in life is for him to stay at the Centre. I'm not going to put him in one of those invisible agencies that the government runs. It'll be my order that Jim stays at the Toronto Learning Centre. Since the parents can't afford it, I direct the municipality to pay the fees. That's $7,400 in four instalments."

It was almost 5:30. Sergeant Crossin stood up. "Your Honour," he said, "I've got baseball. There are fifteen boys waiting for their coach. Me."

"Okay, sergeant," Judge Durham said. "Good luck with the game."

He looked down at Jim. "On the theft from the Canadian Tire store, Jim, I'm fining you ten dollars."

Jim held the judge's gaze.

"That's your own money, remember," Judge Durham said. "Not anybody else's."

Jim nodded.

"All right," the judge went on, "we'll adjourn now till a year from now, June 26, at 9:30 a.m., and we'll see how we've all made out."

He banged his gavel.

In the corridor outside the courtroom, Jim offered a display of dimples. The people from the Learning Centre took turns shaking his hand. They congratulated him on the day. Then they congratulated themselves.

In his chambers, Judge Durham contemplated a puzzle. "Jim's the first kid I've sent to that place, the TLC. Funny, I keep thinking it stands for Tender Loving Care. Anyway," he said, his judge's robe hung on a hook, his shirt undone at the top button, "he's the first, and it's working for him, and Peel's paying the shot. So I wonder how come other lawyers haven't come into my court and asked me to give their kids the same treatment? I thought there'd be a line-up to follow Jeffery Wilson's example. Aren't there any more lawyers out there thinking like him? Beats me why not."

The next day Wilson wrote letters of thanks to each of his witnesses. He wrote to Jim reminding him to pay the ten-dollar fine and to hold on to the receipt. He added a short paragraph to the end of the letter: "I do not have to say anything about a repeat performance with respect to taking things which are not yours. That will only get in the way of your desire to get an education."

At Osler, Hoskin and Harcourt, J. Edgar Sexton waited for instructions from Peel. Wilson waited, too. On July 25 he received word from Osler, Hoskin that they'd be bringing a motion in the Supreme Court to quash both orders of Judge Durham, the one of November 8, 1978, and the other of June 29, 1979, and to ask for leave to appeal the orders. Then silence set in, months of it. Jim went back to the Toronto Learning Centre in the fall, Peel continued to pay his tuition fees, and Osler, Hoskin made no move to pursue the case into higher court, no motion to quash, no motion for leave to appeal.

"It's just temporarily stuck in the works somewhere at Peel or Osler, Hoskin," Wilson said in his office one afternoon late in the autumn. "The day of reckoning is inevitable, the day when we'll get up in court and argue all these points about what a judge can or can't do under the Juvenile Delinquents Act. We'll thrash at everything. We'll go at the Supreme Court's decision in the Viking case. Nothing gets ignored in this business. All the chickens come home to roost eventually."

Wilson was sitting at his desk under the photographs of the laughing children, the *Annotated Alice,* and *Jacob Two-Two Meets The Hooded Fang.* He talked quickly and he was, as always, all energy and tension.

"None of this really matters as far as Jim's concerned," he said. "He's the winner because while the rest of us are sitting around waiting to go back to court, he's at the TLC and he'll get enough education to become what he wants to be in life. A truck driver."

Wilson smiled, a swift smile that came and went, a beatific smile, lighting up his face for just an instant.

"That's my job — right? — getting Jim an education."

Wilson stood up. He had other things to get on with. He was taking part in a public panel discussion that night at the St. Lawrence Hall. The subject was "The Children of Divorced Parents."

CHAPTER SIX

Joe Sedgwick and the Ottawa Spy

Probably he spoke the simile a hundred times in his life. A thousand times. Joe Sedgwick was a storyteller of the old school, never tiring of a good line, willing to polish and refine it, intuiting the optimum moment to drop it into a speech or conversation, calculating its risible impact.

"A counsel is like a loaded blunderbuss," he used to say. "Your opponent hires him and he blows your brains out or you hire him and he blows your opponent's brains out."

He would laugh, guttural and merry, a Sidney Greenstreet laugh.

"A client's best advice is to hire counsel and then keep his mouth shut," he might go on. "No sense having a dog and barking yourself."

All this was delivered in a voice with the timbre of Churchill's. Even in his retreating years — Sedgwick was eighty-three when he died on December 27, 1981 — the voice kept its rolling, mellifluous quality. Even after the operation for throat cancer in 1974, it remained a cathedral of a voice. And the laugh, that glorious rumble, made a proper mate for the voice.

Joe Sedgwick liked the Queen and horse races and Teacher's Scotch topped off with Apollinaris. He liked bow-ties and after-dinner speaking and the Conservative Party, the Anglican Church and trains and the portrait of himself that hangs in Campbell House, the 1833 Georgian home in downtown Toronto where members of the Advocates' Society take lunches of chops and wine and trifle and talk of the fun and triumphs of their courtroom lives. The Advocates' Society is restricted to lawyers whose practices are at least mainly litigious. It was founded in 1964. Sedgwick gave the money, five thousand dollars, that began the fund to preserve and restore Campbell House. He liked the Advocates' Society. He liked the view from the bedroom of his widower's apartment on the thirty-fourth floor of the Manulife Centre in midtown Toronto, a vista south over the skyscrapers to the islands and the summer sailboats. He liked bridge, poker, the military, Chesterton, and his grandchildren. But, most of all, he liked to laugh.

When Sedgwick, in his courtroom prime through the 1940s, '50s, and '60s, used to arrive by train in Ottawa to argue appeals before the Supreme Court of Canada, his suite at the Château Laurier became the unofficial clubroom to all the counsel in town for the Supreme Court sittings. Sedgwick poured drinks. Tensions eased. Sedgwick told stories. Counsel's minds drifted away from their briefs. Sedgwick laughed. So did everyone.

"My great friend Jack Cartwright has always been the very epitome of courtesy," Sedgwick used to say, launching one of his favourite stories about the Honourable J.R. Cartwright, a Justice on the Supreme Court of Canada from 1949 and its Chief Justice from October 3, 1967, to March 20, 1970, when he retired. "Jack is a gentleman. Isn't he *just*. But, you know, there was a single occasion when Jack was seen to display some unkindness. That distinguished but ponderous counsel, Matthews, was before Jack's court arguing a combines case and he was going on in a very dull and long-winded fashion. Jack kept his patience for an hour or so but finally he interrupted Matthews.

" 'May I ask, Mr. Matthews, if this is the nub of your argument?' And Jack outlined Matthews' point in a very few clear sentences.

" 'Yes, m'lord,' Matthews said. 'That is certainly my point.'

" 'Thank you, Mr. Matthews,' Jack said 'I just wanted to know what to do with my mind while you were talking.' "

Sedgwick's laugh and his stories and his availability brought him friends and acquaintances by the lineup. He was one of those men who seem effortlessly to brush up against history. Somehow he found himself next to famous people. When he began to practise law in Toronto in the early 1920s, he took on his first articling student. The young man passed his spare time in Sedgwick's office writing short stories. He was Morley Callaghan. When Sedgwick joined the Ontario Attorney General's Office for eight years, 1929 to 1937, he assisted in the prosecutions of Tim Buck, charged with the then crime of membership in the Communist Party, and of David Meisner, charged with kidnapping John Labatt, the beer tycoon. Buck got five years, Meisner fifteen. In 1935, Sedgwick and David Croll, then the Ontario Minister of Municipal Affairs, put together the Dionne Quintuplets Protection Act and used it to negotiate a series of commercial deals for the girls. "We made them a million bucks," Sedgwick said. "Without us, they'd have been robbed blind." In 1937, Sedgwick was fired from the Attorney General's Office when Mitchell Hepburn, the Ontario premier, who was given to unexplained purges, cleared house of Croll, Sedgwick, and company. "Mitch phoned me years afterwards when he was out of office," Sedgwick later said. "He wanted a favour. Mitch remembered me all right."

So did they all, Callaghan and Buck and the Dionnes. So did Jack Kent Cooke and Charlotte Whitton. Sedgwick defended the two, successfully, when the Province of Alberta charged them with criminal libel as a result of a story that Whitton, later the mayor of Ottawa, wrote about an Alberta child-adoption system in *Liberty* magazine, which was owned by Cooke, later a California sports tycoon. When Canadians with recognizable names and significant connections got into trouble, Sedgwick was summoned to the scene. In one case, he defended Morris Shumiatcher, a prominent Prairies lawyer and Tommy Douglas's number one advisor during his years as premier of Saskatchewan, and in another case, he acted for Ralph Farris, Vancouver business-man and brother of the Chief Justice of the British Columbia Supreme Court. Sedgwick sued Pierre Trudeau and his Minister of Energy, Joe Greene, on behalf of Steve Roman, the president of Denison Mines, who was sore at the federal government for blocking the sale of a piece of his company. As a per-sonal favour to another prime minister, Lester Pear-son, Sedgwick took on a tough chore in 1965, conducting a federal inquiry into the country's immigration policies. A third prime minister, John Diefenbaker, was for a while Sedgwick's *bête noire*.

"Oh, John was all right," Sedgwick said, the lifelong Tory. "He was a loner and that made him difficult. He said he'd put me in the Senate, which I would have enjoyed, but he got cross at me over some imagined slight and never followed through. We were at odds until the day I went up to him and said, 'John, we've known each other for too many

years to carry on in such an undignified manner.'
This was at (former Ontario premier) Les Frost's
funeral, and John and I patched things up."

Sedgwick's conversations were punctuated with
the names of his many prominent friends. One of
these was Tom Fogden, president of Gilbey's Gin,
who went to Sedgwick in the spring of 1946 with a
case that will perhaps be remembered as Sedgwick's
monument. Fogden's brother-in-law — Fogden's
wife's sister's husband — was in trouble. His name
was Eric Adams. He was thirty-nine years old in
1946, a man with the suave good looks and tidy
moustache of a William Powell. Adams had a degree
in electrical engineering from McGill and an M.B.A.
from Harvard. Through the 1930s he worked in
Montreal for Cockfield Brown Advertising Agency,
in the office of the assistant to the president of the
CPR, and for a firm of consulting engineers, Cover-
dale & Colpitts, in New York City. In November
1940 he was summoned to Ottawa to handle a series
of assignments for the Foreign Exchange Control
Board and the Bank of Canada. Both bodies placed
him on loan to various agencies, and he held jobs
with the Wartime Requirements Board, the War
Inventions Board, the National Selective Service, the
Department of Finance, and, beginning in January
1945, the Industrial Development Bank in Montreal.
The jobs put him close to the upper reaches of the
civil service in wartime Ottawa. He came into contact
with mandarins like Norman Robertson, Under-
Secretary of State for External Affairs. He sat on
committees. He was privy to crucial decisions. He
occupied a position of trust and delicacy. And
through it all, during his long wartime service in high
places, Eric Adams may have been, as the Canadian

government now claimed and as Tom Fogden told Joe Sedgwick, a spy for Russia.

Igor Gouzenko began the fuss when he walked out of the Russian Embassy in Ottawa on the evening of September 5, 1945, with 109 documents buttoned inside his shirt. Gouzenko was officially listed at the embassy as secretary and interpreter to Colonel Nicolai Zabotin, who was, in turn, officially listed as military attaché, but Gouzenko served in fact and deed as cipher clerk for Zabotin, who was nothing less than the Soviet's head of Military Intelligence in Canada. Gouzenko and his family were scheduled for return to Moscow in the fall of 1945. However, having grown accustomed to a democratic and congenial lifestyle after their years in Ottawa, they elected to defect, and Gouzenko took along the 109 documents which, he knew, revealed the existence of nine rings of Canadian spies maintained by Zabotin. The rings included several men and women in Canada's civil service. *That*, Gouzenko figured, ought to catch Ottawa's attention.

At first he met rejection. On the night of September 5 and early the following morning, the *Ottawa Journal*, the Ministry of Justice, the RCMP, and Ottawa's crown attorney all turned away Gouzenko along with his story and his documents. But later that morning, word of the Russian who was frantically banging on the doors of official Ottawa reached Norman Robertson. He was sufficiently alarmed by Gouzenko's tale that he carried it to Prime Minister Mackenzie King, whose instant instinct was to reject Gouzenko's plea for asylum. But by a stroke of good fortune for Robertson and Gouzenko, William Stevenson happened to be visiting in the Ottawa area. Stevenson, a Canadian with his base in England, had operated during the Second World War as one of the Allies' master spies, and when Robertson had the presence of mind to tell Stevenson of Gouzenko, his advice was unequivocal. "Take him," he said to Robertson, and on the afternoon of September 7, after speaking again to King, Robertson send out the word to the RCMP. Gouzenko was given asylum.

Robertson and the other Ottawa decision-makers proceeded cautiously and privately on the Gouzenko revelations of Russian spies in their midst. Mackenzie King favoured a tiptoe approach to the whole embarrassing business. Why should Canada, of all Western democracies, be seen as the country to disturb relations between East and West? Why were *we* afflicted with this awkward situation? King travelled to Washington and advised three Americans — President Harry Truman, Secretary of State Dean Acheson, and FBI Director J. Edgar Hoover — of the Gouzenko situation. The United States, for its own diplomatic reasons, urged King to resist any impulse to go immediately public with the news. And, back home, King's own Ministry of Justice pointed out, correctly, that its lawyers needed time to build cases against the people named in Gouzenko's documents that would lead to convictions in court. Tiptoeing, for all these reasons, seemed a wise policy.

In the end, a journalist forced King to act. On February 3, 1946, Drew Pearson broke the story of the Ottawa spies on his radio program. Pearson was a Washington columnist and broadcaster adept at dishing up inside dope, and his tip on Gouzenko had originated with J. Edgar Hoover, who was anxious to get on with the battle against the Red menace. In Ottawa, King fell back on that most Canadian of institutions, the royal commission. On February 5, after telling his full cabinet of the spy troubles for the first time but continuing to keep his electorate in the dark, he appointed a royal commission with an intimidating mandate: "To Investigate the Facts Relating to and the Circumstances Surrounding the Communication by Public Officials and Other Persons in Positions of Trust of Secret and Confidential Information to Agents of a Foreign Power." The two men selected to preside over the Commission, Justices Robert Taschereau and R.L. Kellock of the Supreme Court of Canada, moved swiftly and secretly. On February 13, after steeping themselves in the RCMP's research on the mess, they questioned Gouzenko *in camera* and were, as they later wrote in their report, "impressed with the sincerity of the man and with the manner in which he gave his evidence, which we have no hesitation in accepting."

Two days after the questioning, on February 15, the King government revealed to Canadians the first official news of the spy rings. The announcement took place in the afternoon. On the morning of that day, at seven a.m., RCMP officers had arrested the first thirteen of the alleged spies on charges that weren't specified. Under the Mounties' original plan, the arrests were scheduled for three a.m., but Norman Robertson insisted on a more civilized hour. Three a.m., he thought, smacked of Russian tactics. The way for the arrests had been paved by an Order-in-Council passed in virtual secrecy back on October 6, 1945, by three cabinet members, King, Minister of Justice Louis St. Laurent and one other minister. The Order-in-Council gave the government authority to detain any spy suspects without the usual requirement of formal charges. Bail, right to counsel, contact with family, habeas corpus — all were denied to the thirteen men and women who were spirited away to the RCMP training centre in the Ottawa district of Rockcliffe where they were held in isolation from the outside world, especially from their alleged Russian masters, who would surely advise them to hold silent.

Eric Adams was one of the thirteen.

"Ahhh, Eric wasn't a communist," Joe Sedgwick later insisted. "He was a pinko, nothing more. What they called in those days a fellow-traveller. Nothing traitorous about the man."

Adams' fascination with Russia, even his affection for it, was undisguised. He journeyed through the Soviet Union as a tourist for several weeks in 1934. His library was long on Russian political and economical theory. He saved back copies of such left-wing North American journals as the *Clarion*, the *Canadian Tribune*, and *New Masses*. And he served as an active Ottawa member of an organization, admittedly respectable in the wartime context of co-operation with Russia, called Friends of the Soviet Union.

The Royal Commissioners deduced that Adams' Russian connections were rather more sinister. "We have no doubt on all the evidence," they wrote in their 733-page final report, "but that Colonel Zabotin found in Adams a convinced communist who considered the communication of information to Russia in line with his ardent beliefs as a member of the Party." Some of the Commissioners' "evidence" smacked more of anti-Red hysteria than of hard proof. "Adams' library," they wrote, "was literally full of Communist books, including such authors as Marx, Engels and Lenin." But other facts, especially the information that surfaced from Gouzenko's 109 documents, appeared to be altogether more damning.

Several documents identified one of the Canadian spies as a man operating under the code name of "Ernst." Whom did "Ernst" shield? The documents had an answer: Eric Adams. One of the documents was a page of paper with handwriting on it torn from a notebook and ripped in three. The notebook and the handwriting, in Russian, belonged to Nicolai Zabotin. He had ripped the page on a morning in August 1945 and given the pieces to Gouzenko for burning. Gouzenko instead squirrelled away the three scraps against the day when he walked out of the embassy. The page, when put together, summed up Ernst's contributions to Zabotin's spy ring. "He gives detailed information on all kind of industries and plans for the future," the colonel had written. "Supplies detailed accounts of conferences." Zabotin jotted a few more notes, then described Ernst's value in two devastating words: "Good worker."

The Commissioners marshalled other facts that seemed to point to Adams' involvement in the ring. There was a copy of a mailing list that Zabotin sent to Moscow on January 5, 1945, in which Ernst was credited with furnishing pages of printed material during the preceding year, information on the "Despatch of Munitions to England," on the "Invention of Waterproofing," copies of "Correspondence about contracts." And there was the testimony against Adams given by a woman named Kathleen Willsher, another of the thirteen arrested on February 15. Willsher was English, an employee since 1930 in the Ottawa office of the British High Commissioner, and her job as Deputy Registrar gave her access to most of the confidential papers that passed through the High Commissioner's hands. By her own admission to the Royal Commission she saw to it that the contents of many of those secret documents reached Colonel Zabotin, and one of her contacts, a fellow agent who, she testified, acted as a relay between her and Zabotin, was Adams.

"Adams' conduct and associations with Soviet agents," the Commissioners reported, "his personal sympathies dating back at least to 1934 which made him easily receptive to the suggestions of Zabotin, his endeavors to obtain information of a secret nature, which turned out in many instances to be fruitful, as evidenced by the testimony of Miss Willsher, and the documents from the embassy, leave little doubt in our minds that he has conspired to commit offences in violation of the Official Secrets Act, and that he has also committed the substantive offences of obtaining, for the benefit of a foreign power, secret information, and of inciting others to commit such offence."

Adams hardly helped his own cause in the testimony that he gave to the Royal Commissioners before whom, as was the case for all the suspected spies, he was compelled to appear without counsel. He claimed a misfiring memory in answer to many of the questions put to him by the Commission's counsel. Who attended the "study group meetings . . . discussing Communism and Marxism" at Adams' Ottawa home? "I don't recall any people there." How did he happen to know Kathleen Willsher and who introduced them? "I don't recall." And how did a document prepared for the Labor-Progressive Party, the name under which Canada's Communist Party operated, a document entitled "Draft Outline for Research in Province of Ontario" and described in its first paragraph as "of great political importance to our Party," find its way between the pages of a book in Adams' home library? "I don't recall now." The answers left the Commissioners politely sceptical. "We unhesitatingly accept Kathleen Willsher's evidence with regard to Adams, and indeed Adams does not deny that evidence. He merely does not 'recall' the events to which Willsher deposed. That, of course, is incredible. Such evidence is typical of a mind which recalls the facts perfectly, and, while not prepared to admit, takes refuge in the fancied security of an assumed inability to remember."

The case against Adams appeared to grow more secure through the spring of 1946. In late March the government took Fred Rose to court for a preliminary hearing on charges that he had recruited several of Zabotin's spies and had acted as a conduit in passing on secrets. Rose was a Member of Parliament from Montreal representing the Labor-Progressive Party, and a principal witness against him was Kathleen Willsher, who testified that she began handing over to Rose useful information from the British High Commissioner's Office as early as 1936.

Crown counsel to Willsher: "Subsequently did any other person introduce himself to you for the same purpose?"

Willsher: "Eric Adams in 1942 or 1943." She gave Adams, she told the court, material concerning "a general outline about the war, that there would be a second front, generally the prosecution of the war."

When Rose came to trial in May and June of 1946, Adams was called as a crown witness. He was asked questions about Rose's involvement in spying and about his own connections with Rose and others in the ring. Adams gave the same response to all questions. "I decline to answer on the grounds that it might incriminate me at my own trial." The judge presiding over the Rose trial sentenced Adams to three months in jail for contempt of court. Rose was convicted of spying and got six years in prison.

"It was a good tactic on Eric's part not to respond," Sedgwick said. "It meant that his answers at the Rose trial couldn't be read back to him in cross-examination at his own trial. That might have had the potential to be embarrassing."

It wasn't Sedgwick who advised Adams in the tactic — Adams was on his own as a witness — but Sedgwick had taken up his client's cause earlier in the spring when Tom Fogden first approached him. Sedgwick, ever faithful to his concept of counsel as a "loaded blunderbuss," hesitated not for a moment to accept the case. Some friends, however, needed straightening out on his motivation.

"It was the temper of the times," he later explained. "McCarthyism in its early form. George Drew — he was premier of Ontario then — came to me and said, 'Joe, how can you act for such a man, a *traitor*?' George was a good fellow. He served with my brother Harry in the same brigade of artillery in the First World War. A good fellow but a little stiff. It's been said of the British that they have all the qualities of a poker except for the occasional warmth. That describes George. 'How can you defend this man?' he asked me. George was a lawyer but he had never acted in court. I told him he didn't understand the business of the counsel. 'With the fees we charge,' I said to George, 'we don't get the innocent, but by God, they're innocent once we get them!' "

Sedgwick laughed.

"That may be funny," he went on. "But it's also the truth. Unless you can involve yourself to a personal degree in a client's misfortune, you don't have the right to practise the kind of law I practised."

Sedgwick's major chore before the start of Adams' trial, apart from conferring with his client and building a defence, was to sort out the exact nature of the charges against Adams. The crown had issued two indictments alleging in vague and sketchy wording that Adams had conspired with a group that included six Russians, eight Canadians, and one Englishwoman, the ubiquitous Kathleen Willsher, to collect and communicate information in violation of the Official Secrets Act. Sedgwick needed more. He brought a Motion For Particulars in the Supreme Court of Ontario, and when he succeeded, the crown was compelled to produce a document, called simply Particulars, which succinctly outlined its case against Adams.

The crown alleged that from the beginning of 1942 to the end of 1945 a conspiracy existed in Canada to gather information about the country's military, its war industries and munitions, its development in radar, and its relations with Britain, Russia, and the United States, and to convey this information to Moscow by way of Russian officials in Ottawa. Eric Adams, so the Particulars alleged, joined the conspiracy in 1942 and carried out a number of acts that were conspicuously "in furtherance of the conspiracy." Most especially, he gathered the various pieces of information, correspondence, and research that were set out in Colonel Zabotin's mailing list dated January 5, 1945; he collected information from Kathleen Willsher, usually the contents of letters addressed to the British High Commissioner in Ottawa; and finally, "in furtherance of the conspiracy," in June 1945 he paid Willsher a sum of money, twenty-five dollars, to cover some of her expenses incurred in the act of passing secrets to Adams.

Thus enlightened, Sedgwick pondered his defence strategy.

"As a defence counsel," he always said, "you must have a theory. Otherwise you're up the creek without a paddle. You have a theory, and every question you ask in examination or cross-examination is directed to establishing that theory or demolishing the one on the other side."

Sedgwick went into the Adams defence with a simple theory: when the Canadian government interpreted Adams' actions as traitorous, it was misreading behaviour that could be explained in entirely innocent terms. Adams was not "Ernst." Kathleen Willsher was mistaken in the view she took of her contacts with Adams, which were, for him, merely social. And Adams' fascination with Russia, its economics and politics, sprang simply from his educational and professional interests as a businessman, economist, and civil-service employee.

In the eight days that the trial eventually lasted, Sedgwick's defence — his theory translated to specifics — would not turn on courtroom histrionics and fireworks, or on a surprise witness, or on a piece of sparkling cross-examination. His defence would be a matter of chipping away at the crown's case. It would depend on the manner in which Sedgwick handled the crown's witnesses, casting tiny shadows of doubt on their testimony, shaking their assurance every so gently, raising questions in the jury's mind about those witnesses' veracity and accuracy and judgment. And it would depend, at the very end of the trial, at the eleventh hour, on an unforeseeable piece of good luck that Sedgwick would manage brilliantly to turn to his client's advantage.

The trial was called for October in Ottawa. Much earlier, back in June, Sedgwick had moved for a change of venue. He argued that the report of the Taschereau-Kellock Commission, so condemnatory of Adams, had received such wide circulation in the Ottawa newspapers that he'd have trouble finding a jury of twelve men from the city who weren't already persuaded of Adams' guilt. Sedgwick's motion came before James McRuer, Chief Justice of the trial division of the Ontario Supreme Court. Sedgwick suggested that Toronto might be more safely neutral. McRuer rejected the motion. Adams, the Chief Justice held, was as likely to get a fair trial in Ottawa as anywhere else in Ontario.

Sedgwick wasn't distressed.

"All part of the waltz," he later said. "You take these steps, motions, and so on, to keep the other side slightly off balance. I knew that if the trial proceeded in Ottawa, as I expected it would, I'd ask each prospective juryman whether he'd read stories about my man in the newspapers. If he had, I'd reject him. If he hadn't, I'd take him. Oh, I was always a great believer in the jury system. Chesterton's essay 'Twelve Men' has it exactly right. The basic goodness of juries is what Chesterton says, and I agree. I've been before hundreds of them and never met one that wasn't fair."

The trial began on schedule in the Ottawa courthouse on a Monday in mid-October. A familiar face peered down from the bench, Chief Justice McRuer's. And a more familiar face looked over from the crown's table, Jack Cartwright's. Cartwright was in private practice as senior counsel at the Toronto firm of Smith, Rae, Greer & Cartwright and had been retained by the federal government to take on the special burden of prosecuting the Canadians charged in the spy conspiracy. Cartwright came from an Establishment background: a member of one of

Ontario's oldest families; twice wounded in France during the First World War, aide-de-camp to three generals, awarded the Military Cross; an elected Bencher of the Law Society of Upper Canada; a respected barrister; and a good friend of Joe Sedgwick's. He was slim and elegant and dedicated to linguistic precision. The Oxford English Dictionary was his favourite book. Polite, almost self-effacing, he was, for a barrister, deceptively soft-spoken.

"As a counsel, Jack was deadly," Sedgwick said. "By that I mean he applied himself to the points at issue and didn't wander about. He usually gave his opponents very little to work with."

Cartwright called an array of witnesses for the crown. Most of them were RCMP officers who told the court of their investigations into Adams' activities, their interrogations of Adams and others after the February 15 arrests, the results of their searches of Adams' Montreal apartment and his office when they turned up the "communist" books and other documents that pointed to Adams' leftist connections. The RCMP evidence was largely circumstantial, and it became clear that Cartwright's case would depend for its strength on the testimony of two witnesses who were more intimately linked to the spy ring: Igor Gouzenko and Kathleen Willsher.

Gouzenko, in his late twenties, was short, thick-set, with heavy eyebrows. He testified without the hood over his face that later became his trademark, but, for his protection, four or five Mounties in civilian clothes sat among the courtroom spectators. Another Mountie took his place near Gouzenko in the witness-box. He was Constable Melvyn Black, Russian born, and his job was to help Gouzenko, who wasn't entirely comfortable in English, when he stumbled on counsel's questions or his own answers.

Prodded by Cartwright, Gouzenko told his familiar story. How he acted out a simple masquerade at the Russian Embassy as a secretary and an interpreter. How, as Colonel Zabotin's cipher clerk, he trafficked, at least on paper, in Canadian spies. How documents crossed his desk that had been filched from Ottawa government offices and were headed for Zabotin's masters in Moscow. How the different members of Zabotin's network of Canadian sneaks and spies were assigned code names. How "Ernst" was the code name for a man named Eric Adams, a spy who was, according to the documents that Zabotin had in his possession and that Gouzenko removed from the embassy on the night of September 5, 1945, a "good worker." And how convinced Gouzenko was, given the paper evidence and given Zabotin's enthusiasm for Ernst, that Adams was one of the indispensables among Canadian spies.

Sedgwick rose to cross-examine Gouzenko. He had outlined his approach in a handwritten note in his confidential file on the case: "Gouzenko merely gives hearsay. He can't say who made the file on Adams, who designated him as 'Ernst.' He can't say who gave Zabotin the information on which Z made his memo — which must have been hearsay and which is false."

"I couldn't do much with Gouzenko on cross-examination," Sedgwick said later. "He hadn't met my man and he didn't know anything that wasn't in those damned files of his."

Sedgwick contented himself with attempting to establish the points in his memo, that Gouzenko's knowledge of Adams as Ernst was of a second-hand nature. It was hardly a searching cross-examination, but Sedgwick, rightly or wrongly, felt he'd run up a point or two with the jury in his client's favour.

Kathleen Willsher took the stand. She was, in Sedgwick's description, "not a colourful person." She was in her forties, quiet-spoken, bland in looks, a woman who would blend invisibly into any crowd. She had pleaded guilty to violations of the Official Secrets Act on May 3, 1946, and received a sentence of three years in prison. From the date of her plea, she co-operated with the crown and gave evidence at the trials of the other alleged conspirators with whom she claimed to have had contacts. One conspirator she insisted to have been in constant touch with was Eric Adams.

Adams approached her, she told the court at his trial, as early as 1942 and asked her to pass to him any information from the British High Commissioner's Office that might be "in the interest of the Communist Party." Willsher, fascinated by communism and attracted to Russia's cause, agreed. She provided Adams with details from letters, briefings, and other communiqués on a continuing basis from 1942 to 1945, making the meetings of an Ottawa study group, often held at Adams' home, the usual occasions for relaying her secrets. And what was the subject under study by the Ottawa group? "The theory and practice of socialism and communism and the party program."

Cartwright asked Willsher for examples of the information she had conveyed to Adams. Well, Willsher said, there were the contents of two letters dated November 3 and November 11, 1945, that came through her office for the High Commissioner's attention, letters from the Canadian ambassador in Moscow to the Canadian prime minister dealing with matters confidential to the

Canadian government. And there were other pieces of information. Willsher listed them. Then, also in November 1944, Lord Keynes, the British economist, visited Ottawa to discuss financial arrangements between Canada and Great Britain after the war. Willsher got her hands on the reports of the Keynes meetings and rushed their contents to Adams.

Her contacts with Adams didn't end when he moved out of Ottawa to his job with the Industrial Development Bank in Montreal early in 1945. Adams often met her back in Ottawa for the usual purpose of taking delivery of the High Commissioner's secrets. And on a couple of occasions she travelled to Montreal to meet Adams. Once, Adams and his wife invited her to their apartment for a meal. And another time, Adams gave her twenty-five dollars. What was the explanation for this sum? It was money to cover Willsher's train expenses between the two cities when she was on her nefarious business for the Party, the business of passing on government secrets to Eric Adams.

On cross-examination, Sedgwick took the tack that Willsher was naive, confused about her relationship with Adams, and just possibly intimidated by her dealings with the RCMP and the Taschereau-Kellock Commission. Part of the tone for his approach was set in a memo that Adams made for Sedgwick in the weeks before the trial. Adams referred to the questions put to him by the Commission counsel as "attempts to trick me into false admissions" and speculated that "I found it difficult to combat this kind of attack, so what chance had someone like Willsher?" In a later note, Adams offered Sedgwick more on Willsher's likely state of mind: "A friend of Willsher's saw her since (her) trial and she said the RCMP had frightened her by saying that unless she said exactly what she told them and the Commission, her sentence would be increased."

In cross-examining Willsher, Sedgwick affected his most concerned and tender and understanding persona. He *knew* what Willsher had endured, his manner and voice kept saying, and he felt *compassion* for her predicament. Hadn't her appearance before the Royal Commission unnerved her? Wasn't the prospect of a jail sentence a terribly disturbing influence for her? Wasn't she anxious to please the RCMP and the crown in her testimony? And, oh yes, wouldn't it be true to say that all these forces and factors conspired to help her to misconstrue her dealings with Eric Adams? Willsher held essentially to her story in the face of Sedgwick's display of concern, but his questions, if not her answers, had the effect of placing a hint of doubt in the minds of the jury about Willsher's motivation in testifying, her accuracy and her interpretation of events.

It was Friday afternoon, after nearly five days of trial, when Cartwright told Chief Justice McRuer that with Willsher's evidence he had concluded the case for the crown. McRuer asked Sedgwick whether he intended to call evidence on behalf of the defence. Friday afternoon, Sedgwick knew, wasn't a smart time to open a defence; the jury would have all weekend to forget his opening points. Besides, he wanted a couple of days to review the situation with his client. He asked McRuer for an adjournment until the following Monday. McRuer granted it on condition that, no later than noon on Sunday, Sedgwick would advise Cartwright whether or not he planned to put a witness in the box. If Sedgwick called no witnesses, then Cartwright would be obliged to begin his jury address on Monday. If Sedgwick elected to summon evidence, Cartwright had to prepare himself for cross-examination. Sedgwick agreed to the condition. Court adjourned.

"I spent the next day and a half woodshedding my client," Sedgwick later said. "I went over the story Eric would give if he testified. He'd tell me certain things he wanted to say, and sometimes I would have to warn him. 'Very well,' I'd say, 'you may like to put it that way, but I must warn you that it is probably not wise to use those words.' I didn't *coach* him. I never did such a thing with my clients. I *guided* him as to what would be most appropriate to his defence."

In fact, Sedgwick had little doubt from the beginning that he would call Adams to the witness-box.

"He was the only witness who would do me any good," Sedgwick said. "He was the one person who knew anything. And anyway, in a criminal defence I was always in favour of summoning the accused to the box. If he doesn't testify, the jury wonders what he's hiding. I never believed in calling peripheral evidence. I believed in calling the man himself. The key to making these choices, the key to being a good counsel, is judgment. I once said to John Robinette, 'John, you know a great deal of law and I don't, but one thing we possess in common is good judgment.' What I meant is that John and I know when to call a man and when not to call him, when to cross-examine the other side's witness and when to leave him alone. That is judgment, and it is a rare commodity in our courts."

Promptly at noon on Sunday, Sedgwick phoned Cartwright and told him he'd be placing Adams on the stand. For good measure, he phoned the same news to Chief Justice McRuer.

"Next day," Sedgwick said, "Eric Adams got into the witness-box and he performed like a lion."

Under Sedgwick's shrewd probing, Adams told his story for the first time. He wasn't defensive, nor was he outraged. His memory, which had so disastrously failed him before the Taschereau-Kellock Commission, was now apparently intact. He — and Sedgwick — steered away from evasion. He was straightforward. And he radiated a sense of certainty in his own innocence.

He was an Ottawa bureaucrat, he said, and the very nature of the jobs he held for the civil service meant that he moved in many professional and social circles. He met men and women from all levels of government. Perhaps Kathleen Willsher was at a meeting or cocktail party he attended, but so was Norman Robertson. So were many Ottawa mandarins. Did their presence in the same room with Willsher make them parties to a spy conspiracy? The answers, Adams implied in reply to Sedgwick's questions, was of course negative. Robertson and the rest weren't spies, and neither was he.

Adams conceded in his testimony that Willsher had been in his home on a couple of occasions. Perfectly innocent, he said. Perhaps Willsher perceived meetings at the Adams house as somehow linked to a cell of communists. But they were nothing of the sort. You see, Adams said, he and a few other economists began work in 1943, informally and after hours, on an outline for a history of Canada interpreted exclusively in economic terms. They met monthly at one another's homes over the following year and a half, and at one or two meetings, held in Adams' house, a government economist named Laxton brought along a woman named Agatha Chapman, who was a co-worker in the civil service. Chapman, who was later charged in the spy rings, was a friend of Willsher's, and it was she who introduced

Willsher into the Adams home as a guest at the discussions. Perhaps Willsher and Chapman had something to hide, but for Adams, the gatherings were entirely innocuous affairs.

He had equally ready explanations for his other connections with Willsher. Really, his manner in the witness-box conveyed, is the crown *serious* about these silly matters? Of course Willsher had been in his apartment in Montreal·one late-spring evening in 1945. She had phoned Adams and his wife out of the blue, saying she was briefly in town from Ottawa, and on the basis of their earlier acquaintance with her, the Adamses acted the decent hosts and invited her to dinner. Later in the evening, Adams drove Willsher to her Ottawa train. Nothing to it except playing the good host.

And, yes, Adams had in his possession a couple of pages of notes dealing with Lord Keynes' discussions in Ottawa in November 1944. The notes were in Adams' own handwriting and had been seized by the RCMP from his Montreal apartment. Heavens, Adams said, word of Keynes' views came to him in the normal course of his work, not from Willsher, and he made the notes, using government stationery, to keep himself up to date on current economic thinking. Nothing in the least sinister about the damned memo, Adams insisted, which was a point that Sedgwick took pains to emphasize. "If Adams were preparing an improper document," he wrote as a reminder to himself in his confidential brief, "would he logically place a memo of it on the office pad?"

In the same way, Adams explained away the mystery of the twenty-five-dollar payment to Willsher. Was it to cover her expenses to Montreal on an occasion when she delivered secrets from the High

Commissioner's Office to Adams? Certainly not. Willsher, it seems, was on the executive of the Fellowship for a Christian Social Order, an organization as innocent as its name. Fellowship duties sometimes sent Willsher on missions outside Ottawa, and one such trip took her to a conference in Montreal. The Fellowship, alas, was chronically short of funds, and many of Willsher's expenses, when she didn't absorb them herself, were paid by friends and supporters of the Fellowship. Adams counted himself among the latter group, and the famous twenty-five dollars, the money which Willsher had received from Adams, the cash which the crown claimed to be in furtherance of the spy conspiracy, *that* twenty-five dollars — Adams was unequivocal about his facts — came as recompense from Adams to Willsher to cover a journey on behalf of nothing more threatening than the Fellowship for a Christian Social Order.

So much for Willsher.

Sedgwick ticked off the names of the other indicted and unindicted conspirators. Was Adams acquainted with them? Not the Russians, he answered. Never encountered Colonel Zabotin or any of the gang from the Russian Embassy. What of the other Canadian civil servants who had been charged? David Gordon Lunan? Harold Gerson? Dr. Raymond Boyer? No, no, Adams swore as Sedgwick ran down the list. Agatha Chapman? Yes, Adams had met her, both at work and at the discussions to plan the economic history of Canada. But the acquaintance was fleeting. He had known Frederic Poland, another accused spy, because Poland had been an admirer of his wife's at McGill, and he knew Israel Halperin, also accused, because Halperin's wife and

Mrs. Adams had met through their mutual association with an Ottawa nursery school. Could any connection be more harmless? Yes, he had once chatted with James Benning, another civil servant implicated in the spy ring, when the two men happened to be skiing at Camp Fortune on the same day. And he had become friendly with Fred Rose in the late 1930s through his interest in politics in Montreal where Rose was a well-known Member of Parliament. All wonderfully natural, Adams said as he shrugged his innocence from the witness-box.

What, Sedgwick asked, of "Ernst"?

The name, Adams answered, was unknown to him in any context.

Sedgwick consulted the list of documents that Ernst was alleged to have passed to the Russians, the list that was among the papers smuggled out of the Russian Embassy by Gouzenko, the list dated January 5, 1945, and prepared for Moscow by Colonel Zabotin. "Invention of Waterproofing," Sedgwick read from the list. Was Adams aware of such an invention when he was employed by the Inventions Board in Ottawa? Impossible, Adams answered. He had worked for the Main Examining Committee of the Inventions Board rather than for the Board itself and had no access to the information that Zabotin had credited to Ernst. Sedgwick quoted other documents that, according to Zabotin, had originated with Ernst. Adams denied that he'd so much as laid eyes on such documents. They belonged to a category, he swore, that was beyond his range of interest and accessibility.

"By the way, Mr. Adams," Sedgwick said suddenly, looking up from another of the Gouzenko papers, "are you Jewish?"

No.

Sedgwick drew Adams' attention to the page torn out of Colonel Zabotin's notebook that had been pieced together from three torn scraps. It was the page that described Ernst's contributions to the spy ring and characterized him as a "good worker." Sedgwick pointed to the words at the beginning of the page: "Ernst — Jew."

Yes, Adams said, he'd wondered about Ernst's religion. When the RCMP was interrogating him not long after his arrest, an inspector named Anthony asked Adams if he were Jewish. No, Adams said, but why do you ask? "I didn't think you were," Anthony said, "but my records said you are."

What of the books in Adams' library, Sedgwick asked, satisfied that he had thrown enough doubt on the Adams-Ernst connection, the so-called "communist" books?

He owned two thousand books, Adams answered, and of that great number, the RCMP had taken away a mere one hundred, the works of Marx and Lenin and Engels and other socialist authors. But, Adams insisted, all the books were useful to him simply as research and background for his work as an economist. And, for what it was worth, Adams pointed out, his library included two copies of *Mein Kampf*, one in English and one in German. The RCMP had left them behind.

And the left-wing newspapers and journals that Adams kept at home in back copies?

Oh well, Adams said, the *Canadian Tribune*, *National Affairs*, and others were quite harmless. The Bank of Canada, where Adams had done government work, subscribed to them.

Sedgwick built a climate of innocence, leading his client relentlessly through the accusations, maintaining a low-key atmosphere in the courtroom, asking the jury to appreciate as civilized men that these matters were explainable in terms that the crown, well-meaning but not in possession of all the facts, had had the misfortune to overlook.

Had Adams, Sedgwick asked, kept the oath he swore when he went to work for the civil service, the oath that bound him under the Official Secrets Act not to reveal any of his country's confidential matters to a foreign power?

Yes, Adams answered, calm and firm and unhesitating. Yes, he had observed the oath in letter and in spirit. Anyway, he went on, he was never in possession of information that would be especially valuable to Russia or any other foreign power.

Sedgwick sat down.

"On cross-examination," he said later, "Jack Cartwright couldn't budge my man. Eric stuck to his story in every particular and Jack couldn't trap him. He was a tower of strength in the witness-box."

With Adams' testimony, Sedgwick rested his case, and since he had called evidence, he was compelled to go first in addressing the jury. He spoke for over an hour. "That was a long address for me," he later explained. "I don't like to bore a jury with too much material. But in the Adams case I had a great number of points to cover." First, Sedgwick touched on the danger that Adams had faced in the apparently incriminating findings that had come out of the Taschereau-Kellock Commission and the RCMP investigation. He quoted from *Alice in Wonderland*. "'Let the jury consider their verdict,' the King said. 'No, no,' said the Queen. 'Sentence first, verdict afterwards.'"

That, Sedgwick said, is not our system.

And again: "'Give your evidence,' said the King,

'and don't be nervous or I'll have you executed on the spot.'"

Nor that.

Then Sedgwick underlined for the jury his major arguments: that Gouzenko could offer the court only information that arrived in his files from outside sources; that Willsher's testimony was demonstrably suspect; and that Adams had successfully explained away the evidence against him. The crown, Sedgwick concluded before he gave way to Cartwright, had not proved its case.

Cartwright took forty minutes to address the jury, coming down hard on the impact of Gouzenko's testimony and of Willsher's. The evidence of Gouzenko alone was enough to convict Adams, Cartwright argued, and he asked the jury to record a conviction. It was the end of the afternoon.

The next morning, October 26, 1946, the last day of the trial, Chief Justice McRuer wheeled around his chair to face the jury-box. "What Mr. Cartwright has told you is well and good," he said in effect, beginning his instructions to the jury, "but now I will tell you the *whole* story." He differed from Cartwright on one specific. Gouzenko's testimony was not sufficient on its own to convict Adams. No, the jury must find corroboration in the testimony of one of Adam's fellow conspirators. That corroboration, he said, was providentially offered in the evidence of Kathleen Willsher. It seemed to Sedgwick at the time that McRuer concentrated on the crown's case. As he listened to the Chief Justice, Sedgwick came to the view that McRuer was pointing out the crown's strengths and accentuating its persuasiveness. The Chief Justice went on at length, three hours in all. That proved to be a burden in time to one juryman.

He fell asleep. McRuer, noting that he'd lost one-twelfth of his audience, called a short adjournment to allow the unhappy man to recover his wits. After the ten-minute break, McRuer continued his remarks until he was satisfied that no element of the Adams case remained unexamined. Content, he sent the jury away to consider its verdict.

"Mr. Sedgwick," the Chief Justice said when the jury-box was emptied, "do you have any comment on my instructions to the jury?"

Sedgwick hesitated for a moment. As he told the tale of the trial in later years, he was convinced the Chief Justice had not sufficiently put the defence's case to the jury. He thought McRuer had leaned to the crown's side and not allowed enough weight to the evidence that may have pointed to Adams' innocence.

"It's an old defence counsel's ploy," Sedgwick said later, "to object to a judge's summation on the grounds that he's slighted our side. I thought the Adams case gave me an opening to raise that objection, and I may say I was very sly about it."

Sedgwick stood up slowly from his chair in response to the Chief Justice's question, and affecting a manner that was just a trifle weary and wounded, immaculately understated, he spoke of his quibbles with the jury instructions.

"I tried to get across the impression," Sedgwick later recollected, "that his lordship may not have adequately impressed on the jury that there was a presumption of innocence in favour of the accused."

No man with as much experience on the bench as McRuer would have overlooked so basic an element in a justice's jury instructions, but Sedgwick pressed his point.

"Well, Mr. Sedgwick," the Chief Justice finally said, "do you wish to have the jury rcalled?"

"Yes," Sedgwick said.

The jury returned, and once again, for a few minutes, the twelve jurymen listened to the words of James McRuer. But this time, as Sedgwick told the story in later years, it was a point or two in favour of Eric Adams that demanded most of their attention. No one dozed off, and at the end of the fresh instructions, with new information in their heads, they returned to their deliberations.

"Oh, it was glorious," Sedgwick said years later. "What you must remember about a jury is that they are not permitted to take notes. And nobody can possibly retain everything from a trial in his head. So the jury has to rely on the addresses of the crown and of the defence counsel and ultimately on the cooling words of the presiding judge. That's what they mainly remember. Well, in the Adams case, what I perceived as Jim McRuer's clear slant in the crown's direction opened the door for me, and the result was that the last words ringing in the ears of the jury as they left the courtroom for the final time were to the good of my man."

The jury was out for only ninety minutes longer than it had taken McRuer to deliver his original summation. It was gone for a mere four and a half hours, and when it returned, it presented to the stilled and wondering audience in the courtroom a unanimous verdict.

Not guilty.

Eric Adams, as reserved and contained as he'd been through the trial, immediately left the court for his home and family in Montreal. Sedgwick left for a few drinks at the Château Laurier. In a hall of the hotel he ran into Chief Justice McRuer.

"Joe," McRuer said, "I congratulate you."

"M'lord, I thank you," Sedgwick said. "And may I also say that I am grateful to you."

"Why is that?"

"M'lord," Sedgwick said, "I believe that if you had left things alone after Jack Cartwright sat down, my man would undoubtedly have been convicted."

McRuer nodded and turned away.

In the years after the Adams trial, its principals moved to fates that were almost predictably inevitable. J. R. Cartwright, a winner in most things in life except his prosecution of Adams, was invited to sit on the Supreme Court of Canada in 1949. The court was expanding from seven judges to nine, and for reasons of tradition, politics, and cultural balance, the two new members had to be a French-speaking Quebecker and an English-Canadian lawyer from Ontario. Gérard Fauteux accepted the Quebec appointment. He had served as a counsel to the Taschereau-Kellock Commission, a relentless adversary whom Eric Adams regarded as his most diabolical tormentor. Cartwright was the choice from Ontario, but before he accepted, he called on Joe Sedgwick. It seemed that a year or two earlier, Cartwright had promised his Toronto firm, Smith, Rae, Greer & Cartwright, that he would stay with it for another five years. He was the firm's senior counsel and couldn't abandon it without an expert in litigation. Would Sedgwick, Cartwright asked, give up his one-man practice and join the firm in Cartwright's place? Sedgwick agreed, taking a drop in earnings in the process but enabling Cartwright to move to the Supreme Court, where he remained until 1970. At the farewell dinner on his retirement from the court, it was Sedgwick, so at home before an audience he considered august, who gave the farewell speech.

"The motto of your old school, Upper Canada College," he said in his grand voice, plummy and orotund, "was borrowed, I believe, from Lord Nelson's arms. 'Palmam qui meruit ferat.' My lord, you have brought honour to that old school, and like that greatest of sailors, you bear the palm that your merit has earned."

Igor Gouzenko was another alumnus of the Adams trial who heard a Sedgwick address in later years. After his defection, Gouzenko displayed a wide range of talents. He painted pictures in an attractive, realistic style and he wrote two successful books. The first, an autobiography called *This Was My Choice*, earned him $150,000, and the second, a novel based on the life of Maxim Gorky, *Fall of a Titan*, won him the 1954 Governor General's Medal for fiction. During these years, Gouzenko and his family, protected by the RCMP, lived a difficult undercover existence, and it was on one of his rare excursions into the outer world that Gouzenko encountered Joe Sedgwick.

The occasion was a libel action. A dozen years after the Adams trial, Gouzenko felt that Blair Fraser, the Ottawa correspondent for *Maclean's* magazine, had libelled him in an article that looked into Gouzenko's career in the post-defection years. The matter came to trial, and it was none other than Sedgwick who argued the case for *Maclean's*. This time, his arguments to the jury weren't persuasive enough, and the trial ended with a verdict in Gouzenko's favour.

Kathleen Willsher served her term in prison, then vanished, leaving behind a mystery that persisted into the 1980s. The puzzle arose out of the identity of "Elli." That was the code name used by Colonel

Zabotin for one of the most prized spies in his Ottawa ring, a spy who was somehow plugged into the British High Commissioner's Office. The Taschereau-Kellock Commission concluded that Willsher was Elli, and this view was adopted by most students of the Gouzenko affair. Montgomery Hyde, in his apparently definitive book *The Atom Bomb Spies*, took it for granted that Elli and Willsher were one, and so did Phillip Knightley, a British journalist specializing in espionage, when he re-analysed the Ottawa episode for the *Sunday Times* in mid-1981.

But other experts lined up on the opposite side. An English author named Chapman Pincher was one. In his 1981 book *Their Trade Is Treachery*, he arrived at a more shocking identity for Elli. It was Sir Roger Hollis, who headed MI5 from 1956 to 1965. MI5, the British intelligence network, dispatched Hollis to Ottawa in 1945 for a debriefing of Gouzenko on revelations that Russians had placed agents inside the highest British institutions, including MI5. According to Pincher, Hollis took steps to ensure that the elusive Elli was never uncovered. Why? Because Hollis *was* Elli.

"The records showed," Pincher wrote, "that Hollis had reported the minimum amount of information from Gouzenko, who later complained that no proper notice had been taken of his Elli disclosure and that he had obviously made a big mistake in reporting the MI5 penetration to MI5 itself."

If Gouzenko complained that no notice was taken of Elli, then Elli could not be Willsher, who had plenty of notice taken of her — she went to prison. Sir Roger Hollis couldn't respond to the 1981 claims that he was Elli. Hollis died in 1973. Willsher has never responded either. But in the fall of 1981, another possibility surfaced when previously secret testimony given before the Taschereau-Kellock Commission was finally made public. In it, during Gouzenko's testimony, he raised in passing the notion, never followed up in his questioning, that there might exist two Ellis. Willsher was one, and, in Gouzenko's words, "there is also a cover name Elli and I understand that he or she, I do not know which, has been identified as an agent in England."

For Joe Sedgwick's part, no matter what the confusions and puzzles, he had arrived at one firm conclusion of his own about Elli's identity back in 1946 during his preparation of Eric Adams' defence. He compared a list of the secret documents that Elli passed to Colonel Zabotin with a list of documents that would — and wouldn't — have come to Willsher's hand. The lists didn't match.

"This would indicate," Sedgwick wrote on page 23 of his brief for the Adams case, "that 'Elli' is not Willsher — at least in this instance and probably not at all."

Agatha Chapman, Frederic Poland, Israel Halperin, and James Benning were four of the accused spies whom Adams admitted that he had met, sometimes socially, sometimes in the course of his civil-service duties. Chapman, Poland, and Halperin were acquitted of spying charges at their trials. Benning was convicted, but his conviction was overturned on appeal. He, too, went free. Two of the several others who were charged pleaded guilty; Willsher was one of the two. Eight others pleaded not guilty but were convicted at trial and lost their appeals. Their penalties ranged from a five-hundred-dollar fine for a civil servant named John Soboloff to six years in penitentiary for Fred Rose and for another long-time member of the Communist and Labor-Progressive parties, Sam Carr.

As for Eric Adams, after the trial he settled again in Montreal, where he set up his own engineering consulting firm. He maintained his interest in events behind the Iron Curtain, and in 1951 he took his wife and two young daughters to live in Prague, Czechoslovakia. He disappeared from Western view, but some time, many years later, he must have returned to Canada, because in the late 1960s Sedgwick spotted him on King Street in downtown Toronto. The two men nodded from across the years, spoke briefly, and passed on.

"Eric was never a friend of mine," Sedgwick said much later. "But I knew him enough to recognize that he was a brilliant man. Clever, educated, well-spoken, excellent at engineering and economics. The charges against him, the accusations of spying, ruined all of that. They ended his career, and the one thing I remember from the short meeting on King Street is how he looked."

Sedgwick paused.

"Very shabby indeed."

Joe Sedgwick did not laugh.

CHAPTER SEVEN

The Hockey Player and the Marine Drive Socialist

Mike Robitaille didn't mind when the New York Rangers hockey club took him away from home. It meant he'd escape the tension of life with his mother. The family scraped by in Midland, Ontario, in tough financial circumstances, and Geraldine Robitaille was a woman whom middle age had visited with demons. She suffered two nervous breakdowns, and when her moods were at their blackest, it was Mike who was the special target of her wrath. He was the youngest, a change-of-life baby, born nine years after the next last in line of the eleven Robitaille children, and his youth left him isolated and vulnerable. Ernie Robitaille, husband and father, was a saint, as Mike always said, patient with all the kids, but he couldn't stand up to his wife's demons. Mike was hardly sad to leave the house on the wrong side of the tracks in Midland. He was bound to be moving into a more promising world. It was the autumn of 1962 and Mike was fourteen years old.

The Rangers sent him further south in Ontario to play junior hockey in Kitchener. He and a teammate rented a tiny basement apartment where they shared a double bed behind the furnace. Mike didn't log many sleeping hours, mostly because the other boy led parades of girls and beer through the apartment. He was a sophisticate, five years older than Mike and the bragging possessor of a couple of arrests for car theft. Mike was intrigued by the hint of danger that the teammate brought into his life. He dropped out of classes at St. Jerome's College, a school in Kitchener for proper Catholic boys, and might have been headed down the fast road to trouble.

Mike had two rescuers. One was hockey. Mike recognized it as his ticket to fame and fortune. He was obsessed with the dream of climbing away from the hard and money-poor times he'd known in his parents' home, and he drove himself to make a career in hockey. His other salvation was the love of a good woman. Her name was Isabel, blonde and lovely and strong-minded, and he met her in February 1967 at St. Mary's Hospital in Kitchener, where she was a medical secretary and he was receiving treatment for a hockey injury. Isabel's family took to Mike. "They practically adopted me," he later said. The couple became engaged in May 1968 and were married at the end of the hockey season a year later, May 24, 1969. Stability entered Mike's life.

His hockey skills improved steadily. He played defence. He was a big kid, an inch short of six feet and five pounds shy of two hundred, and he had long, flat, hard muscles that looked as if they'd been layered on his body by a sculptor. His face, square and handsome in the jock style, gave off waves of determination and dedication. He played tough but, perhaps surprisingly, not dirty; in his 382 National Hockey League games, he would receive only 286 minutes in penalties, a remarkably low figure for a defenceman. His forte was the hip check. He could take a forward out with it in one brief, bruising instant, and any opposing player who carried the puck into Robitaille's zone learned to keep his head up. He also possessed an excellent right-hand shot from the point and he was gifted at moving the puck briskly out of his own end. He gave honest work in every game and qualified as somewhere above average among professional players, not a superstar but much more than a journeyman.

In 1968 the Rangers promoted him from the Kitchener juniors to Omaha in the professional Central Hockey League, where he spent two years. In his second season with Omaha, he scored fifty-eight points and was named the league's most outstanding defenceman. He played a few games for the Rangers, then went through a couple of trades, first to the Detroit Red Wings and eventually to the Buffalo Sabres, where he settled in as a solid NHL defenceman. He put in three good seasons for Buffalo until the fall of 1974 when the Sabres traded Robitaille and Gerry Meehan for Jocelyn Guevremont and Bryan McSheffrey of the Vancouver Canucks. Mike was on his way to the west coast and he was taking with him a contract that quoted impressive figures. At the end of the 1973-74 season, he had signed a three-year deal with the Sabres calling for salaries of $75,000 in 1974-75, $85,000 the next season, and $90,000 in 1976-77. The Canucks would, of course, assume the contract. Robitaille, unhappy to be moving away with Isabel and their baby daughter, Anique, from friends among the Buffalo players, nevertheless looked forward to a flourishing career with Vancouver. He was only twenty-six years old, and he was approaching his prime as a player and, maybe more important, as a money-earner.

To be sure, he was paying a price for the success he had driven himself to achieve. He suffered from anxiety attacks. They had begun when he was nineteen and they were brutal, sometimes giving him the sensation that his chest was being crushed. "You would think you were having a heart attack," he later described the feeling. "Your mind would be playing a big game on you, and you were very fearful that death or something was going to happen and everything inside was going to let loose, like your heart might fly apart." Mike fought off the attacks with Valium. Some doctors for NHL clubs freely handed out Valium capsules in the dressing-rooms, and Mike was rarely without a supply in his pocket. Some days he might take as many as eighty milligrams, almost four times the maximum dosage that a sensible doctor would allow a patient. But for Mike they seemed at those terrifying times his only defence against the fear that his heart might burst out of his chest.

The dependence on Valium contributed to a crisis for Robitaille that peaked in September 1976. He felt, as he would later say, under the gun with the new hockey season growing nearer. He had given an excellent performance during his first year with the Canucks, 1974-75, and had put in an accomplished enough season in 1975-76, though an ankle injury near the end of that year meant that it closed on a down note. (He was accustomed to enduring injuries and playing hurt: in his NHL career, he survived three shoulder separations, a broken wrist and finger, torn rib cartileges, and ripped ligaments in one knee.) But the upcoming season, 1976-77, was the last under his three-year contract, and Mike sensed pressure building inside him to produce a superior year of hockey that would yield him the upper hand in negotiating an even more lucrative deal. "I promise to give you one hundred per cent this season," he wrote to Phil Maloney, who was both coach and general manager for Vancouver, in a letter before training camp. Still, Mike was torn. He recognized that his best hockey might elude him unless he freed himself from his Valium addiction, and at the same time, in the early days of training camp, the familiar attacks of anxiety grew in such intensity that he found himself struggling against inexplicable bouts of weeping.

Early in September he consulted a Vancouver psychiatrist, Dr. Eric Termansen, who recommended that Mike check himself into a hospital long enough to shake the need for tranquilizers out of his system. Mike, desperate, told his troubles to Maloney, left training camp, and entered the Lions Gate Hospital in Vancouver as Termansen's patient. The cure was a swift success. In ten days Mike's Valium habit had vanished, replaced by a program of relaxation exercises and transcendatal meditation that seemed to hold his anxiety in check. Reassurance washed over him, and he felt comforted, too, by a series of tests that the Lions Gate psychiatric staff ran on him.

"They showed I'm not neurotic," Mike told Isabel, proud that he had managed to hang on to his marbles in spite of a turbulent adolescence. "And they showed I've got a high IQ."

Not everybody was so convinced, not Phil Maloney and not Bill Hughes, the Canucks president. They weren't entirely persuaded of the soundness of Mike's health, especially of his mental health.

"I met with both Maloney and Hughes to explain Mike's situation," Dr. Termansen later recalled. "They thanked me, but I wasn't sure the message had gotten across. Maloney wanted to know whether Mike could fulfil his contract. Was he going to go freaky? Was Mike just using the emotional trouble as a way of copping out of his obligations to the team?"

Mike missed the first three games of the season, all of them on the road, but he dressed for the Canucks' home opening game on October 13. He played with such skill and élan that he was named one of the game's three stars. His confidence — and the calibre of his performance — shifted to a higher plateau. Mike was flying. And he flew for a couple of weeks until, as if fate had decided that Robitaille must be parcelled good fortune in small doses and bad luck in generous portions, he came out of a game in St. Louis with a shoulder that was throbbing and inflamed. And it was at this point that Dr. Michael Piper arrived on the scene as a crucial performer over the next four years in the drama, on and off the ice, of Mike Robitaille's life.

The Canucks had three doctors on their payroll. Michael Piper was the most active, an orthopedic surgeon from New Westminster just down the highway south of Vancouver. None of the doctors took the job for the money, a measly $2,500 per season. They got their satisfaction from the perks; a pair of season tickets in the coveted red section at the Coliseum where the Canucks played their home games, free parking in prime space, and the heady chance to mingle on the inside of big-league hockey. Piper was a fan. In his early forties, he was tall and dark, trim and fit, smartly turned out in blazers and white shirts. His career in orthopedics was escalating at a satisfactory rate, and the post with the Canucks, which he had accepted in that fall of '76, came as one more indicator of his upward progress.

When Robitaille returned to Vancouver from the St. Louis game, Dr. Piper took X-rays of his right shoulder.

"Bone chips," he told Mike. "Bunch of them floating around in there. It's such a mess you're going to need an operation. But that's some time down the road, maybe at the end of the season.''

For now, Piper told Mike, he should take a short rest from hockey until the inflammation receded. Not long. Maybe a few games. Be almost as good as new. Piper cheered Mike on his way.

Mike accepted the advice — he'd been knuckling under to hockey doctors, to coaches and general managers and owners, since he was fourteen — but unease nagged at him. There was something else wrong, something besides the bone chips in the shoulder. It was this strange numbness in his right arm. It wasn't entirely new. He'd felt it a few times the season before, but thirty minutes of hot packs from Patty Dunn, the Canucks' trainer, had always cleared away the tingles. Mike asked again for the hot-pack treatment, explaining to Dunn that the numbness from last year was acting up. Dunn lathered balm on Mike's neck, right shoulder, and arm and put him under a heat lamp for twenty minutes. The numbness retreated, but somehow Mike couldn't shake his uneasiness. Maybe — he didn't articulate his worry so much as intuit it — he had a problem that was beyond the temporary relief of Patty Dunn's balm and heat lamp.

Mike recognized he had troubles of another sort when he picked up the *Vancouver Province* on November 1 and read Eric Whitehead's sports column. Whitehead was writing about the Canucks' efforts to climb higher in their NHL division, closer to eventual playoff contention, and he quoted Phil Maloney's views on the team's recent lack of success. "Of course," Maloney told Whitehead, "we were short a defenceman with Robitaille out (sore shoulder). I don't know how bad it is but I can tell you he'd better start playing. If he doesn't, I'm going to have to consider suspending him."

"You really mean what you told the papers," Robitaille said to Maloney later that day at the Coliseum.

"Damn right."

"*Suspend* me? Suspend me when all I'm doing is resting a bad shoulder?"

"Listen, Mike," Maloney said. "There was this guy who played with me in the NHL years ago. The 1950s is when I'm talking about, only six teams in the league and you had to work your butt off to stay up there. This guy had the most rotten shoulder I ever saw, but he played. He strapped up his shoulder and he played. That's what you got to do. Tough it out or I'll suspend you."

Robitaille played. What choice did he have? His career was on the line, the money, the future, the new contract, the long climb out of Midland, Ontario. He missed three games while he rested the sore shoulder. Then he played. Dr. Piper had been correct in his diagnosis of the chips inside the shoulder, but Piper raised no objections when Mike returned to hockey action. At least Piper said nothing to Mike. Maloney spoke to Mike and so did Bill Hughes, the Canucks president, and their message was clear: *play*. Mike played. He tended to labour on the ice, not flying the way he had in mid-October. But nobody could make noises about suspending him. He was playing.

Robitaille's ancient devil, anxiety, began to surface again. To hold it off, he stepped up his program of relaxation exercises and transcendental meditation. Before each game he spent ten or fifteen minutes in the team's steam room putting himself through a series of exercises. He carried a tape machine and some cassettes on road trips, and sitting on planes and buses he'd plug into his machine, soaking up the soothing message of relaxation that kept his anxiety at bay.

To his teammates, Mike's dedication to the tapes and the TM and the curious relaxing regime marked him as a mild figure of fun. They kidded him, Mike the weirdo. The Canucks management took notice, too, of Robitaille's unorthodoxies. Hockey players weren't supposed to rely on such foreign gimmicks as TM. It smacked too much of another culture, too effiminate for a real man. "Mike Robitaille. Tape recorder. Bus. Van. Seattle," Patty Dunn wrote in his team diary in an entry for December 2, 1976. The note was a reminder to Dunn that he'd observed Mike tuned into one of his funny tapes during a team bus ride from Vancouver to connect with a plane at the Seattle airport. Dunn kept the diary as an informal record of the players' physical condition, and he thought it worth noting Robitaille's behaviour. Mike was acting strange, not like a head case exactly but like someone whose mind was working differently from the other guys'. Dunn thought so. Maloney did, too, and Bill Hughes. Piper was coming around to the same opinion. And Orland Kurtenbach was willing to go along with whatever the others thought. He had been promoted on December 22 from his coaching job at Vancouver's farm team in Tulsa to take over as coach of the Canucks in order to let Maloney concentrate on his general manager's duties, and Kurtenbach wasn't going to challenge the thinking in the front office, not on the issue of Mike Robitaille's health.

His first up-close introduction to Mike's complaints came at a Holiday Inn on Long Island, New York, on the morning of New Year's Day 1977. The Canucks had left Vancouver the previous day for a gruelling road trip, six games in eight days, beginning with a January 1 game against the New York Islanders in Nassau, Long Island. Mike woke up that morning with pain reaching down his back on either side of his spinal column and spreading over his right shoulder as far as the elbow. It felt, he later said, "like somebody took a ball peen hammer and banged away at the points around my shoulder and elbow." He'd been experiencing the old numbness, the pain and the tingles and the fuzziness on his right side, at an intensified degree ever since early December. He noticed that his skating had been growing clumsy. He fell down when no one was near him. All of this frightened him, and when he mentioned the numbness and the awkwardness and the hurts to Dunn, Patty shrugged and gave him the usual treatment, the balm and the heat lamp and the hot pack. Their curing effect was minimal, and on New Year's Day morning the pain had reached a new and excruciating level.

"I don't know if I can play tonight, Kurt," Robitaille said to Kurtenbach when he saw him in the Holiday Inn lobby.

"Get yourself some heat," Kurtenbach said after he'd heard Robitaille's trouble. "We'll leave it till game time. Then we can talk about playing or not."

But Kurtenbach said nothing to Mike that night, and he played. He moved cautiously on the ice and took care not to run into anybody, no body checks, no skirmishes, no hitting. And back on the bench, the right arm throbbing between shifts, Mike sat with his head hung low, below his shoulders, and the right arm held flat along the boards. It was the only posture that offered comfort.

No relief came the next day when the Canucks travelled into Manhattan for a game against the

Rangers at Madison Square Garden. Mike complained again to Dunn and asked to see a doctor. It wouldn't be Piper, since team doctors rarely hit the road. "After the game," Dunn said, "we'll get the guy from the Rangers." Midway through the game, Mike came to more grief. A big, tough New York forward named Nick Fotiu slammed him to the ice with a ferocious check. A shock ran through Mike's body, and his right leg turned to rubber. When he tried to skate, the leg barely responded. Mike couldn't generate any speed. No quickness. No drive. It was as if he were skating in a thick, inhibiting fog. He explained the feeling to Dunn in the dressing-room after the game. Dunn summoned the Rangers doctor, who examined Mike for a minute or two. "Pulled muscle," he diagnosed. "You pulled a muscle somewhere in your back." Dunn said he'd give Mike some heat. That always helped a pulled muscle.

The rest of the road trip was like a nightmare for Mike. He caught a cold, and each time he sneezed or coughed, pain flashed down his right side. He played badly in the January 4 game in Pittsburgh. After the January 5 game in Atlanta, another poor effort for him, the Flames team doctor gave him a five-minute examination and decided Mike had stretched a back muscle. "That," Mike later recalled, knowing his trouble amounted to more than a back muscle gone wrong, "pissed me off." In the January 7 game against Cleveland, a humiliating 8-4 loss for Vancouver, Mike couldn't muster the strength in his right arm to pass the puck. He'd shovel it ahead. Kurtenbach shook his head at the sight, and in the January 8 game in St. Louis, yet another embarrassment to Robitaille, Kurtenbach benched him during much of the last period. Mike hardly cared. The pain pounded through his right arm and leg, and on the flight home to Vancouver, he reminded Dunn to make an appointment for him to see one of the team doctors.

"I'm in trouble, Patty," he said.

On Monday morning, January 10, Dunn reached Dr. Piper. Robitaille might be a little strange, Dunn thought, the tapes and the exercises and all, but maybe this time a doctor ought to have Mike over to his office and check him out.

It would keep till Wednesday, Piper indicated on the phone to Dunn. Wednesday was the next Canucks home game, January 12, against the Minnesota North Stars.

"Somebody'll see Mike at the game," Piper said.

Mike arrived early for the Wednesday game. He took the usual massage and heat treatment from Dunn and waited for a doctor. None appeared. Mike dressed and played, and late in the third period, with barely two minutes left in the game, he found himself skating backwards alongside his defence partner, somewhere close to the Canucks blueline, waiting to check an on-rushing Minnesota forward. The North Star was a rookie, and he pulled a manoeuvre that only an inexperienced player would attempt, cutting into the centre of the ice and diving head-on between the two Vancouver defencemen. All three players smacked the ice. Two of them didn't get up. The North Star's wind was knocked out of him and he rolled on the ice in a temporary spasm. Robitaille lay beside him, writhing under the impact of an inner shock that made him feel, he would later say, "like I'd stuck my finger in an open light socket." His right leg had gone dead. He pushed himself to his feet, and with the one leg unable to hold its share of his weight, he spunt around in a series of half circles. Dunn arrived on the ice and helped Mike to the dressing-room. The right leg jerked out of control. "It looked the way a fish does when you haul it out of the water," Robitaille described it. He felt sick at his stomach and he sat on his stool in the dressing-room, almost in a trance of suffering, willing a doctor to come to his aid.

Shortly after the end of the game, Dr. Piper opened the dressing-room door. He crossed the floor, passing among the players and looking straight ahead. Mike watched him silently as he went into Patty Dunn's private quarters at the back of the main room. When he's talked to Patty, Mike thought, when he's heard about my leg, he'll take care of me. He will. He'll check my back and arm and leg. He'll do something about the pain. A few minutes later, Piper reappeared from Dunn's room. He walked purposefully through the dressing-room and out the door. Robitaille stared, disbelieving, at the closed door.

"I felt so discouraged," he would later say of the moments in the dressing-room. "I'd been seeing myself as a kind of saint because I went out and played hockey when I was practically dying from the pain. But nobody cared. None of these people cared about me."

Isabel drove Mike home, and he lay awake most of the night, twisting to find a position in the bed that didn't aggravate the throb on his right side. The next day, he visited Dr. Termansen for one of his regular sessions of psychiatric therapy. Although Termansen felt that Mike's emotional problems had stabilized, he continued to see him as part of a regular ongoing program of therapeutic support, as is common with many psychiatrists and their patients. Termansen wasn't treating Mike's body, but he made a note in the Robitaille file about events of the previous night.

"1-13-77. Injured in game last night. Complains of severe neck pain radiating down right leg." The talk with Termansen, just a talk, gave Mike a measure of comfort, and to his relief in the days that followed, the leg seemed to recover strength, at least enough to allow him to practise with the team. He skated gingerly, avoiding fast stops and sharp turns, and he managed to get through a home game on January 15 against Cleveland. It helped that Kurtenbach used six defencemen rather than the usual four or five. That meant Mike had longer rests between shifts on the ice, and he figured that his play didn't shame him. The leg was better, but not the neck and not the back. They buzzed and tingled and ached, and suggested to Mike the sensation of a decayed tooth that had spread through all the tissues of his body.

When Mike left home in the afternoon of January 19 for a game against the Pittsburgh Penguins at the Coliseum, Isabel told him not to worry if he looked up into the stands to the section where she sat for the games and couldn't spot her.

"Don't be upset, Michael," she said. "Those stairs are getting too much for me. I'll probably stay in the wives' lounge for the second period."

Isabel was six months pregnant, and her condition made her one of the few people in the Coliseum that night who didn't see Dennis Owchar of the Penguins hit her husband with a blind-side body check. Mike took a two-minute minor penalty in the second period, and as he stepped on the ice at the end of the two minutes, the puck came loose and squirted in his direction. He was a couple of strides from a breakaway, and he pushed toward the Pittsburgh goal. The crowd roared. Mike thought the noise was a celebration of his breakaway. It wasn't. It was a collective shout of warning. Owchar, a rugged winger, was making a wide U-turn, lining up Robitaille for a check. Mike, intent on the puck, skated ahead unaware of Owchar's motion. The Pittsburgh player closed in on Robitaille at a speed of almost twenty-five miles per hour. Bodies and pads collided. The crunch echoed over the crowd noise and reached up into the press box. Mike took Owchar's shoulder in his chest and the side of his face. The hit to the face was immediately visible in a wide scrape across Robitaille's cheek, "one huge raspberry," as he later described it. The scrape didn't bother Mike, not as much as the buzzing in his right arm and leg, the shock to his body, the sense of oblivion that overwhelmed him.

"Help me," he said, lying on the ice and looking up at the player nearest him, a Pittsburgh defence-man named Don Awrey. "Please help me."

The hush in the Coliseum was so complete that the building might have been empty. People sucked in their breath and held back their fears for Robitaille. One fan spoke, a well-dressed, grey-haired gentleman sitting in a red seat three rows above ice level. "That man is seriously hurt," he said. He was Dr. Gordon Thompson, a Vancouver neurosurgeon, and he was speaking to the person in the seat next to his, Michael Piper. "You'd better get down there, Mike," Thompson said. Piper had lit a cigarette a moment before the collision on the ice. He didn't seem to Thompson to be in a hurry to leave his cigarette or his seat.

Down below, Patty Dunn skidded across the ice to Robitaille.

"I can't get anything to work," Mike said.

"Let's try and get you up," Dunn said.

Robitaille flopped over, pushing with his left arm and leg, while Dunn got a grip on his body. A Vancouver player, Chris Oddleifson, swung one of Robitaille's arms over his own shoulder and the other over Dunn's. The two supported Mike by grabbing the seat of his hockey pants and steered him toward a gate in the boards. Robitaille's legs cut grooves in the ice as they dragged behind him. The three-man procession moved in an agony of slow-motion, and the crowd, angry that Robitaille hadn't been placed on a stretcher, broke their silence to boo and jeer at Dunn.

Piper was waiting at the side of the boards by the gate. So was a stretcher. Dunn and Piper supervised Robitaille's shift on to the stretcher. Mike fell from their grip as he was manoeuvred through the tiny gate. He sprawled half on, half off the stretcher. The awkwardness of the position sent pain screaming up Robitaille's arm and leg. The minutes between the Owcar check and the stretcher seemed like an eternity.

In the dressing-room, Dunn ripped out the laces of Mike's skates and pulled off skates and stockings. His feet were bare, and Piper ran a sharp object across the soles; there was no reaction. Another doctor arrived in the dressing-room, an older man named Walter Brewster who had been Piper's predecessor as a team doctor. "Something is really wrong," he said, but he deferred to Piper for diagnosis and decisions. Piper continued testing for five or six minutes. He finished and gave Mike a look that Piper intended to be reassuring.

"When you get home," he said, "treat yourself to a shot of Courvoisier and you'll be fine, Mike."

Piper left the dressing-room.

"Don't let the other fellas see you like this," Dunn

said to Mike. "Don't let them think Pittsburgh's hurt you bad."

He helped Mike into his training-room off the back of the main dressing-room. Mike took two ammonia tablets to give his body a lift and sat on a table wrapped in a blanket.

No one spoke to Isabel about Mike's injury, and when she returned to her seat for the third period, she was puzzled that her husband was missing from the Canucks bench. She made her way to the Vancouver dressing-room and knocked. The door opened quickly. Piper and Dunn stood inside the entrance. Guilt flickered over Dunn's face, and he spoke swiftly and anxiously.

"We didn't take him off on a stretcher," he said, "because I didn't want to worry you, Isabel."

"What are you talking about?" Isabel asked.

"Mike's okay," Piper said.

The news was coming at Isabel in terrifying fragments. She groped for a question.

"Does Michael have to go to the hospital?"

"No, no," Piper said. "He'll be out of the dressing-room in a while. Why don't you wait for him in the lounge?"

Isabel obeyed. She waited through the rest of the third period and past the end of the game until Piper appeared at the door of the lounge.

"What's happening?" Isabel asked. "Does Michael need X-rays?"

"I'll see him in the morning," Piper said. "For now, just take him home, tuck him into bed, and give him a shot of Courvoisier."

Isabel stood outside the team dressing-room with Patty Dunn's wife, Marie. Inside, Mike tried to shower, but the splashes of water felt like pellets of pain to his body. He put his clothes on in the dressing-room which had now been emptied of everyone except himself and Dunn. Dunn asked Mike to come out for a drink, the two men and their wives. Funny, Mike thought, Patty's never gone drinking with me. Nice of him to ask, but strange. Robitaille agreed to the drink.

As Mike and Dunn emerged from the dressing-room, the lights were dimming in the arena. Only Isabel and Marie Dunn waited in the darkened corridor, and Isabel, seeing her husband for the first time since early in the game, his shoulders now hunched over and his right leg dragging, couldn't control a burst of panic.

"Oh, Michael, what's *wrong*?"

"Wait for now," Robitaille said, flashing annoyance. "We'll talk later."

The invitation to drinks surprised Isabel as much as it had Michael. The Dunns and the Robitailles never socialized together, and the party at the bar in West Vancouver turned out to be brief and grim. Mike couldn't grip his glass. He experimented with a couple of makeshift techniques and settled on clutching the glass between both wrists and lifting it to his lips. He made a mild joke about his problem. Only Dunn laughed.

"Listen, Mike," Dunn said as the unhappy group was leaving the bar, "I'll pick you up first thing in the morning and drive you for X-rays."

At home, Robitaille fretted over Dunn's offer.

"He never does that kind of job," he said to Isabel. "What's he being so attentive for, the drinks and everything? Something must be really wrong with me."

Isabel undressed her husband and brought him a bowl of soup in the bedroom. She left when he tried to eat it, too embarrassed to watch. Mike couldn't hold the soup spoon.

"Dr. Piper said something about a shot of Courvoisier," she said to Mike later.

"Yeah," Mike said. "I heard that line, too."

Robitaille was awake most of the night, shuffling back and forth to the bathroom. He vomited. He had diarrhea. And when he lay on the bed, he couldn't bear the pressure of a sheet on top of him. Its touch sent tingles of pain through his body. He rolled and sweated away the hours, and he would always remember this as the most wretched of all his terrible nights.

The next morning, January 20, Dunn picked Robitaille up at eight o'clock in the Canucks team truck and drove him to the Royal Columbia Hospital in New Westminster. Mike stayed there for nine days. It was a time of loneliness and secrecy and confusion. The loneliness grew out of Robitaille's realization that the rest of the Canucks, his teammates, had come to look on him as someone whose company was dangerous. Whatever management figured Mike had, the players reasoned, it might be catching. Just a single one of Robitaille's fellow Canucks, Dennis Kearns, dared to visit him at the Royal Columbia.

The secrecy came from the doctors. And they were responsible, too, for the confusion. Dr. Piper set the tone for Mike's treatment at the hospital when he phoned Dr. Termansen on that first day, January 20.

"What I think Mike has," Piper said to Termansen, "is conversion hysteria."

Termansen paused in disbelief. "Conversion hysteria" is medical jargon to describe a physical paralysis that originates in emotional troubles.

"Mike's beyond that," Termansen said. "I've been seeing him for months and he's responded positively to our sessions. Whatever he's complaining of is in his body. It's physical."

"Emotional," Piper said before he hung up.

Piper phoned Isabel.

"Mike's going to be under observation for a few days," he told her. "I don't know what's wrong, but we can't overrule the fact it may be psychosomatic."

Piper sent Robitaille to the X-ray room and asked Dr. Richard Grosch, a neurologist, to examine Mike and his X-rays.

"Well, the neurological signs are confusing," Grosch said. "But the problem could be essentially psychosomatic."

Next day, January 21, Piper dispatched another specialist, a neurosurgeon named John Porayko, to look at Mike. Porayko's diagnosis was different from Grosch's and Piper's. It was a diagnosis that was later to be confirmed by other specialists, a diagnosis that would haunt the debate over Robitaille's condition. But it was also a diagnosis that was almost immediately lost in the shuffle by everyone associated with the Canucks. It looks, Porayko said, as if this hockey player has a problem with his cervical cord. A contusion maybe, a severe bruising of the cord up near the C-5 or C-6 level, about mid-neck. Grosch considered what Porayko had to say and took another look at Robitaille's X-rays. He withdrew his view that Mike's injury was psychosomatic.

No one mentioned Porayko's diagnosis to Robitaille. No one reviewed his condition with him. No one offered satisfactory instructions or information or encouragement. Mike was left in the dark until the evening of his ninth day at the Royal Columbia when a nurse arrived at his door with instructions for him to move out within the hour. The hospital was short of beds. Mike went home, and all he had to show Isabel was a case of the blues and an appointment at Piper's office on February 3.

The day before the appointment, Piper made another of his phone calls to Dr. Termansen. Piper moved swiftly to the point.

"Robitaille," he told Termansen, "better get it together or he's going to find himself traded away from the Canucks."

Mike kept the February 3 appointment. Piper didn't. His associate, Dr. Richard Loomer, saw Robitaille. Loomer was, like Piper, an orthopedic surgeon. He was also, like Piper, a club doctor for the Canucks.

"These doctors," Mike said to Loomer, "they're not paying attention to what's wrong with me. They gotta quit thinking of me as some kind of head case. I'm a *patient*."

"You can't blame people for feeling the way they do when you consider all the circumstances," Loomer said.

"Huh?" Robitaille said.

Loomer tried to take a clear-eyed look at Robitaille's problems. He prescribed a program of physiotherapy. He told Mike to stay away from hockey. And he wrote on Mike's file that he should be "closely followed."

The words — "closely followed" — would strike Robitaille as ironic and cruel when they were repeated to him many months later.

One afternoon, during the time when Robitaille was in the Royal Columbia, Bill Good dropped into Greg Douglas's office at the Coliseum. Good was a veteran sportscaster around town, the anchorman for the CBC's telecasts of Canucks games, and he made it a habit to touch base regularly with Douglas, a former reporter who now worked as Phil Maloney's assistant in charge of publicity and media relations. Douglas kept Good up to date on events around the team, feeding him material that sounded newsy on television. But this January afternoon, Douglas offered a tidbit that he asked Good to keep under his hat.

"The reason Mike Robitaille's not playing is kind of confidential, Bill," Douglas said. "He's undergoing psychiatric treatment. He's got emotional difficulties, and I'd really appreciate it if you held this in confidence. Don't broadcast it, Bill. It might hurt his family."

Good wasn't surprised. He'd been hearing the same whispers about Robitaille in the Canucks front office for a few weeks. Robitaille had mental problems. It seemed to be what Maloney and Hughes and Douglas and everybody were saying. But to play it safe, Good checked with a couple of other sports reporters. Oh yeah, Denny Boyd from radio station CJOR said, Robitaille's supposed to be in bad emotional shape, or anyway that's what they're giving out at the Coliseum. Okay, Good thought, I'll accept it. And I'll keep mum.

Robitaille stuck to the physiotherapy program that Dr. Loomer had prescribed. It helped. The pain remained in his back and shoulder, and the leg still lacked strength and co-ordination, but at least the exercises gave him a soothing sense of progress. He needed small encouragements. At home, he spent much of his time in front of the television set. His right hand kept clutching up. It was difficult to lift a glass or the car keys or the TV guide. Despair threatened him. He was cut off. No communication from the club. Nothing from Piper or Loomer. Porayko's diagnosis of a cervical cord contusion remained a secret to Robitaille. No one acted on it. No doctor checked his progress. Mike was on his own.

One day he laced up his skates at the Coliseum. He moved gingerly to the ice. This, he told himself, was an experiment. He began to push off in his familiar skating position. Nothing happened. He couldn't stride on his skates. It was the right leg. The only way he could make it function was to throw it ahead of the left. Almost grab it with his hands and force it to move in the way it had done automatically for twenty years of hockey. Mike fell down. He got up. And fell down again. He looked like a clown on the ice. But Mike wasn't laughing. Nor was the man who was watching the performance from the stands. Phil Maloney.

In mid-February, Mike's pay cheque was a few days late. He phoned the Canucks office and reached Larry Popein, an assistant to Maloney. Popein had been Robitaille's first coach in pro hockey, back at Omaha in the late 1960s, and Mike regarded him with respect and affection.

"I'm looking for my cheque, Larry," Mike said into the phone. "Hasn't come yet."

Popein measured his answer in one sentence that devastated Robitaille. "We got cheques around here," Popein said, "only for guys who want to play hockey."

"Larry, you mean you feel just the same as the rest of them? *You*, Larry?"

"I guess I do," Popein said and hung up.

Robitaille drove to the Canucks offices in search of his cheque. He spoke to Dunn, who referred him to Orland Kurtenbach, who told him to see Maloney. Mike was in for his second lecture of the day from the Canucks management on the ethics of effort in hockey.

"I've been watching you skate," Maloney said to Robitaille when the two men were seated in Maloney's office. "What are you trying to prove? How come you're not trying? Who do you think you're kidding?"

"I can't help it," Mike said. "I'm trying to get back in shape. Maybe I can help the club later in the season."

"You're a con artist," Maloney said. Robitaille couldn't tell whether Maloney's anger was real or whether it was faked for Mike's benefit. Feigned anger was a favourite motivating tool among hockey coaches and managers.

"You're cheating your family," Maloney went on, rolling on the heat of his performance. "You're cheating your wife and the fans and your teammates. Jesus, the stuff you're pulling."

Maloney reached into a drawer of his desk and waved a familiar piece of stationery at Robitaille.

"Recognize this?" Maloney asked. It was the letter that Mike had written to Maloney before training camp several months earlier. "You promised me in this letter you were gonna give one hundred per cent. You said you wouldn't let me down. You know what you are? You're nothing but a con artist."

"Don't say those things," Robitaille said, furious. "Don't call me a liar."

Mike couldn't bear any more of Maloney's wrath.

As he left the Canucks office, someone handed him the pay cheque. Mike hardly noticed.

Two days later he called on Kurtenbach at the Coliseum. Maybe, Mike thought, he'd understand.

"Well, y'know," Kurtenbach said, "sometimes you gotta learn to play with pain."

Not him too.

"Believe me, Kurt," Mike said as patiently as he could manage, "I want to play for you. I think the world of you. It's just that I can't work my right leg."

"Okay," Kurtenbach said, "here's what I want. I want you to come out with the guys tomorrow and practise with us."

Next day, Robitaille put on his skates in the Canucks dressing-room and took his place on the ice for the practice session. Kurtenbach called the first drill, a series of skate sprints. The team divided into two groups, half behind one goal, half behind the opposite goal, and when Kurtenbach blew his whistle, one player from each end would skate for the opposite end, pumping at maximum speed. Robitaille's turn came. He pushed off and floundered almost instantly. His right leg held like an anchor, and he'd reached only as far as the blueline in his own end when the player from the opposite end flew past him.

"Never mind, Mike," Kurtenbach called from across the ice. "Pack it in."

Kurtenbach's expression showed no anger. It was disgust that was written across his face. Anguish showed on Robitaille's.

Isabel let a few days go by, days of watching her husband in isolation and torment. Enough, she decided.

If the club doctors weren't helping, she'd find someone who would. Mike was reluctant to turn to an outsider. There were channels to these things in hockey, a player gets hurt and he speaks to the trainer and the trainer calls in the team doctor. That's the traditional route, an order of priorities that a player learns from his first years in the game. But Isabel prevailed, and on February 21 she phoned Dr. Rod McGillivray. He was a general practitioner and had seen Mike for checkups and other minor medical matters over the previous year. Isabel arranged an appointment, and when Dr. McGillivray had examined Mike and listened to his description of the pains on his right side, he decided that a specialist's attention was called for. He referred Mike to Dr. Brian Hunt, a neurosurgeon.

Early in the last week of February, Mike took a phone call from Calgary. It was Joe Crozier on the line, Mike's old coach at Buffalo and now the general manager of the Calgary Cowboys in the World Hockey Association. Crozier said he'd heard from the Canucks. They were interested in working out a deal to send Mike to the Cowboys.

"Joe, I'd be honoured to play for you," Mike said. He couldn't make up his mind whether to laugh or cry. He opted for the laugh. "If you got a need for paraplegics on Calgary, I'm your guy."

"What?" Crozier said. "You kidding me or what?"

"Joe, I can't even *move* my right leg."

"What?"

"I can't skate."

"What's Vancouver trying to pull on me?"

"I tried, Joe, and I can't skate."

"Well, *shit*."

On February 25, Greg Douglas, the Canucks assistant general manager, phoned the Robitaille house. Mike was out and Isabel answered. *Douglas?* He was like the rest of the Canucks people, insensitive to Michael, and Isabel went cold when she heard his voice. But his message to her didn't come from the front office. It came from Douglas's conscience.

"I just want to warn you that you ought to consider getting a lawyer for Mike," he said. "There's a lot of shit flying around down here, and I think Mike's gonna get hurt."

"Aren't you going out on a limb or something?" Isabel said. "I mean, should you be telling me this?"

"At this point, I don't care," Douglas said. "Mike's gonna be made the scapegoat. That's all I'm saying. The rest is up to you and Mike."

Bruce McColl, in his mid-thirties, was a lawyer in a Vancouver firm, Macaulay, McColl & MacKenzie, where the others were like him, young and bright and gung-ho. He acted for a number of Vancouver players in negotiating contracts with the Canucks management. He'd handled a few matters for Robitaille and would be working out the new deal for Mike as soon as his original three-year contract expired over the next few months. McColl liked Robitaille, and when Mike phoned him with his troubles on February 26, his mind latched immediately on to legal tactics.

"More medical information," he said. "Mike, the only way we can deal with the Canucks people is if we have solid medical information."

"Something bad's going on," Robitaille said. "I heard from Joe Crozier. Maybe they're trying to trade me. But more likely they're gonna suspend me. That must be what Greg Douglas is talking about."

"All right, Mike, okay," McColl said. "Think about the medical stuff. You got to see an orthopedic specialist or a neurologist, somebody like that. Brian Hunt? Is that the specialist Dr. McGillivray wants you to go to? He's good. Get a report on your real condition, and I'll take care of business with the Canucks."

At last, Mike thought, *somebody*'s listening to me.

On February 28 Dr. Hunt examined Robitaille. His diagnosis was a rerun of Dr. Porayko's. Mike had sustained a severe injury to his spinal cord and was suffering from a physical disability that ranked in the critical category. Hunt couldn't be immediately certain of the disability's nature or origin, but he could draw a couple of obvious conclusions. One was that Mike needed long-term treatment. And the other was that he shouldn't put his body under the strain of physical activity. No hockey. No skating.

On Friday, March 4, Bruce McColl got on the phone. He talked to Dr. Hunt, who ran through his diagnosis and offered the opinion that Robitaille shouldn't have played in the game of January 19. His troubles in the spine probably predated the January 19 check from Dennis Owchar. "God knows," Hunt said to McColl, "what would happen if Robitaille fell on the ice again." McColl phoned Dr. Termansen. Of course, Termansen said, growing exasperated over his constant repetition of the obvious, Mike has no more emotional problems. It's his *body*. McColl phoned Phil Maloney at the Canucks offices. Maloney was on the road with the team. McColl left a message. Greg Douglas spotted it and returned McColl's call. He knew that if Bruce McColl had phoned, something heavy was in the air.

"I've been doing a lot of work with the doctors," McColl told Douglas, "and I think we're into matters that are very serious for Mike and for you people."

Douglas reached Maloney in Toronto, and later that day, four o'clock Vancouver time, Maloney phoned McColl.

"What's Robitaille's doctor say?" Maloney asked.

McColl sketched Dr. Hunt's preliminary diagnosis.

"Look, Mike Robitaille's a con artist," Maloney said. "Nothing but a crybaby."

"What concerns me in this business, Phil," McColl persisted, "is that Mike was made to play a game when he was already suffering from some injury. I'm talking about the January 19 game. That really concerns me."

Maloney began to retreat. "It wasn't me. The pressure comes from the top. Bill Hughes wants his players on the ice. I won't put any more heat on Mike if he's really hurt bad."

"I'm gonna get Dr. Hunt's written report," McColl said. "When it's ready, I'll get back to you people, and we'll go at the whole thing again."

McColl had pushed the Robitaille situation one long step closer to confrontation.

Al Davidson represents the Howard Cosell tradition of sports broadcasting in the Vancouver area. He insists on calling them the way they are, and on his sportscast over radio station CKNW on March 4, he spoke out fearlessly on the Mike Robitaille case. "Some hockey players like the great Frank Mahovlich and Mike Walton had the same thing happen to them, nervous breakdowns," Davidson told his listeners. "I have known Mike Robitaille for a couple of years now and he's a fine boy. Let's get everybody behind him and hope some day he'll be normal."

Robitaille didn't hear the broadcast, but a friend paraphrased it for him. Mike phoned Bruce McColl, and next day the two went to CKNW and listened to a tape of Davidson's words. McColl arranged a meeting with Davidson and asked for a retraction. On his next broadcast, Davidson took it all back. Robitaille wasn't like the great Frank Mahovlich or Mike Walton. He'd not had a nervous breakdown. His trouble was physical. Mike listened to the retraction and felt weary. He appreciated Davidson's apology, but he knew the word was out that hockey people thought of Mike Robitaille as a head case.

The Canucks were playing a home game on March 9, a Wednesday, and an hour before the start of the first period, Bruce McColl arrived at the Coliseum. He was carrying Dr. Hunt's written report on Robitaille's condition, and he took it to a meeting in Maloney's office. Maloney, it was immediately clear to McColl, had returned to his familiar stand on the whole bothersome Robitaille mess. There was no more mention of "pressure from the top" and of "not putting heat on Mike."

"I don't know this guy Hunt," Maloney said to McColl, "but I know Mike Robitaille. I've been in his house. He's got all these medical journals that he reads, and if you ask me, he simulates the injuries you're talking about. I wouldn't be surprised if he conned your Dr. Hunt."

"Phil, the main reason I'm here discussing this with you is to avoid a lawsuit," McColl said. "Unless somebody pays attention to Mike, we're going to end up in court. I'm telling you, there could be a basic problem of negligence here. Negligence by the Canucks.''

It was the first time a legal term — "negligence" — had been used in connection with Mike Robitaille's problems.

Maloney lost his cool. "I'm used to your types," he told McColl. "You're not interested in Mike Robitaille. You're not interested in the Canucks. You're not interested in anything except yourself. You want to make a big public deal of this thing. You want to flog it out there."

Maloney left to watch the hockey game, and between the second and third periods McColl returned to Maloney's office for a second meeting. Dr. Piper was in the room. So were Greg Douglas, Maloney, and the third team doctor, a general practitioner named Lough. Piper took the spokesman's role.

"I hear you're making allegations of negligence," he said to McColl. "Maybe you should just wait a minute and hear our side of the story."

"Well, first," McColl said, "I might suggest that you should speak to the Canucks lawyers before you go any further."

"Never mind the lawyers," Piper said. "The point is that Mike Robitaille has deep psychological problems and he's under treatment right this minute."

"Wait, wait," McColl said. "I spoke to Mike's psychiatrist. I spoke to Dr. Termansen and he says there's no psychological problems at all."

Piper had a curious answer. "Eric Termansen tends to get carried away with himself."

"But what about the lack of treatment that Mike got?" McColl said. "I understand you saw him on different occasions, Dr. Piper, and you heard him making complaints. I'm talking about January 12 and later on. What about the lack of treatment?''

"On that point," Piper sad, "we go back to the question I raised in the first place. As far as I'm concerned, Michael's problems are all in his head.''

"Dr. Hunt told me that Mike might never play hockey again.''

"Well," Piper said, giving a reprise to a favourite line. "Brian tends to get carried away with himself.''

McColl shifted his approach. "Okay," he said, "why don't we get another opinion beside Dr. Hunt's? How about that? I know Barbara Allan. She's a neurologist, and she's on a top team at the Vancouver General. We get her and then we see what Mike needs, an operation or what.''

"We'll go along with that," Piper said.

The buzzer had already sounded to signal the beginning of the third period, and the meeting in Maloney's office broke up.

On April 4, Isabel gave birth to a baby, a second daughter for the Robitailles. They named the little girl Sarah.

On April 17, Dr. Barbara Allan, a practitioner in clinical neurology, submitted Robitaille to the most thorough examination that he had so far received. She recognized symptoms of trouble, enough to offer a diagnosis that she would stand by. From that moment of decision, Dr. Allan became a major protagonist in the debate over Robitaille's condition. She emerged as Mike's medical voice in the struggle with the Canucks that was to stretch over another four years. The hockey team later came forward with other medical voices that sought to put the lie to Dr. Allan's diagnosis of April 17. But she held firm, and it was her word that formed the small, hard core at the centre of Mike Robitaille's cause.

"This man," Dr. Allan wrote in her report, which was dated April 27, "has symptoms of cervical spinal-cord abnormality, the first symptoms of this that one can be definite about occurring during the game of 12 January 1977, but prior to this time from January 1 on, he had symptoms of neck pain with cervical root irritation judging by the radiation of pain to the right arm."

What Mike must have suffered in the January 12 game, she concluded, was a hemorrhaging or severe bruising of the spinal cord. The electrical-shock sensation that Mike had felt earlier in the season, the pain in the elbow and shoulder, the shooting spasms down his arm and leg — all of these indicated that he was already suffering some sort of protrusion in a cervical disc. But the bang he took in the January 12 game was the clincher. If she had seen Mike's condition after the game, Dr. Allan would have immediately admitted him to hospital. She would have ordered a myelogram, a painful process in which dye is injected inside the spinal canal and the canal photographed. She would have kept him away from hockey, and certainly she would have forbidden him from playing in the game of January 19 when Mike was patently at risk.

Her April 26 report drew a line under the dangers Robitaille faced in the later game:

"How did the injury on January 19, 1977, relate to the injury on January 12, 1977?

"Answer: It made it considerably worse according to his history; on January 12, 1977, he had relatively transient and less severe symptoms of cervical cord abnormality while on January 19, the symptoms suggested more extensive cervical involvement and the symptoms failed to clear.''

The body check Mike took from Dennis Owchar on January 19 aggravated the injury of January 12. The blow was to the very same area of the spinal cord, at the C-5 and C-6 level in mid-neck, that was giving Mike such excruciating pain, and what happened was the precise injury that Dr. Allan, if she'd seen Mike on the twelfth, would have set out to avoid by keeping Robitaille away from hockey. Now Mike was paying a penalty in pain and suffering. It would take extensive rest and treatment to relieve his agony, and he would never be free of some disability for the rest of his life. Would he play hockey again? Not a chance.

The 1976-77 NHL season ended in late April. The Canucks had sixty-three points, a total that tied the team with the Chicago Black Hawks for third place in its division. But Chicago had managed to show one more game in the win column than Vancouver and took the last spot in the Stanley Cup playoffs. A few weeks later, the Canucks fired Phil Maloney as general manager. He found a job in Vancouver as a car salesman.

In the summer of 1977, Mike and Isabel and the two little girls moved from Vancouver to Buffalo. It was good to get away from a city where people thought of Mike as some kind of nut. The Al Davidson broadcast had hurt his reputation. The Canucks players were avoiding him. And he felt isolated in Vancouver. Buffalo, on the other hand, was a city where Mike had played good hockey, a community where, as he said, ''I feel socially comfortable.'' Physically,

Mike was in agony. His right hand would fold involuntarily into a painful claw. His right leg turned inward and developed a tremor. Simple activities — a short walk, an hour of driving around the city — left him exhausted. He kept up sessions of physiotherapy that brought some relief. But the strength he took such pride in during his career in hockey had fled from his body.

The Canucks sent Mike a letter in early August. The team was releasing him because, as Robitaille's own doctors advised, he was incapable of playing hockey. The release took Mike off team medical coverage, and when his hospital bills came back unpaid, he turned to his savings.

"I had to use money from the bank account," he said. "I mean, a job? I couldn't even dial the phone to ask anybody for a job."

Robitaille was bitter.

"You're an NHL hockey player and people you meet promise the sun and the stars," he said. " 'Sure, Mike,' they'd tell me, 'when you quit hockey, I'd like you to work for me at my restaurant, in my business, public relations stuff.' Those people, what I thought of as friends, they've vanished out of my life."

Meanwhile, Bruce McColl chased after legal remedies for Robitaille. He flew to Toronto for discussions with Alan Eagleson, the lawyer who runs the NHL Players' Association. The situation was dicey, Eagleson said, and a court case, if that's what it came to, wasn't the association's proper role. McColl negotiated with the Canucks. The talks yielded nothing, no offer of settlement, no admission of an obligation to Robitaille. It was becoming clearer to McColl with each frustration that action in the courts was reaching the stage of inevitability. He organized his weapons. He instructed Mike to submit himself to one more examination, and in November at a Buffalo hospital a neuroradiologist named Kenneth Kaan and a neurosurgeon named Lawrence Jacobs X-rayed Mike's spinal canal and put him through the ordeal of another myelogram. The Kaan-Jacobs report confirmed in every major respect Dr. Barbara Allan's earlier analysis of Mike's condition. With that news, McColl decided it was time to take the Canucks to court, and as counsel for Robitaille he briefed a Vancouver barrister. His name was John Laxton.

When John Laxton talks, he runs his right hand through his hair in a gesture that's decidedly sensuous. The hair is thick, black turning grey, and would inevitably be described in a man more pretentious than Laxton as leonine. He's in his late forties, medium height, wears smart moustaches, and has the sturdy good looks of the hero of a Thomas Hardy novel. His style, at work or play, is casual. The receptionist in his firm, Laxton, Pidgeon, calls him by his first name. So does everybody who has known him for at least five minutes.

Laxton's office is in a ten-storey building in downtown Vancouver that opened in 1980 and cost ten million dollars to put up. Laxton raised the money, and the building reflects his tastes and inclinations. Designed by the celebrated Vancouver architect Arthur Erickson, it slopes away on three sides in a series of pyramid-like levels. Plants tumble from the tiered balconies and look lush against the building's concrete and glass. A YWCA branch, sleek and fully equipped, takes up most of the third floor. Its presence was arranged by Laxton, who is a fitness freak and marathon runner. His devotion to a sound body does not stop him, however, from pointing out in an aside that's both proud and puckish that his Y is the only branch in the world boasting a beer and wine bar.

Laxton, Pidgeon occupies the building's top floor, and the view from Laxton's office through the window that fills the entire north wall looks across Coal Harbour and its traffic in freighters and seaplanes to the mountains, Grouse and Seymour, that define the boundary between Vancouver and the wilderness. Inside, the office runs to maroon walls, black furnishings, and light-grey carpeting. A wood fire burns in the grate, and invisible behind the panel to the right of the fireplace there's a bar that is stocked to meet everybody's drinking preference. Laxton's is Scotch, and each Friday, come five o'clock, he breaks out the drinks and the conversation.

"Maybe the muff-diver case was the craziest I ever took," he might say with very little prompting. "Back around 1970, Vancouver was death on hippies, really hated them, and I acted for the *Georgia Strait*, which was the hippie newspaper of the day. One of the guys in the crown attorney's office used to lay charges against the *Strait*, out of some sort of wild moral fervour, at the rate of about one a week, and I'd parade back and forth to court trying to fight off the attacks.

"Things got utterly ridiculous when this crown slapped the paper with an obscenity charge on the basis of an ad that ran in the *Strait*'s personal section. The ad read something like 'Young man wants to meet young woman for muff diving, etc.' So we went to court, and the crown and the police pretended to be scandalized by the printing of the phrase 'muff diving,' which everybody knows, but nobody was coming out and saying, is a colloquialism for cunnilingus. All right, what was I supposed to do for a defence? By great good fortune, about the time of the trial I happened to run into an old friend from back in my Lancashire days, Fred Bowers, who was teaching English at UBC. He told me his specialty was the structure of the English language. Marvelous, I said, you're my expert witness in the muff-diving case.

"Fred was fantastic. He got on the stand and he talked for two hours. He told the court he'd researched the word in question, 'muff diving,' through every source available to him. He reviewed ancient slang and the modern vernacular, obscure sources and serious literature. It was a virtuoso performance. He gave a bloody lecture in his thick Lancashire accent that he's never lost, and the judge, my god, he was absolutely enthralled. He hung on every word that Fred uttered. Fred said the faintest trace he could find of the word was from an eighteenth-century source that described 'muff' as a term for female private parts. But that in his considered opinion 'muff diving' had no identifiable and established meaning in the English language.

"The judge loved it. He said in his judgment he adopted the views of the expert witness in whole. He found that 'muff diving' was without meaning and that therefore the *Georgia Strait* had committed no crime in publishing the said non-word.

"Case bloody dismissed."

John Laxton's first job in Canada was as a Montreal vacuum-cleaner salesman. He and his wife Valerie had paused on a bumming-around trip to the South Pacific. They'd come from England, where Laxton grew up in Lancashire, the son of a coal miner who read Karl Marx. When Laxton headed out from his home country, he took along his father's affection for socialism. He also packed a degree in law from King's College of Durham University. He and his wife drifted west from Montreal and the vacuum-cleaner business, and as soon as their eyes fell on Vancouver, they decided that the South Pacific could wait.

"Vancouver looked like paradise," Laxton says in a voice that has shed most of the Lancashire accent. "What I remembered about home was the chimneys. Everywhere you looked in Lancashire, you saw those goddamned dirty, smoking chimneys. But in Vancouver it was open and clean and free and beautiful."

Valerie Laxton took a job — $200 a month — and the couple rented a humble apartment — $70 a month — while Laxton went through the tedious one-year routine of meeting the educational requirements for the British Columbia bar. He got his call in 1960 and went to work with a Vancouver firm, Shulman & Company, that had a lock on labour cases up and down the coast. In the atmosphere of the Shulman firm, knocking over the establishment on behalf of the workers, Laxton blossomed.

"There was a grand Irishman in the firm, Tom Hurley, who taught me one of the great secrets of arguing in court," Laxton says. "We used to have these Saturday-morning sessions in the office. One of the lawyers would have to be on deck the following Monday for a case in the Supreme Court, and we'd sit down and try to cover all the legal points to help the guy get a handle on his case. Talk'd fly around the table, stuff about precedents and theories and cases on point. Hurley used to sit in his chair, very quiet at first, absorbing all the babble, and then he'd go to work. His method was to distil an argument by putting it forward as if, right there in the office on Saturday morning, he was actually talking to a judge. He'd get past the academic junk and set the scene in the courtroom. It was amazing how that technique focussed the mind. Tom had the facility for conceiving wonderful phrases that would sum up an hour's argument and put the shaft to the other side. It'd be all wrapped up in a single sentence, and the lawyer who was due in court on Monday would write it down and construct his whole argument around the one sentence. Ever since those days, in my own office, I've followed Hurley's approach. I imagine I'm addressing the judge, and I don't waste words or build silly ideas. And I usually win the case."

Whatever his technique, Laxton developed into a persuasive counsel. He was made a partner in the Shulman firm in 1963, stayed another eleven years, then left to found his own firm in 1974. Labour law still keeps most of Laxton, Pidgeon's partners and associates busy, but Laxton has branched out to take on criminal charges, compensation work, and negligence cases. Away from the office, he has worked for the NDP and served as the party's B.C. president through the late 1960s. At the same time, socialism hasn't prevented him from turning a big dollar. Laxton exudes style and the golden touch. In the mid-1960s, he and Valerie spotted a piece of lovely seaside land on a sloping lot on Marine Drive in West Vancouver. Laxton picked it up for $10,000, persuaded Arthur Erickson to design a house that would blend into the setting, and hired a friendly contractor to take on the building job at a bargain price. The home, graceful in the laid-back west coast manner, cost less than $50,000, and today, when Marine Drive is a showcase for some of the most spectacular domestic architecture in Canada, it would go cheap at a million and a quarter. And Laxton has been just as astute in his ventures into commercial-land investment. In all things, he's a dealer with good instincts, disciplined follow-through, and an eye for the main chance.

Case number C782249 in the Vancouver Registry of the Supreme Court of British Columbia: Michael Robitaille and Michael Robitaille Investments Ltd., plaintiffs, and Vançouver Hockey Club Limited, defendant.

Laxton issued the writ in August 1978, and legal language took over from sports jargon. The plaintiff claimed damages in loss of income and in pain and suffering from the defendant for an injury that ended the plaintiff's hockey career and left him permanently disabled to a serious degree. The injury resulted from the defendant's negligence, which took a variety of forms: failure to respond to the plaintiff's complaints and to his clear symptoms of injury, failure to keep the plaintiff out of hockey games, and the ultimate failure to provide the plaintiff with proper medical care.

Laxton brushed up on his negligence law. In order to prove his claim that the Canucks were responsible for Robitaille's injuries through their negligence, he would first have to satisfy the court that the Canucks owed Mike a "duty of care." That concept — duty of care — is fundamental to a plaintiff's claim in the law of torts, running through Canadian cases on negligence and further back to the leading cases in British courts which established the first principles in tort law. "First," Lord Wilberforce, a law lord, wrote in *Anns* v. *London Borough of Morton*, a leading English appeal case on duty of care, "one has to ask whether, as between the alleged wrong-doer

and the person who suffered damage, there is sufficient relationship of proximity or neighbourhood
such that, in the reasonable contemplation of the
former, carelessness on his part may be likely to
cause damage to the latter, in which case a prima
facie case of duty of care arises.''

It made perfect sense to Laxton that the Canucks
knew their failure to provide proper protection and
medical attention for Robitaille would inevitably
expose him, an employee who was in a position of
relying on their protection, to the reasonable
possibility of injury. It made sense, but, alas, there
were no earlier cases that offered a comforting precedent in Robitaille's special set of circumstances. No
factual situation in any reported case, Canadian or
English, approached the facts in the Robitaille case.
It was unique. On just a single previous occasion had
a professional athlete sued his team alleging that its
negligence left him vulnerable to physical harm. The
case was American, a football player named Dick
Butkus versus the Chicago Bears of the National
Football League, but it had been settled out of court
with a payment of $50,000 to Butkus and therefore
gave Laxton no assistance in judge-made case law.
He was on his own, blazing legal trails, up against the
establishment of professional hockey. For Laxton, it
was hardly a new role.

He researched the law, interviewed witnesses, and
began to build a case that would, in fact and in law,
establish the Canucks' negligence. He leaned on
Robitaille in a series of interviews, ransacking Mike's
memories for every detail of his long ordeal. In the
course of two years, Robitaille made nine plane trips
to Vancouver for sessions with Laxton. The journeys
were arduous, but they gave Mike a sense of ongoing
accomplishment, something that was missing from

his life in Buffalo. He had tried a couple of jobs that cost him in finances and pride. He lost money in a wine-and-cheese importing operation, and he abandoned a plant and tree business when he couldn't handle its modest physical demands. He found a job as a salesman with a machinery firm, earning $12,000 a year plus commissions, but it tired him, the car-driving and the socializing, and he would knock off work each day, exhausted, by two in the afternoon. His body was a burden to him — the lack of co-ordination, the tightness and pounding in his right arm and leg, the extreme sensitivity in parts of his body that often made sex with Isabel a painful impossibility. Life came hard for Mike, and while helping Laxton build his case, he opened himself to one more blow.

Laxton asked Robitaille to contact a group of players from his NHL years and persuade them to testify on his behalf at the trial. Laxton needed evidence that Mike wasn't a malingerer who was likely to fake injuries and that, except for the career-ending injury, he had the skills to play in the NHL for several more money-making years. Robitaille wrote letters to thirty of his former teammates and waited for the answers to roll in. But of the thirty, only two players volunteered to testify, Syl Apps, Jr., and Ab DeMarco. Two more, Jim Schoenfeld and Jerry Korab, came forward on their own, volunteering support in court. The rest shied away from Robitaille, and one player let him know that, if he were subpoenaed to testify, he would give evidence in a way to deliberately hurt Mike's case. Robitaille's morale was shattered.

"These were guys that Isabel and I spent Christmases with," he said, uncomprehending. "I thought of them as my special friends. But they were scared of what the hockey owners would do to them. The guy who said he'd testify to hurt me, he was trying to get a job as an NHL scout. He'd never get it if the owners thought he was on my side. The guys figured my friendship wasn't worth bucking the big shots.''

Robitaille soldiered on.

So did Laxton, and as he moved further into his research and deeper into his construction of the case, he grew confident that he would lick the Canucks in court. A breakthrough came with his examination for discovery of Phil Maloney. Discovery is a pretrial process in a civil action that permits lawyers for plaintiff and defendant to question the other side's witnesses under oath before a court reporter. Though Maloney was a potential witness for the Canucks, he had no axe to grind for the team that had fired him, and he willingly yielded pages of valuable material under Laxton's examination. He admitted that he considered Mike's problems more mental than physical and for that reason had ignored Robitaille's cries for help. This view, Maloney testified, wasn't exclusive to him. It was shared by others around the Canucks office, by people like Michael Piper. Maloney's testimony amounted to an admission of negligence, and, buoyed by the revelations, Laxton approached the Canucks lawyer and offered to settle the case before it went to trial.

"We'll take $350,000," Laxton said.

Barry Kirkham was acting for the Canucks. He's a short, slim, good-looking man in his late thirties. He has a high-pitched voice and his manner speaks of an establishment background. He practises with Owen, Bird in Vancouver, a firm that Laxton had plenty of reason to remember. The very day after he was called to the B.C. bar in 1960, Shulman & Company dispatched him to his first court appearance. He was to argue the appellant's case in the Court of Appeal, and on the other side, for the respondent, was a senior Vancouver counsel, Walter Owen, who had two juniors in tow. "The case," Laxton says, "represented twenty-four hours' experience at the bar against sixty-seven years'." Laxton had one strong point that he put to the three appeal-court justices in his argument, but when Owen's turn came to speak, he refused to address himself to the point, even under the prodding of the three judges. "He was courtly and wise and very evasive," Laxton remembers. "He talked for a day and a half, and eventually the court gave up trying to bring him around to my one point." The judges in effect said to hell with Laxton's point and found in favour of Owen's client. Owen bestowed a patrician smile on Laxton, and a few years later he retired from practice to be named British Columbia's lieutenant-governor.

"Three hundred and fifty thousand," Laxton said.

"Out of the question," Kirkham told him. "I've already assured my people we're going to win."

As events later unfolded, $350,000 may not have been an offer that deserved to be refused.

On April 10, 1979, Dr. Gordon Thompson re-entered the Robitaille case and came close to destroying it for Laxton. It was Dr. Thompson who had sat beside Michael Piper at the Coliseum on the night of January 19 when Robitaille took the infamous check from Dennis Owchar. Now the Canucks were calling on him to examine Robitaille on their behalf. They had the right to satisfy themselves as to Robitaille's condition, and on Piper's recommendation they chose Dr. Thompson for the job. He possessed the qualifications. A man close to sixty, grey-haired and ruddy, distinguished and imperious, he ranked as the leading neurosurgeon in Vancouver. He was neuro-surgeon-in-chief at the Vancouver General Hospital, taught the subject at UBC and served as chief examiner in his specialty for the Royal College of Physicians and Surgeons. He also enjoyed close connections with the Canucks. He'd been a season ticket holder since the team entered the NHL in 1970, and after he performed a successful operation on Coley Hall, a former Canucks owner, he was rewarded by having his season tickets moved into more exclusive territory in a row just above ice level next to seats that came to be occupied by Michael Piper.

Thompson's examination of Robitaille on April 10 didn't err, as such medical matters go, on the side of length. "We got talking about hockey," Mike remembers, "and the actual check-up and everything else lasted about an hour." That was time enough for Dr. Thompson to arrive at some opinions that brought him into a head-on difference of diagnosis with Dr. Barbara Allan.

"I do not think there is any question in my mind," he wrote in his report to Kirkham, "that this man sustained his injury to the cervical cord on January 19, 1977, when he was heavily checked. He sustained a hyper-extensive injury to the cervical spine at the time with attendant contusion of the underlying cervical cord, the residual of which is present today. I am of the opinion that his complaints prior to January 19, 1977, in the region of the neck and shoulder are unrelated as a pre-existing condition to the incomplete spinal cord injury sustained on that date."

So, Dr. Thompson was saying, the January 19 injury was independent of earlier injuries. It had no connection with the bang that Mike took to his back on January 12. There was no casual link between the two. It was, Thompson insisted, "most unusual" for one cervical-cord injury to be aggravated by another. That view contradicted Dr. Allan, who concluded that the blow of January 19 had been to the same area of the spinal cord as the blow of January 12, with the obvious disastrous consequences. No, no, Thompson said, staking out his territory, the Dennis Owchar body check of January 19 was isolated as the sole and only cause of Robitaille's troubles.

From the Thompson version, one major consequence flowed that spelled death to Laxton's case. If the January 19 incident stood alone, then Robitaille was in no jeopardy when he went into the game. He was free of serious symptoms that doctors or trainers should have been treating. No red flags had gone up, putting Dr. Piper on alert. Hence, there was no negligence on his part in allowing Mike to play, none on Patty Dunn's part of Phil Maloney's or any other Canucks agent. No negligence. And no case against the Canucks.

Dr. Thompson's opinion formed the basis of the argument that Barry Kirkham considered with good reason to be his most convincing. Still, he prepared other, necessarily lesser points in his client's favour. He would argue that Robitaille, in his own relentless play, was sadly the author of his own misfortune. He'd contend that the Canucks provided Mike with the services of team doctors and if they failed to treat him properly, then the club was not at fault. It had carried out any duty of care it owed Robitaille, and whatever action he had at law lay against the doctors, not the Canucks. Kirkham would argue, touching all the alternatives available to him, that Maloney alone should shoulder the blame, that other Canuck officials and employees acted honourably toward Mike, all but Maloney, and that Robitaille must seek his relief against him. Kirkham would raise all of these arguments in his defence of the Canucks, but ultimately it would be Dr. Thompson's diagnosis that he depended on as the most persuasive of his submissions. Dr. Thompson would shoot Laxton out of the water.

On the evening of the day after he examined Robitaille, Dr. Thompson went to dinner with his brother-in-law and the two men's wives at the Arbutus Club, a members-only club for sports and dining that caters to Vancouver's upper crust. The couples settled first in the lounge, sitting over drinks at a large L-shaped sofa. Thompson dominated the early conversation, and it was Mike Robitaille who was on his mind.

"This chap Robitaille is seriously hurt, you know," Thompson said. "I've examined him and he isn't good for anything. I doubt if he could drive a garbage truck."

Directly opposite Thompson, about twenty feet away at a matching L-shaped sofa, another man, much younger, sat with his wife. The young man came alert when he heard Robitaille's name dropped into the neighbouring conversation.

"Bruce McColl's dumped Robitaille as a client," Thompson went on. "He went somewhere else, and now he's in the hands of this Laxton. You know him, the socialist lawyer who drives the big car?"

By an astounding coincidence that Dr. Thompson would come to regret, the young man opposite him, in easy earshot, in the wind of Thompson's pronouncements, was a lawyer named Robert MacKenzie. His firm was Macaulay, McColl & MacKenzie. He was Bruce McColl's partner.

"I was at that game with Piper," Thompson continued. "I saw the hit and I heard the crack as he went down. I said, 'That man has been seriously hurt. Somebody should go down right away.' I said this to Piper. I was sitting at the game talking to him and I nudged him. Piper had just lit a cigarette."

Robert MacKenzie felt gauche. What did social protocol demand in the situation? He was sitting in the Arbutus Club twenty feet from a man who was skirting close to insults directed at one of his law partners and the partner's client. The man was talking about fairly confidential matters that touched on a trial scheduled to start in a couple of months. MacKenzie decided to assert himself. He stood up and walked across to the Thompson group.

"I don't mean to be rude," he said, addressing Thompson, "but I'm Bruce McColl's partner."

He got no further. Thompson gave MacKenzie what he later described as "the coldest stare I ever received."

"We're not talking about that," Thompson said.

The freezing look, the clipped tone, Thompson's forbidding manner, and the intimidating atmosphere of the setting — nobody raises a voice in the Arbutus Club — combined to discourage MacKenzie. He felt his face go pale, and he turned away without speaking again.

"Who is that man?" he heard Thompson ask his brother-in-law.

"He's Rob MacKenzie," the answer came.

Thompson shifted the topic of conversation, and while they finished their drinks, the four people talked of tax matters.

The day after the encounter, MacKenzie repeated the details of his bizarre evening at the Arbutus Club to

Bruce McColl. *Fantastic*, McColl said, and phoned Laxton.

"What's he mean 'socialist lawyer with a big car'?" Laxton said. "It's a 1972 Jaguar that I got for a thousand dollars, and it spends most of its time going from garage to garage for repairs."

After Laxton had given his indignation a mild and comic workout, he told McColl that he could envision a situation down the line in the trial where he could use MacKenzie as a witness. Yes, he said, it wouldn't surprise him at all if Rob contributed valuable testimony. It was looking like a rough case up ahead.

Mr. Justice William Esson drew the assignment at the spring non-jury assizes for *Robitaille* v. *Vancouver Hockey Club Ltd.*, a choice that came as a mild surprise. Esson had been appointed to the B.C. Supreme Court only within the previous year, and the case, which would clearly take the court into uncharted legal regions, was made to order for a veteran member of the bench. Esson was in his mid-forties, strait-laced, diligent, and plucked for the court from a large downtown Vancouver firm. He blocked out the month of June 1979 to hear the Robitaille case, and when his clerk called the court to order on opening day, Monday, June 4, 1979, he was feeling a few butterflies of nervousness. Nobody in the courtroom on that day was entirely calm.

Laxton called his first witness, Dr. Barbara Allan. She told the story that Laxton knew by heart. How, as her examination of Mike two years earlier had revealed, he showed symptoms of nerve-root irritation at different levels of his spine at least as early as January 1, 1977. And how hemorrhage or severe bruising of the spinal cord occurred initially during

315

the game of January 12 and to a more marked extent in the January 19 game. Under Laxton's careful questioning, Dr. Allan spelled out her analysis of Mike's condition and its causes for Mr. Justice Esson. She repeated her declaration that if she'd seen Mike's symptoms on January 12, she would have hustled him to hospital care. He was, she said, clearly in trouble by that date. Laxton was satisfied that Dr. Allan's voice gave off the ring of conviction. She appeared confident but not pushy or overbearing. She seemed believable, Laxton thought, and surely the frightening opinion with which she ended her examination-in-chief must have moved Esson to sympathy for Robitaille's plight. It was unlikely, Dr. Allan testified in her level-headed way, that Mike's present disabilities would ever grow less painful and inhibiting, not in all the years that were left to him.

On cross-examination, Barry Kirkham couldn't budge Dr. Allan from her views. He presented her with the defence's thesis, the notion that Dr. Thompson would introduce later in the trial. "I suggest to you," Kirkham said, "that the mechanism that caused this man's spinal-cord injury was what happened on January 19 and only what happened on January 19." Dr. Allan countered with *her* thesis, that the January 19 body check aggravated the existing injury from the January 12 game. Dr. Allan held firm, and Laxton had successfully planted with the court the seed of his case.

In the next few days, Laxton summoned thirteen more witnesses. First came three hockey players, Jim Schoenfeld, Syl Apps, Jr., and Ab DeMarco. "One of the best hip checks in the league," Schoenfeld said of Robitaille. He ought to have lasted with an NHL club till he was thirty-four or thirty-five, and his next contract should have given him, minimum, a half-million dollars over five years. Apps and DeMarco spoke of other financial possibilities for Robitaille, playing in the European leagues, coaching in minor hockey, perhaps working a job behind an NHL bench. Mike had the right temperament to handle other guys.

Alan Eagleson, the head of the NHL Players' Association, flew from Toronto to speak for Robitaille. He testified two days after the June 11 issue of *Sports Illustrated* hit newsstands with a feature article entitled "Playing Hurt — The Doctors' Dilemma." The piece dealt at length with the role of the team physician: "Is his paramount concern the health of the athlete or is it the welfare of the club?" And Laxton used it as a jumping-off point in his examination of Eagleson. Athletes feel pressure to play when they're hurt, Eagleson said, pressure from management and sometimes from physicians. But there's a distinction to be made. On a hockey-team roster of twenty players, the top five don't take the heat. "If Darryl Sittler says he doesn't feel like playing tonight," Eagleson said, "there's no question from management." But, he went on, "if the others from five to twenty say the same thing, then the question from management is, why? Those players feel if they don't do what management says, they won't be around long."

And where did Mike Robitaille fit in the range of players? Top five? Or five to twenty?

"Five to twenty."

Next came the doctors. Rod McGillivray, Mike's general practitioner, told of Robitaille's medical background and of his examination of Mike in early February of 1977. Eric Termansen ran through Mike's psychiatric history and the positive ways in which he took to Termansen's treatment. And Brian Hunt testified to his diagnosis of Mike's cervical injury, his examination of February 28, 1977, supporting Dr. Allan's later diagnosis.

Two sportscasters, Bill Good, Jr., and Denny Boyd, told the court of the word that Canucks management had been spreading through late 1976 and early '77, that Robitaille was in deep emotional trouble, a head case. Bruce McColl, the lawyer, relived his encounters with the Canucks officials, with Phil Maloney and Michael Piper, and testified to their intransigent attitudes toward Mike. Isabel took the stand and traced the events of early 1977, focussing on the horrors that her husband endured when he returned home, hurt and baffled, after the January 12 and January 19 games.

Mike Robitaille limped across the courtroom to testify on his own behalf. He made a compelling witness, speaking in great swelling rushes of sentences, the words tumbling over one another. Mike was eager after years of frustration to get out his version of all that had happened to him. He began with his earliest ambitions: "I knew I had to do well because I saw my dad and I didn't want to have the life he led. I was going to be a special player because that was my only way out." And he didn't finish, after almost three days of testimony, until he'd reached the circumstances of the end of his life in the NHL: "Nobody, not management, wants to listen to stuff about injuries. Just win the hockey games and tell me your excuses afterwards. You're getting paid a lot of money. You should be able to perform like the Almighty out there."

As Robitaille spoke, and Isabel and the doctors and players and sportscasters, a piece of magic unfolded in Mr. Justice Esson's courtroom, no less dazzling because of its familiarity. It happens in all courtrooms in all trials when gifted counsel are at work, the magical transformation of cold facts into a tale as gripping as a piece of fiction. Characters emerge, heroes and villains and innocent bystanders, and the elements of story-telling fall into place, cohesion and plot development, a climax that's logical and human. The story comes in many voices and falls from a variety of points of view, and yet one man, the counsel, arranges the sequence of paragraphs and chapters. He asks the questions that evoke the answering lines, but in the end, the questions are rubbed out, and all that remains is the flow of the narrative, the story in its simplicity and drama.

So John Laxton acted as amanuensis in the recounting of the Mike Robitaille story. Disparate events from years earlier were woven into a piece of wonderful consistency. It started at young Mike's torturous boyhood and skipped forward, touching on the essences of his hockey career to the point when, in the autumn of 1976, life and career began to come unravelled.

Encounters and conversations clicked into the story. Bill Good's conversation with Greg Douglas, Michael Piper's conversations with Eric Termansen, Phil Maloney's with Robitaille, Larry Popein's one-sentence talk with Robitaille ("We got cheques around here only for guys who want to play hockey"). Perhaps one party to the conversations may have lost them in the swirls of memory, but the words survived and were brought back to life in the courtroom. And they made, as Laxton intended them to, an insistent point: that the Canucks management had adopted throughout a view of Robitaille that he was a faker, a man whose emotions were in disarray, sicker in mind than in body, a player unique for being, in Maloney's indelicate phrase, "a con artist."

Nothing from the past escaped the story that Laxton coaxed from his witnesses. Al Davidson's radio broadcast. Dr. Piper's stroll past the aching Robitaille in the Coliseum dressing-room after the January 12 game. His advice following the January 19 game, given once and repeated a second time, to take a shot of Courvoisier. Maloney's disparagement of Bruce McColl at the Coliseum on March 9, 1977 ("I'm used to your types"), and Piper's challenge to McColl on the same night. Incident piled on incident. The Canucks' efforts to trade Robitaille to Calgary when they were aware he couldn't skate. The doctors' neglect to follow up on Dr. Porayko's January 21 diagnosis, correct as it turned out, of Mike's cervical problems. Did Laxton leave out any stray fact? Mr. Justice Esson could hardly have imagined so. Piper's January 20 phone call to Isabel ("We can't overrule the fact it may be psychosomatic"), and the team's failure the night before to carry Mike from the ice on a stretcher rather than on the shoulders of a trainer and a player. It was all in place, every last word of the story.

"When I finished," Laxton said later of his presentation of the plaintiff's case, "I was at least sixty per cent certain we'd win everything we asked for. Probably seventy per cent."

The story had been long and complex and colourful in the recounting, but Laxton's request of Mr. Justice Esson was simple: he must hold that the Canucks, in ignoring Robitaille's real symptoms because of their dismissal of him as a sort of charlatan, had caused Mike's crippling and permanent injuries, for which they must recompense him in a sum covering his suffering and his loss of past and future income.

When Barry Kirkham opened for the defence, he called Michael Piper as his first witness. Piper promptly lobbed a bombshell into Laxton's case.

KIRKHAM: "What do you know about the evening of January 12, 1977?"

PIPER: "I know I wasn't at the hockey game on that night."

KIRKHAM: "How do you know that?"

PIPER: "Because I was at a meeting of the board of directors of the Westminster Medical Building of which I was member of the board at the time and that meeting was held at the office of Touche, Ross, and the meeting began at eight o'clock and adjourned at 11:30, and I was in attendance at it."

KIRKHAM: "All right, were minutes kept at the meeting?"

PIPER: "Yes."

KIRKHAM: "When did you obtain such minutes?"

PIPER: "The minutes would have been mailed out, you know, a week or two after and filed."

KIRKHAM: "You produced them to me last week?"

PIPER: "That's correct."

KIRKHAM (showing Piper some sheets of paper): "Are these the minutes in question?"

PIPER: "Yes."

KIRKHAM (turning to Mr. Justice Esson): "May the minutes be the next exhibit?"

ESSON: "Any objection, Mr. Laxton?"

The minutes came as a shock to Laxton. They represented a piece of eleventh-hour evidence that placed Piper miles away from the Coliseum on the night when Robitaille had suffered the first of his two crucial injuries. It was of course Piper who, according to Laxton's case, had walked through the Canucks dressing-room after the game and ignored Robitaille's obvious distress. This was one of the principal instances of the Canucks' negligence. But if Piper wasn't in the dressing-room, or even in the building, then a substantial section of the plaintiff's case lost its persuasive power. So much for Piper's negligent behaviour on January 12.

Laxton objected that Kirkham was introducing the minutes at an improper time. They should have been produced to the plaintiff months earlier when the rest of the defendant's documents had been handed over. "It makes it a bit late in the day," Laxton told Esson, "for us to check on whether Dr. Piper did attend the meeting." Kirkham countered with the point that Piper had revealed the existence of the minutes only a week before. "Dr. Piper," he said, "obviously forgot about them, and they came up when I was trying to pin down whether there was any way he could say he was at the game of January 12 or not." Mr. Justice Esson considered the lawyers' points and ruled that he'd order the minutes marked for identification by the court clerk and would then hold them, not yet admitted as an exhibit, until both lawyers could prepare more arguments on the admissibility question. Laxton was given breathing-space.

But, he fretted, what good would it do him even if he kept the minutes out of the trial? As Kirkham himself had indicated, he had at least one other way of establishing Piper's absence from the Coliseum on January 12. He could call to the witness-box the other directors of the Westminster Medical Building, a bunch of doctors presumably, and they'd testify that Piper had attended the meeting until 11:30, long after the end of the hockey game. Laxton was already beginning to write off the evidence of Piper's negligence on January 12.

The day's testimony ended, and Laxton, his optimism dampened, sat at the plaintiff's table gathering his papers. The courtroom had emptied of everyone except Laxton, his junior, and the court clerk.

"Let me show you something you'll be interested in, Mr. Laxton." It was the court clerk.

"I used to be a policeman," he went on, "a detective, and I'm kind of fascinated by this case of yours."

"Yes," Laxton said. "So?"

"So I was looking pretty close at the minutes, the ones you were arguing about today. Show you what I mean."

The clerk put the minutes on a light-box that had been set up in the courtroom to illuminate X-rays of Robitaille's spinal cord. The box blew the typing on the minutes into large, transparent letters and figures. Laxton studied them.

"Get my point?" the clerk asked.

Laxton got it. The numerals "11:30 p.m.," indicating the time when the meeting was supposed to have ended, had been rubbed out and typed over, and the original time, under the "11:30 p.m.," shone through as "7:30 p.m." The earlier hour gave Piper plenty of time to drive to the Coliseum for the hockey game.

Laxton considered the series of possibilities. Someone had tampered with the minutes. Someone had pulled a small forgery job. Someone was lying. Someone was trying to run a bluff past the court. Or it could have been something as innocent as a typist's error.

"What is this?" Laxton said. "A trial or a Sherlock Holmes mystery?"

He thanked the clerk and tucked away the revelations of the light-box for future reference.

As Barry Kirkham continued to present his defence over the next few days, the court's attention swung to two dominant issues. One had to do with medical matters and the other with credibility. The defence's doctors, Michael Piper and Gordon Thompson, figured in both.

Almost unwittingly, Laxton set a challenge for Piper and the believability of his version of events when he cross-examined him on his actions on the night of January 19. Laxton was dealing with an ace up his sleeve. He already knew what Piper had said and done on the nineteenth. He had Thompson's word for Piper's actions, Thompson who had spilled the story of the nineteenth at the Arbutus Club on an evening when Rob MacKenzie was unexpectedly privy to Thompson's conversation. Laxton had no notion of putting Piper's credibility to the test when he began his cross-examination. His intention was in a sense more innocent — to establish that Piper had been slow to react to Robitaille's injury on the ice, that he lingered over his cigarette before going to Mike's aid, that he had therefore been negligent. Laxton began cross-examination on the point by asking a simple question — who was Piper sitting beside at the January 19 game? — and he got an answer he didn't expect, an answer that would later get Piper in deep waters.

LAXTON: "Were you sitting beside Dr. Thompson at the game of January 19?"

PIPER: "No, I was not."

LAXTON: "Who were you sitting with?"

PIPER: "I imagine probably my wife. I know it was not Dr. Thompson because his seats were about six rows behind ours at that stage. I imagine Dr. Thompson was probably sitting about six rows behind us and ten or twelve seats over. I wasn't aware of him at the game."

LAXTON: "Well, I suggest you were sitting next to Dr. Thompson or very close to him when this accident happened on the nineteenth of January."

PIPER: "Well, I assure you I was not sitting next to him because the seats I was sitting in at that time were row three and Dr. Thompson's, I think, are in row nine."

Slightly baffled, Laxton let the point pass, but he returned to it a few days later when his turn came to cross-examine Dr. Thompson. He zeroed in on Thompson's whereabouts on the nineteenth.

LAXTON: "You were sitting next to Dr. Piper on January 19 when this incident happened, weren't you?"

THOMPSON: "Yes."

Once having made the admission, however, and put the lie to Piper's earlier testimony, Thompson lit out for the hills in the questions that followed. He wouldn't deny that Piper was next to him, but he would fudge on Piper's behaviour in the minutes immediately after Robitaille was crushed to the ice by Dennis Owchar's check.

LAXTON: "You remember seeing the accident, don't you?"

THOMPSON: "I really don't know that I did."

LAXTON: "Well, I suggest to you that you noticed how serious the accident was and you said to Dr. Piper, 'Mike, that man has been hurt. You better get down there.' "

THOMPSON: "Well, if I did, I don't recall."

LAXTON: "Why not?"

THOMPSON: "I don't know. I suppose there are many aspects to watching a hockey game."

LAXTON: "Didn't you nudge Dr. Piper and say, 'Mike, you better get down there. He's really hurt.' "

THOMPSON: "I don't recall."

LAXTON: "And didn't Dr. Piper continue to sit there?"

THOMPSON: "I really don't know."

LAXTON: "That's possible, though, isn't it?"

THOMPSON: "I don't know. That's two years ago and I don't know."

LAXTON: "Mike Piper didn't go down to the ice immediately, did he?"

THOMPSON: "I don't know that."

LAXTON: "You mean you can't remember?"

THOMPSON: "I really don't know. I can't remember. That really wasn't of any concern to me."

Laxton decided it was time to slip the ace from his sleeve. He hadn't yet introduced Rob MacKenzie's name to the court. Now he'd spring him on Thompson.

LAXTON: "Doctor, did you attend the Arbutus Club on April 11, 1979?"

THOMPSON: "I really don't know. I could have been."

LAXTON: "Do you remember that someone came over to your table when you were sitting there on April 11, 1979, and introduced himself as Mr. Rob MacKenzie?"

THOMPSON: "No, no one introduced himself as Rob MacKenzie."

Laxton persisted, and Thompson eventually allowed that *someone* had approached his party at the club.

THOMPSON: "I remember someone coming up and asking if we were doctors, and I said, it just happens the person here happens to be a lawyer, and that was the end of the conversation. He didn't introduce himself. He didn't say anything else."

The chase was on, Laxton hounding Thompson with questions about his words and actions at the Arbutus Club and Thompson stepping a stride or two ahead with his denials. Then Thompson slipped.

LAXTON: "Did you say anything to (MacKenzie) in respect of we were not talking about Robitaille's case?"

THOMPSON: "I didn't say anything about that. He came and introduced. . ." Thompson caught himself in `mid-stumble. "At least he didn't introduce himself. He just spoke to me and wanted to know if we were two doctors."

Thompson was off again, just out of reach of the pursuing questions. The purpose behind Laxton's line of interrogations was plain — to show that Thompson had talked in MacKenzie's hearing at the Arbutus Club and had described Piper's behaviour on the nineteenth in terms that brought Piper close to negligence. Piper was the ultimate target, but Thompson, denying memory of any such conversation, acted as his shield. Thompson remained unyielding, and Laxton at last gave up the pursuit. He abandoned his questions about the great Arbutus Club run-in. He shoved the ace into his deck of cards and held it there for a few days until Barry Kirkham told the court that he had concluded the defence's case. Laxton rose and asked Mr. Justice Esson's permission to call one more witness for the plaintiff, a witness whose evidence would go to the delay of Dr. Piper to attend to Robitaille on the ice on the nineteenth and would also bear on the credibility of Dr.

Thompson in parts of his testimony. Kirkham objected that Laxton had closed for the plaintiff and wasn't entitled to reopen his case. The judge listened to the arguments and came down on Laxton's side. The new evidence was admissible, he ruled, because it would apparently deal with a prior inconsistent statement by an earlier witness, Thompson. Laxton's ace was out of the deck. He called Rob MacKenzie to the witness-box.

"We were sitting in what might be described as the lounge area in the Arbutus Club," MacKenzie began, "which is like a livingroom with chesterfields in an L-shape. Every twenty feet away there is another chesterfield in an L-shape. The end result is I am facing Dr. Gordon Thompson. . . I didn't pay any attention to anything except all of a sudden I hear the name Robitaille. . . ."

Mackenzie told his story, the tale of the astounding coincidence, a version of events that differed dramatically from Dr. Thompson's memory of them, a stunning piece of contradiction. Laxton was content that MacKenzie came across as a formidable witness, unfaltering and detailed in his recollections of an encounter that had, after all, taken place a mere ten weeks earlier. Mr. Justice Esson listened in silence to the testimony. Neither Laxton nor Kirkham would know what Esson made of it until many months later when he analysed it in his written judgment. Kirkham wouldn't care for the analysis. Neither would Dr. Thompson.

Dr. Thompson found himself at the storm centre of another controversy that took over the trial for several more tense and critical hours. The issue this time was medical, though it ultimately turned on a point of credibility, and it surfaced during the course of the proceedings, not as something that Laxton could anticipate and prepare for. The issue grew out of the examination at the trial of two sets of X-rays that had been taken of Robitaille's spinal canal, the first at the Royal Columbia Hospital in New Westminster in the days after Mike's last game on January 19, 1977, and the second at a hospital in Buffalo in November 1977. During Dr. Barbara Allan's testimony, she looked at the X-rays and gave it as her view that Robitaille's spinal canal was abnormally small. In a written report that was prepared at Laxton's request as the trial was proceeding, Dr. Kenneth Kaan, the Buffalo neuroradiologist, agreed with Dr. Allan's assessment. The spinal canal is the channel that encloses and protects the spinal cord, and its normal width is about eleven millimetres. Robitaille's was narrower, critically narrower at approximately 8.5 millimetres. The reason for the narrowness couldn't be determined — a congenital condition perhaps or the result of degenerative change — but its significance was apparent and crucial. When the canal is narrow, the cord is crowded for space, and if the canal takes a blow from the outside, then the chances are greater for the cord to come into such jarring contact with the hard surface of the canal that it will suffer serious damage. Thus, the narrowness of Robitaille's spinal canal increased the odds on injury to his spinal cord. More than that, given Dr. Allan's contention about the connection between Robitaille's injuries of January 12 and those of January 19, it stepped up the odds on two *related* injuries to his cord.

For the defence, Dr. Thompson studied the X-rays and pronounced himself satisfied that there was nothing dangerously narrow about Robitaille's spinal canal as revealed in the January 1977 X-rays. If there were signs of narrowing in the later X-rays from Buffalo, then the degenerative changes had taken place in the ten months from January to November 1977. Thompson was firm, defiant even, in his interpretation of the X-rays, and Laxton swooped in to cross-examine him on the point. He had no difficulty in getting Thompson to agree that eleven millimetres was a normal width for the spinal canal and that anything under nine millimetres was "in the critical area." Then Laxton had the January X-rays placed on the light-box. They showed Robitaille's spinal canal in a blow-up that had been examined by Dr. Kaan in Buffalo in preparing his report for the court. Dr. Kaan had written a measurement of the canal on the X-ray: eleven millimetres. Laxton asked Thompson to confirm the measurement. Thompson stepped up to the light-box, worked his measuring instrument, and announced that he agreed with the figure Kaan had written in: eleven millimetres.

LAXTON: "Do you see narrowing of the diameter of the spinal canal?"

THOMPSON: "No, I don't see any narrowing. I see a measurement that he's got there of about eleven millimetres. But I think that's within acceptable limits. I don't call that narrowing."

LAXTON: "Now you say there is a measurement there that shows eleven millimetres but that is not evidence of a narrow canal?"

THOMPSON: "I would accept that within my range of normal."

Laxton was proceeding at a slower rate than the one at which he usually conducted his cross-examinations. He was repeating himself, going over the same territory one or two times more than he needed to. The repetition and the leisurely pace weren't the product of any confusion on Laxton's part. They sprang from excitement. Thompson, Laxton recognized, had dug himself into a hole. Laxton knew that the eleven millimetres shown on the X-ray in Kaan's handwriting, the eleven millimetres confirmed by Thompson's own calculation, wasn't an absolute measurement. It was a preliminary figure. It didn't take into account something essential called the magnification factor. Before the real width of Robitaille's spinal canal could be computed, a figure had to be worked into the equation that allowed for the amount by which the width had been magnified by the process of X-raying. When that factor was thrown into the mathematics, the final, authentic, physical width of Mike Robitaille's spinal canal came to a measurement close to 8.5 millimetres. Dr. Thompson had not mentioned the magnification factor to the court.

"When I realized what Thompson was doing," Laxton recalled long after the trial, "I got so excited I almost blew it. These Perry Mason things aren't supposed to happen in real trials. Here I had this witness clearly trapped in a contradiction and I couldn't believe it was happening."

Laxton pulled his excitement under control and put the direct question to Thompson.

"How," he asked, "could you work out the true or absolute measurement without knowing the magnification factor?"

"Well, this is what I said about the Buffalo film," Thompson began, looking for solid ground and not finding it, "and I don't know about the ratio, the multiplying." He stopped and started again. "I don't know what the ratio is, the multiplying factor is."

LAXTON: "You would have to go to an expert like Dr. Kaan, wouldn't you, to know the fixed rate of magnification?"

THOMPSON: "Well, I would expect I would have to go to the area or the place where the radiograph was done, that's correct."

LAXTON: "What you're telling me, doctor, is that you can't look at that film and work out the true spinal cord measurement because you don't know the ratio of magnification."

THOMPSON: "You can't work out the true diameter of the spinal cord."

LAXTON: "You can't do that?"

THOMPSON: "No, there is a multiplying factor on all magnification."

LAXTON: "You say you looked at that and it showed eleven millimetres and that's normal."

THOMPSON: "No, I didn't say that. I said there's a number written on there, eleven millimetres."

LAXTON: "And that's within normal? You're satisfied with that?"

THOMPSON: "I accept a measurement of that."

Laxton was still struggling to control his excited delight and to nail Thompson once and for all. The focus of his questions wavered. Then, finally, again: "Do you know that you had to take into account the magnification factor?"

THOMPSON: "Always, that's correct."

LAXTON: "Now, when you take into account the magnification factor, that eleven millimetres comes down to 8.46 millimetres. Does that sound reasonable?"

THOMPSON: "Yes, that sounds reasonable."

LAXTON: "Because the magnification factor is 1.3 times actual size?"

THOMPSON: "That sounds quite reasonable."

Laxton worked over the same ground with two or three additional questions, and then pounced on what he considered the gap in Thompson's earlier testimony.

"You see, the impression you gave me," he said to Thompson, "was that you looked over the X-ray, you made a measurement, you assumed eleven millimetres was right, and that was the width of the spinal canal."

"I said," Thompson told Laxton, "that was the number written on the film."

LAXTON: "Yes, and you assumed that was within normal limits?"

THOMPSON: "No, I didn't assume that. I said that was the number written on there and I measured it, and it was eleven millimetres, and I know there is a magnification factor."

Mr. Justice Esson seemed satisfied that the fly had been pinned. He interrupted Laxton's questions with one of his own.

"Well," he said to Thompson, "was there any meaning to your saying it was within normal limits if you didn't know the magnification factor?"

THOMPSON: "No. All I mean, it would be less than the eleven millimetres that was on there but, and I made this point about the Buffalo films because they are not comparable films to the Royal Columbia's."

Thompson's testimony on the point fizzled to an end.

Barry Kirkham's case was developing pock-marks. Piper and Thompson were caught in contradictory testimony. When Kirkham summoned another witness, John Chessman, the Canucks' comptroller, he gave the plaintiff more ammunition by conceding under cross-examination that, sure, it was common practice to attempt to peddle an injured player, Robitaille for example, to another team, the Calgary

Cowboys, without mentioning the injury. With Chessman as his vehicle, Kirkham's own witness, Laxton scored an easy point: the Canucks were callous. Kirkham was treading water, in danger of going under. He called fewer witnesses than he had indicated to the court at the outset of the trial that he would call. And he failed to return to Dr. Piper's alibi for January 12. He didn't offer witnesses to vouch that Piper was at a meeting in New Westminster rather than at the hockey game, and it never became necessary for Laxton to trot out the revelation of the light-box. Had Kirkham cottoned on to a possible forgery? Laxton couldn't be certain. All he knew was that his fears for the twelfth had fled. And his confidence about the outcome of the trial took a quantum leap.

"If I felt seventy per cent positive I'd win after my own case went in," he said later, "I felt one hundred per cent sure after the defence's case was finished."

The last three days of the trial were devoted to counsel's argument, and Laxton took most of the hours in those days, Kirkham preferring to present the bulk of his argument in written form. Laxton was assured as he waded through his presentation, and if he'd been more alert during a curious and possibly telling exchange with Mr. Justice Esson at the beginning of his third day of addressing the court, he might have been fairly bursting with certainty.

"I'm making a supreme sacrifice," he said to Esson in an offhand remark as he organized the documents in front of him for the day's session. "The principal where my twelve-year-old daughter goes to school asked me to come to the prize-giving today: She's going to receive the top prize for academics, sports, and citizenship."

ESSON: "Please convey my regrets and congratulations."

LAXTON: "Thank you, my lord."

ESSON: "Hopefully I can do more for you than that."

Had Esson signalled his verdict? Was he saying his decision would bring a few smiles and a few bucks for Laxton and Robitaille? Laxton had no idea. He wasn't listening.

"I was so busy getting my papers in order," he said later, "that I didn't pay attention to what Esson was saying. It wasn't until months later, a year and a half later, when I read over the transcript that I realized what he'd told me. Even then, I wasn't really sure that he was sending me a particular message."

Laxton was his thorough self in serving up the case for the plaintiff, ticking off the strengths in his own argument and the weaknesses in Kirkham's. He covered all witnesses, all events, but it was in his third day of presentation, near the end of the time on his feet, that he grew most passionate. He put a unique request to Esson. He asked that exemplary damages be awarded to Robitaille. Exemplary damages go beyond simple damages for pain and suffering and loss of income. They're special and rare punitive damages that are given only when the court decides to censure a defendant for its outrageous conduct or for the cruel way in which it has harmed the plaintiff. Laxton argued that the Canucks had behaved so abominably in their treatment of Robitaille that this, of all cases, was an appropriate occasion to invoke exemplary damages. He listed the outrages: the careless handling of Robitaille on the night of January 19; advising the press on the sly that Mike's problems were caused by a faulty psyche; branding him a "con artist" and subjecting him to a variety of indignities. Even in the conduct of the case itself,

Laxton argued, the defendant was shown to be un-cooperative and contemptuous. He cited the abortive try at developing an alibi for Dr. Piper on January 12. "I was astonished," Laxton said, taking a poke at Barry Kirkham, "that when my friend closed his case, he didn't call the people at the January 12 meeting." Laxton hardly missed a bet. How much should Esson award in exemplary damages? Laxton cited the highest amount that had so far been given under that head in a British Columbia court, $30,000, against the International Association of Bridge Structural & Ornamental Ironworkers Union for their high-handed conduct in dismantling a challenging union, the Canadian Ironworkers Union No. 1. Laxton knew the case intimately. He had acted for the plaintiff, the Canadian Ironworkers, and he'd secured the exemplary damages. He asked Esson to give at least as much to Robitaille.

Once done with the special plea, Laxton wound up his argument in *Robitaille* v. *Vancouver Hockey Club Ltd.* with a small flourish. "The case itself," he said, "is a classic one." Why, he went on, "it could maybe form the basis of a great Canadian novel."

Mr. Justice Esson, as his law clerk for 1978 remembered, "sweated blood over the writing of the Robitaille decision." He kept at it, evenings and weekends, through much of the six months after the end of the trial. He wrote and rewrote. In one draft, he came down hard on the defence's medical witnesses. Then he reconsidered and softened the passages that dealt with the doctors. The decision was ready by December, but even then, Esson was revising the judgment, a fat 143-page document, up to the last possible moment. Finally, he released it to the waiting plaintiff, defendant, and public. The date was December 18, 1978, and Mr. Justice Esson's hard-wrought words arrived at last as a glorious triumph for Mike Robitaille — and for John Laxton.

Legal judgments are rarely works of literature. They're pragmatic documents, delivered in prose that's usually plodding, sometimes fussy, and always painstaking. Esson's judgment was no exception. Its major virtue was its clarity. The wording may not have been elegant, but the meaning was forever plain, and the judgment represented a remarkable display of cool control. Occasionally Esson's natural indignation popped through the flow of legalese, through the laborious construction of sentences and paragraphs. But for the most part he kept a proper rein on his emotions and concentrated on conveying fact and interpretation — *his* interpretation — in language that no one, plaintiff or defendant or appeal court, could misread.

By necessity, Esson made the issue of credibility one pivot of his decision. Who was he going to believe? Robitaille and his fellow witnesses for the plaintiff? Or the representatives and agents of the Canucks? Which set of doctors would he accept? Dr. Barbara Allan and friends? Or Piper, Thompson, and company? Esson arrived almost effortlessly at his choice.

Of Robitaille he wrote: "He has not been shown to have been wrong to any significant extent in the course of the lengthy evidence in relation to any veritable fact to which he testified, i.e. those facts which relate to events external to his feelings, sensations and injuries and which were capable of being checked."

The Canucks' witnesses, on the other hand, especially the doctors, offered evidence that Esson found less than acceptable, and he handed out rebukes that ranged from mild to stern.

On Dr. Piper's alibi for January 12: "At trial, an attempt was made to establish that Dr. Piper was elsewhere on the evening of January 12. That attempt did not succeed. After considering all the evidence on the point, I find that Robitaille was right in saying that it was Dr. Piper who walked through the dressing room."

On Piper's seat at the Coliseum on the night of January 19: "Dr. Piper denied in his evidence that he was sitting beside Dr. Thompson at the time of the injury to Robitaille. On that conflict, I prefer the evidence of Dr. Thompson who could have no reason to be wrong on that point."

On Dr. Thompson's testimony with the width of Robitaille's spinal canal: "He said that the measurement was eleven millimetres and 'within acceptable limits,' anything over ten millimetres being outside the range of critically narrow. That was a misleading answer because, as he must have known, the eleven millimetres figure involved a magnification factor and indicated an actual width of under nine millimetres. The matter of magnification had not been mentioned to that point in the trial. I concluded that this could not have been a matter of oversight or forgetfulness but was a matter of the witness taking a chance on not being caught out rather than admitting a fact unfavourable to his basic thesis."

On Thompson's conversation at the Arbutus Club on the night when Rob MacKenzie was sitting in earshot: "(Dr. Thompson denied) having made at a dinner party certain statements as to the conduct of Dr. Piper, who was sitting beside him as a spectator at the January 19 game when Robitaille was injured, and as to his opinion as to the seriousness of Robitaille's injury. The occasion was within a day or two after Dr. Thompson had examined Robitaille in preparation for giving evidence. He denied making those statements. I do not accept that denial in face of the evidence led for the plaintiff, which evidence I find was true as to what was said on that occasion.''

Esson seemed downright shocked by Dr. Thompson's testimony on the Arbutus Club incident, and he used it as ground for throwing doubt on much of the rest of Thompson's evidence. ''Had that false denial (of the Arbutus Club statements),'' Esson wrote, ''been motivated only by embarrassment at a social and professional faux pas, it might have little importance in relation to the question of the weight to be given to the witness's opinion in the field in which he is so highly qualified. But it goes beyond that. I find that he was motivated, at least in part, by his desire to protect the defendant, with the owners of which he had a friendly relationship, and by his desire to protect Dr. Piper, who incidentally was the person who arranged on behalf of the defendant for him to act. Whatever the reason, I find that he allowed himself to become a partisan on behalf of the defendant and allowed that attitude to affect his opinion evidence.''

Thus, with Dr. Thompson's credibility as an objective witness shot to pieces, wherever his medical testimony differed from Dr. Barbara Allan's, Esson accepted the Allan version. Robitaille's January 19 injury *was* an aggravation of the injury that dated back to January 12 and probably earlier. The Canucks, through their doctors, general manager, and other agents and employees, had been negligent in their treatment of Robitaille, blaming his non-existent emotional troubles for his real physical ailments. The defendant, Esson held, owed the plaintiff a duty of care, and it had failed to carry out the duty. The defendant must pay damages to the plaintiff, and by page 119 of his judgment, Esson was ready to add up the bill.

Loss of opportunity to earn income as a major-league player after the 1976-77 season: $175,000.

Loss of opportunity to earn income for the rest of his life: $185,000.

Damages for pain and suffering and loss of enjoyment of life: $40,000.

Then Esson took up Laxton's request for exemplary damages. Yes, he wrote, he agreed with Laxton. Indeed, in the strongest language of his judgment, he may have exceeded Laxton in announcing his wrath at the Canucks' treatment of Robitaille. "The conduct of the defendant can fairly be described as high-handed, arrogant and as displaying a reckless disregard for the rights of the plaintiff. . . . In carrying through their chosen treatment (the management and medical team of the defendant) showed a callous disregard for his feelings and his well-being — they ignored the dictates of common decency as well as commonsense." After unloading his blast, Esson proceeded to award Robitaille the highest amount for exemplary damages in B.C. judicial history, topping the award in Laxton's old Ironworkers case by $5,000: $35,000.

Total damages for the plaintiff against the defendant: $435,000 plus costs.

Esson dangled the award in front of Robitaille. Then he snatched some of it back. Robitaille, he wrote, must bear partial blame for his own misfortune. Esson recognized that a professional hockey club puts such pressure on its players that they surrender much of the will to act on their own. Still,

Esson ruled, Robitaille should have begun taking steps to protect his health and his interests in the week before January 19. In not doing so, not consulting a doctor on his own hook, he must be faulted. The passage in Esson's judgment dealing with Robitaille's lack of initiative was sketchy, a mere four pages out of 143, but Esson was satisfied that Mike had contributed his own negligence to the mess and horror he found himself engulfed in. Esson estimated the contributory negligence at twenty per cent and reduced the award by that amount, or $87,000.

Total damages: $348,000, plus Robitaille's court costs.

Every Christmas season, Laxton takes his wife and three daughters to Hawaii for a combined holiday and birthday celebration. Laxton's natal day is December 25, and all his Vancouver friends, the lawyers and politicians and old pals who make the islands the scene for their winter break, know that Christmas Day is open house at the Laxton retreat.

Christmas of 1978, shortly after the publication of the Robitaille judgment, was no exception to the family tradition, and all the Laxtons flew to Hawaii, where they sunned, swam, jogged, and partied. The head of the house, husband and father, was especially ready to unwind. It had been a long year in the courts, what with Robitaille and a couple of other demanding cases, but in a few days Laxton was feeling tanned and relaxed. He liked to take his ease on the balcony of the family's hotel suite, and one afternoon when he was surveying the horizon from his favourite perch, he spotted a familiar figure in the driveway below. It was none other than Mr. Justice William Esson of the B.C. Supreme Court. Laxton had the notion that Esson was deliberately hanging around, keen to run into Laxton but reluctant to approach him directly. Just about everybody from Vancouver knew where Laxton stayed, and it would be no trouble for Esson, another vacationer from the mainland, to locate him. Laxton shouted down and invited Esson up to the balcony for a drink.

"Naturally we didn't talk about the case," Lawton remembers of the amiable hour or so he passed with Esson. "We couldn't because it was still open for appeal. But I think Bill felt the way I did, that it was nice just to sit and kind of bask in the memory of the trial. Both of us had performed pretty damn well through all those weeks in court. We took pleasure in that even though we didn't dare say anything much about the case. God knows I kept thinking that Bill Esson had done a hell of a fine job of running a trial and writing a judgment."

Barry Kirkham wasn't so sure of the quality of Esson's work, and he elected to take the Robitaille decision to the B.C. Court of Appeal. Laxton cranked up and went back to court, arguing with Kirkham before a three-man appeal court that was headed by Chief Justice Nathan Nemetz. The three listened patiently to the two counsel's arguments, pondered their points over several months, and on April 10, 1981, handed down a 42-page decision that offered bad news to the Canucks and a slight increase in damages to Robitaille. The appeal court agreed in every particular but one with Mr. Justice Esson's decision. They accepted his findings of negligence, his doubts of the defence doctors' credibility, his apportionment of damages. They adopted all his findings and rulings, all except his reasoning on exemplary damages. Yes, the appeal court said, the defendant's despicable actions entitled the plaintiff to exemplary damages. Of course. But Robitaille should get *more* under that head, *more* exemplary damages. The trial judge, according to the appeal court, erred when he applied Robitaille's contributory negligence, twenty per cent, to all damages. The twenty per cent shouldn't bear on exemplary damages. "There is no evidence," the court held, "that Robitaille's negligence contributed to the conduct of the Club which gives rise to the award under this head of damages." The Court of Appeal added $7,000 to Robitaille's bill, and the Canucks now owed him $355,000 and costs.

On May 14, 1981, the Canucks announced that they would not take the case on appeal to the Supreme Court of Canada. Almost three years after John Laxton had issued the writ, four and a half years after Mike Robitaille had felt the first pains shooting down his back and leg, *Robitaille* v. *Vancouver Hockey Club Ltd.* had dwindled to its conclusion.

Near the end of the first week in July 1981, Mike and Isabel flew from Buffalo to Vancouver. It was their first trip to the coast in years that wasn't burdened by a lawsuit and anguish. They planned to visit friends, the ones who'd survived the Canucks days. They'd call on John Laxton. And they would pick up a cheque from the Supreme Court of British Columbia written on moneys that the Canucks had delivered into court in settlement of Mike's judgment against the club. Payment in full.

"The money came at the right time," Isabel said. "After all the years of suing people, we were running out of cash."

What the Robitailles weren't going short on, given the bleak times, was optimism. The world had begun to break Mike's way shortly after his trial. He took a public relations job with the Buffalo Stallions indoor soccer team that suited his gifts for talk and sports and enthusiasm. He found himself growing closer to his family and his church. "I understand people better now, my wife and kids and everybody, after what I went through," he said. "And I go to mass every day." His strength and stamina began to return. He couldn't play hockey, not with the right hand that clutched up when he was tired, not with the right leg that turned inward and developed a tremor. But he could coach hockey, and in the winter of 1979-80 he spent his nights and weekends with the Lockport Wolves, a junior team in a suburban Buffalo community. He coached, he managed, he led the cheers, and he blossomed into a personality around Lockport. Everybody knew Mike Robitaille. Everybody warmed to his open ways. When he ran the Wolves again the following season to the same reaction from everyone in town, a large group-insurance company in the area — "a good Christian business," as Isabel describes it, Isabel who sets the family's religious and psychological tone — took a calculated look at Mike's local popularity and made him an offer. They'd set him up in his very own insurance agency. He accepted, and in the late spring of '81, Mike Robitaille Insurance opened for business in downtown Lockport.

"Look at *that*!" Mike's older daughter, Anique, said when he drove her past the spanking new office. "Daddy's name's up in lights!"

Mike felt high in Vancouver, the lawsuit behind him and a fresh career ahead. And then the call came from Toronto. Geraldine Robitaille had died at St. Michael's Hospital on Wednesday, July 8. Mike's mother was dead, the woman who had, years earlier, been the victim of two nervous breakdowns, the woman who had brought disorder and tension into the childhood of her youngest. It was a difficult period for Mike. His lawsuit was finished and his mother was dead.

"It was okay," Isabel said later of the news from Toronto. "Mike was deeply saddened. Of course he was. But he'd made his peace with his mother. He understood that his anxieties as an adult had grown out of his experiences with her as a boy. He'd come to grips with all of that before she died."

As for John Laxton, the Robitailles didn't see much of him in Vancouver. He was busy. An NDP Member of Parliament named Ian Waddell was suing the Governor General and all the members of the federal cabinet. He contended that orders-in-council passed by the cabinet which made certain alterations in the construction of the Alaska Highway natural gas pipeline had usurped the role of Parliament. Waddell retained Laxton to take the matter to court. Laxton was back in his natural element.

Books by John Mortimer From Penguin

☐ **Clinging to the Wreckage** $5.95

The creator of Rumpole, the best playwright to ever appear for a murderer at the Central Criminal Court, the son who immortalized a parent in *Voyage Round My Father*, John Mortimer now gives us his funny, astringent and tender autobiography.

As seen on PBS television

☐ **Rumpole and the Golden Thread** $3.95

Horace Rumpole deftly juggles the vagaries of law, the ambiguities of crime and the contradictions of the human heart in his death-defying performances on behalf of justice.

☐ **The First Rumpole Omnibus** $11.95

Horace Rumpole's legal triumphs are celebrated here in this first omnibus edition which includes *Rumpole of the Bailey*, *The Trials of Rumpole* and *Rumpole's Return*.

These books should be available wherever books are sold. They can also be ordered by mail. Please indicate the titles required and fill in the form below.

NAME _____

ADDRESS _____

_____

_____

Enclose a cheque or money order payable to Penguin Books Canada Limited to cover the total price of books ordered, plus $1.00 per book for postage and handling, and mail to Penguin Books Canada Limited, 2801 John Street, Markham, Ontario, L3R 1B4.

Prices subject to change without notice.